BIGFOOT

John Napier

BIGFOOT

The Yeti and Sasquatch in Myth and Reality

E. P. DUTTON & CO., INC.
New York 1973

First published in the U.S.A. 1973 by E. P. Dutton & Co., Inc.
Copyright © 1972 by John Napier
All rights reserved. Printed in the U.S.A.
Second Printing, May 1973

SBN: 0-525-06658-6
Library of Congress Catalog Card Number: 71-179857

We gratefully acknowledge permission to reproduce the following: the lines from 'The
Yak' by Hilaire Belloc, from *Cautionary Tales,* published 1941 by Alfred A. Knopf, Inc.;
and the extract from *The Long Walk* by Slawomir Rawicz (New York, Harper & Row,
1956).

Contents

Illustrations

Acknowledgments

In this book I have leaned very heavily on other people's published experiences, experiments and opinions, and the acknowledgment of my indebtedness appears in footnotes which are numbered in the text and listed collectively at the end of the book. These footnotes also provide a bibliography of the principal works consulted.

Apart from published sources, a great deal of my information — though not the opinions, which are my own except where stated — has been derived from conversations and correspondence with a great many people who have generously given me their time and help. In particular they include the following: Don Abbott, Frank L. Beebe, George Berklacy, T. S. Blakeney, Peter Byrne, Rene Dahinden, L. W. Davies, James Ellis, John Green, Don Grieve, Christoph von Fürer-Haimendorf, Bernard Heuvelmans, J. E. Hill, Dr W. C. Osman Hill, Lord Hunt, Grover S. Krantz, Charles Manning, Jim McClarin, Robert W. Morgan, Roger Patterson, S. Dillon Ripley, Ivan T. Sanderson, Eric Shipton, Lawrence W. Swan, Odette Tchernine, Michael Ward, Don Whillans and E. S. Williams.

I am indebted to the following for their practical help with the manuscript, literary criticism and downright good sense: Michael Day, Barbara Dickson, Gemma Forster, John Green, Peter Lattin, Gilbert Manley and Alison Richard.

Prue Napier was responsible for the research that provided the data for table 4, and in addition, of course, has been involved in countless ways with the preparation of this book.

If there are errors of judgment or factual inaccuracies, the fault is mine alone.

JOHN NAPIER

Explanatory Note

'Bigfoot' is my collective name for the giant-sized man-like creatures that are believed to dwell in the boreal forests of north-west America and in the snowfields of the Himalayas. I am using the American Indian name 'Sasquatch' for the Bigfoot in British Columbia, across the 49th parallel in the north-west states of the U.S.A. and in Northern California. In the Himalayas, the creature is called the Abominable Snowman or the Yeti.

Although Sasquatches and Yetis differ quite considerably in details of their structure and habits, both are, very broadly speaking, man-like inasmuch as they are said to walk on two legs and are credited with a human shape.

The footprints of both geographical varieties are indubitably big—hence the name 'Bigfoot'.

1. Man and his Monsters

I cannot remember exactly when I first became interested in the legend of the Yeti, but it really all started with a photograph. I had been fascinated by footprints for a long time. Part of my early research interests were concerned with the normal and abnormal walking patterns of human beings through the study of footprints and by such unromantic devices as the analysis of wear on the soles and heels of boots and shoes. The photograph that set me off was taken by the well-known mountaineer, Eric Shipton.

In 1951, accompanied by Michael Ward, Shipton was returning from an Everest Reconnaissance Expedition when he came across a line of footprints at the edge of the Menlung Glacier; Shipton photographed one of these prints. The heavy publicity that this photograph received was, I believe, instrumental in introducing the Yeti to a world-wide public. Certainly no one was more surprised than Eric Shipton when the stewardess on his flight from Karachi told him that a posse of reporters were waiting for him to step off the plane. Their questions were not about the problems of climbing the highest mountain in the world but about the mysterious being whose footprints he and Michael Ward had photographed. From this moment on the Yeti became news.

In mountaineering circles, peculiar footprints in the snow were common talk; Howard-Bury, Tilman, Hunt, Smythe, Shipton and many others had already reported the discovery of mysterious tracks in the high Himalayas. To most people these earlier reports, which had received scant publicity, appeared simply to be typical travellers' tales of no particular moment. But with the publication of Shipton's picture—sharp, undistorted and precisely exposed—the legend of the Yeti took a giant step forward and entered the public domain. What had been familiar for centuries to the Sherpas of Nepal, the Tibetans, the Bhutanese and the Sikkimese, suddenly, overnight, became a matter of acute interest at a million breakfast tables. With this one photograph, the Yeti joined the long line of traditional monsters.

The image of the Yeti is so firmly entrenched in Western culture that it is hard to believe that in terms of public awareness it is only just over twenty years old. It seems that the legend has been with us always—which in one sense it has: monsters and ogres are the backbone of folklore. During the last few decades man has added quite a crop of assorted monsters to the list. The Loch Ness Monster is a classic example of the genre. With a snapshot taken by Hugh Gray in 1933 it became a national figure and a tourist money-spinner, and is virtually assured of a permanent niche in folklore. Then there are the Unidentified Flying Objects, which we have taken tentatively to our bosoms. Monster comics, monster games, monster TV serials and do-it-yourself monster kits are part of young-teenage culture in America, though in Great Britain and, so far as I know, Europe, teenagers are not so forcibly fed on this demoralizing diet. A monster of a sort has even penetrated the advertising world: in the Jolly Green Giant of the canned and frozen vegetable kingdom we have a debased twentieth-century version of the ancient folk figure of the Green Man; but now he is gentle and strong, a child of nature with the face of a Middle-West farm boy—simple, pure and quite unbearable.

My task in this book is to disentangle what is rational from what is irrational in current monster stories—particularly the man-like monsters of North America and the Himalayas. In the face of many difficulties, as will later become clear, I propose to subject the evidence to the sort of critical analysis that science demands.

Scientists have taken a bad beating over the subject of monsters. They are in fact the whipping boys of the monster establishment. These enthusiasts hold that scientists are suppressing information. Why? You may well ask. Scientists are supposed to know all about these things, but because their biological and evolutionary theories would be shattered if the *real truth* were known they have formed a conspiracy of silence.

From one point of view, scientists should be flattered that they are credited with such superhuman control over their tongues. My experience of scientists is that they are inveterate talkers and compulsive gossipers and that, perhaps with the exception of those employed by national organizations with tight security, they will tell you all that they know—and much that they don't know—at the drop of a chairman's gavel. Thank heaven that this is true, for the philosophy of science would be a mockery otherwise. But nevertheless it has become a boring cliché of the monster establishment that scientists are afraid that the frailties of their own doctrines would be exposed should they so much as admit the existence of unknown animals or unknown forces.

On the contrary, I have found that nothing intrigues a scientist more than monster tales. Most of my colleagues in Britain and the United States delight in speculating on possible theories, and often come up with ingenious solutions that seem to owe more to science fiction than to the principles and methodology of science. This is the stuff of which coffee-breaks are made, and I can assure the monster establishment that their suspicions of the fraternity are quite without foundation. If there is a conspiracy of silence, it derives at best from scientific caution, and at worst from sheer ignorance of the issues, but certainly not from a desire to hush up the truth.

It has been said that the problems of the Yeti, the Sasquatch and all the rest are ignored because they are below the scientific salt. But the truth is that scientists are simply not interested in investigating problems for which there is not sufficient evidence to justify launching an expensive time- and energy-consuming research project. There is no shortage of problems to tackle, and it is hardly surprising that scientists prefer to investigate the probable rather than beat their heads against the wall of the faintly possible. Their reluctance to become actively involved in such matters has no sinister overtones, reflects no fear of ridicule from their peers, but expresses a wholly practical attitude of mind—an attitude which, incidentally, most scientists are paid to pursue. Sir Peter Medawar, F.R.S., has summed up the situation (in a separate context, let me hasten to add) in supremely simple terms: 'Good scientists study the most important problems they think they can solve. It is, after all, their professional business to solve problems, not merely to grapple with them.'[1] However, while admitting the aptness of Medawar's definition of research when matters at the shadowy end of the scientific scale like Bigfoot (or U.F.O.s. for that matter) are at issue, I am disturbed at its implications for research in general. It seems to me that the 'art of the soluble' is a cynical kind of philosophy and a stultifying directive. To establishment scientists obliged to toe the line drawn by the terms of a research grant or by the dictates of the teamwork of departmental policy, it must provide comforting reassurance, but as a clarion call for the venturesome it sounds dismally flat. Solubility is surely not the principle by which great discoveries have been made. Newton, Harvey, Faraday, Darwin, Mendel and Einstein would never have tolerated the implied restrictions of such a definition and would scornfully have disassociated themselves from such an abysmal expression of low-key ambition. Their discoveries owed little to caution or to the fear of the spectacle they would make of themselves if their hunches hadn't come off. I can only see the 'art of the soluble' as a sad reflection of the conformity of many scientists for whom a secure future, or tenure, is recompense enough for the loss of intellectual initiative. The regimentation of scientists makes one long for the days when science was the hobby of the amateur, of the gentleman of leisure, when ethology and ecology were called natural history and when physicists and chemists were the uncommitted and unsalaried masters of their own adventurous minds.

Medawar has expressed a clear warning to potential deviationists: 'The spectacle of a scientist locked in combat with the forces of ignorance is not an inspiring one if, in the outcome, the scientist is routed.' I fail to see the ignominy of this situation unless the scientist has so sequestered himself from the people who pay him that his only concern is what his colleagues think of him. The general public are delighted when science is routed; it makes their day. It also makes the scientist human and fallible, which is no bad thing even at such a price. Science costs the citizen a packet; at least he should have a share of the fun. To me it does not seem an unreasonable request that at least a tiny proportion of the money spent on lasers and quasars should be re-allocated to the study of ghoulies and ghosties and other fringe sciences, if only for the satisfaction of the shareholders. Ordinary people take the soluble for granted; it is the great insoluble problems that really interest them.

It is up to the grant-giving foundations and research councils (without whose help research would surely grind to a halt) to devote a proportion of their budgets to students (in the widest sense of the word) who wish to investigate the insoluble, the outrageous and the offbeat. Surely there is enough evidence that mad ideas in the history of science have paid off handsomely to justify a small annual expenditure. It is in the spirit of 'fools rush in where angels fear to tread' that I am approaching the subject of Bigfoot. It is a supremely complex affair because it concerns both fact and fantasy; it deals with physical truths and hypothetical concepts; it involves the mind of man, with all its genetic and environmental influences and motivations, with its cultural idiosyncrasies, and its plain 'ornery' capacity for coming up with an independent idea.

For these reasons in the succeeding pages it will become intellectually necessary from time to time to abandon the real world and, like Persephone, enter the dark regions of another world which I like to call the Goblin Universe.

It is simple enough to apply reason to what is reasonable, but it is much more difficult to argue logically about the illogical. However, there comes a time when it is necessary to do so in order to demonstrate the illogicality of a major premise. I shall consider evidence for the existence of Bigfoot which for a number of reasons is equivocal or poorly documented. In other circumstances I would dismiss it. The rules of logic of our world forbid the drawing of inferences from hypotheses, but this is the currency the monster establishment commonly deals in. In writing this book I am necessarily tackling them, as well as the subject of Bigfoot, and so I shall sometimes have to resort to their logical method.

If you see me disappearing down a mental rabbit-hole from time to time you will know where I am headed. I will be travelling unwillingly into the Goblin Universe.

Bigfoot, the living animal, if it exists must be part of nature. Bigfoot, the legend, which undeniably exists, is part of human culture. Thus there are two sorts of evidence to consider, natural and cultural, and both have material and theoretical components.

Natural evidence concerns the animal itself: its size, its structure, its zoological affinities, its diet and, to some extent, its behaviour. These characteristics can be assessed from material evidence, which ideally should take the form of the living animal, its dead body or its skeleton. Unfortunately, as far as Bigfoot is concerned, we have virtually no material evidence. Fragments of 'evidence' such as scalps, mummified hands, droppings, scraps of hair and so on, have been produced from time to time, but without exception all have been shown to be either fakes or irrelevancies. The only form of material evidence available to us is footprints, and although they can provide a moderate amount of information, at best they have only a circumstantial value.

The theoretical component of the natural evidence is the matter of ecology. Francis Bacon wrote, 'About Nature, consult Nature herself,' which is sound advice. One rule of nature is that in order to survive, animals must be adapted to the environment in which they live. This is very relevant to the problem of Bigfoot; it provides a theoretical yardstick by which the probability of such a creature living in such-and-such an area can be assessed.

Cultural evidence concerns what people think, write and say about Bigfoot. The material components are the eyewitness accounts which are the real lifeblood of the Bigfoot phenomenon. Without this type of human involvement, the affair would never have got off the ground. Footprints are all very well, but they have relatively little emotive value compared with sightings. However, eyewitness accounts must be treated with considerable caution. Man is too much a slave to his cultural environment to be wholly trusted in matters of this sort. Although we don't always know what we see, we tend to see what we know. The theoretical component of cultural evidence is the role that myth and legend has played – and still plays – in the life of man. What biological purpose, in the widest sense, does it fulfil?

The irrational element in the Bigfoot stories is labelled myth, legend or folktale. Do the tales belong to these categories, or are they simply distortions of natural history? The main question – whether Bigfoot is fantasy or fact – cannot be answered until the evidence has been examined and the probabilities assessed, but whatever the answer, strong elements of fantasy are involved.

On the face of it, the Bigfoot tales do not qualify for a place in the triumvirate of legend, myth or folktale because they are not really tales at all. There are no complicated constructions or sequences of events in the Bigfoot sagas, there is no social purpose, no fulfilment element, no fertility symbolism, no ingenuity or trickery. Bigfoot stories are rather static affairs, in which the narrative style of myth and legend is absent. Sherpas will recount an incident when their father, brother or a cousin met with a Yeti, or when they themselves saw one on the hillside near his village (though the personal experience is rather rare). The nearest approach to the story-line of a legend or a folktale is the unelaborated anecdote of a little girl carried away and reared by a Yeti, or of the grateful Yeti which brought a mountain goat to reward a Sherpa who had removed a thorn from its foot.[2] The poverty of these stories is in striking contrast to the richness of traditional tales from other parts of the world, particularly of Hindu mythology, which is highly elaborate and literate. This state of affairs could indicate either that the tales are a recent development and have therefore not acquired the patina of centuries of re-telling, refinement and elaboration, or that the tales are so close to the truth that they are no more fantastic than the fisherman's tale of the size of the fish that got away: no one suspects the fisherman of inventing the fish, merely of exaggerating its length. Bigfoot tales are a form of folklore which on account of their association with journeying might be called travellers' tales. I see travellers' tales as folktales in the making. I am not in a position to assess their status in academic terms so from now on I shall play safe and use the terms myth, legend and folktale in a non-technical sense.

If Bigfoot should simply be a traveller's tale, then it must be judged entirely on its merits. Do the Bigfoot stories contribute anything to the survival of mankind? As monster 'worship' seems to be an ancient and primitive possession, and a characteristic of human societies of all grades of technological evolution, it is fair to assume that it has some adaptive function, in a Darwinian sense, for human survival. If this is the case, then no rational exposé is going to have the slightest effect on what people need to believe. If myths and legends continue to have survival value for mankind, then myths will continue till the end of time and people will go on believing in the illogical and the irrational, and benefit thereby, and there is nothing that anybody can do about it.

On the other hand, if myths and legends confer no benefit but simply clutter the minds of men with superstitious dogma to the exclusion of more rational thoughts, then perhaps a dispassionate analysis would be not only educational but comforting. The curious part of mythology is that its hold on mankind has apparently little to do with intellectual ability; it permeates all classes and grades of society in one form or another; and it is this universality above all that argues in favour of the Darwinian interpretation that myths and legends are as adaptive for man as his possession of an opposable thumb.

Stories of monsters are universals of time and space. The principal strongholds of contemporary monster myths are the mountains of the northern hemisphere: the Caucasus, the Pamirs, the Tien-Shans, the Altai mountains, the Karakorams, the Kunlun-Shans, the Himalayas and the Kailas range. In North America the coastal ranges of British Columbia and the north-west United States, the Cascade Mountains, the mountains of Guatemala in Central America, the Colombian Massif and the Guyana Highlands in South America are splendid breeding-grounds for monster myths. In this book I shall be concentrating principally on the monsters of the Himalayas and North America, although various other monsters and 'wild men of the woods' will not be totally ignored.

Supposing the Bigfoot story to be wholly mythical, then there is no reason why even as a myth Bigfoot should not be sub-divided into several types. For instance, the three types of Cyclopes recognized in classical Greek mythology are: (i) Cyclopes that built the walls of Mycenae, (ii) Polyphemus and his like and (iii) Cyclopes that made the thunderbolts for Zeus. Alternatively, supposing that the Bigfoot stories are based on events that actually took place in the past, then a classification into types is quite understandable. Finally, if the tales are derived from the misidentification of a living animal, it is likely that several creatures are involved.

Ivan T. Sanderson,[3] a writer and zoological scientist with many years' field experience of primates and other animals, classifies four groups of man-like monsters which collectively he refers to as A.B.S.M.s It is a formidable array, an eye-opener for anyone who imagines that the Yeti of the Himalayas is the only manifestation of the genre:

1 Sub-humans, of central and eastern Asia, e.g. Almas

2 Proto-pigmies, of Asia, Africa and South America, e.g. Teh-lma, Duendi, Sedapa, Orang-Pendek of Sumatra and Agogue of East Africa

3 Neo-Giants, of Indochina, Asia, North and South America, e.g. the Dzu-teh of the Himalayas and Tibet

4 Sub-hominids, of central Asia, e.g. the Meh-teh (the Yeti) of the Himalayas and Tibet.

It rather makes the mind boggle that there should be a whole *Systema Naturae* of unknown, living monsters, as is suggested by Sanderson's classification. However, Sanderson wisely presents his classification in the form of a simple list, eschewing the obvious dangers of a formal zoological check-list which would have involved him deeply in the problems of present and past zoological relationships. He uses common regional names to identify types, and avoids the ultimate crime in systematic zoology of providing a Latin name for an animal of which there is no formally designated type-specimen.

Later in this chapter I shall be discussing, briefly, the Sedapa or Orang-Pendek of Borneo, the Orang-Dalam of Malaysia, the Agogue of East Africa, the Duendi of the Colombian Andes and the Almas of central Asia. These creatures, which belong to Sanderson's first two categories, come under the heading of 'wild men of the woods'; they are essentially human. The Yeti and the Sasquatch, however, are altogether too big, too bizarre, too remote and too ape-like to be anything but nonhuman monsters. This book is really about the Yeti and the Sasquatch, and I shall be using the collective term 'Bigfoot' for both, just as I might use a family name in zoology, such as Felidae (the cats) or Pongidae (the great apes), though to do so is to stretch the correct meaning of 'Bigfoot', which properly applies only to the giants of Northern California.

On the face of it the Yeti is a more attractive subject to investigate than the Sasquatch. Bigfoot in some quarters of North America has become Big Business, a commodity to be exploited to the full. It can no longer be considered simply as a natural phenomenon that can be studied with the techniques of a naturalist; the entrepreneurs have moved in and folklore has become fakelore. For example, in the township of Willow Creek, California, there is an eight-foot statue of Bigfoot carved in redwood in the town centre; each year carnivals are held called 'Bigfoot Daze'; footprints are emblazoned on the sidewalks and Bigfoot ashtrays and Bigfoot rings are for sale in every local tourist trap. All towns cash in on their favourite sons, if they can scrape one up. One only has to think of Stratford-on-Avon, for instance, or Nottingham, where the Robin Hood Fish Bar holds pride of place. Naturalists don't expect to have to contend in the field with professional publicists and carnival showmen; indeed, by their training, they are exceedingly ill-equipped to do so.

Although this fakelore element tends to destroy faith in the Sasquatch, I have no doubt whatsoever that some of the testimonies of eyewitnesses from the American Pacific seaboard are both truthful and zealous. As I well know, there are sincere and accomplished investigators like Rene Dahinden, John Green, Jim Mclarin and Peter Byrne, to name but a few, whose opinions are worth listening to and whose integrity is beyond doubt. It is not so much that I question the veracity of the hundreds of eyewitnesses as that I mistrust the ambiance in which they live. Man tends to perceive the conceivable and there must be few citizens of the states concerned who are not indoctrinated by the news-media with the image of what they should be on the look-out for.

The name 'Bigfoot' derives from the dimensions of the most consistent item of objective evidence in the whole curious story — the footprints. These range in length from eight inches to at least twenty inches, but it is their width, above all, that justifies the epithet: imagine a footprint *twice* the length of the human average and *three times* its width.

Usually monsters have certain basic characteristics apart from size. First, they hail from uncharted territory: inaccessible mountains, impenetrable forests, remote Pacific islands, the depths of loch or ocean — even the centre of a maze. Whether they are called Abominable Snowmen, Sasquatches, Kaptars, Dzu-tehs, Meh-tehs, Yetis, Almas, Cyclopes, Minotaurs or just plain ogres, is immaterial; the essential element of the monster myth is remoteness.

Monsters are usually ugly. Monsters are always big. We are constantly being persuaded (by big men, of course) that bigness is strength, bigness is fitness and it is the big that survive; that bigness is power, influence, and value for money. The Western world is enjoined to respect Bigness and ignore quality. But for all this, our attitude towards bigness is ambivalent; we both fear and admire it. On the one hand we are delighted when bigness is overthrown, be it the small and good overcoming the big and bad (David and Goliath) or the small and female overcoming the big and male (Samson and Delilah) or simply Man putting a monster in its place (St George and the dragon). It gives us great satisfaction to see financial barons topple, commercial empires dissolve, bosses dismissed, boxing champions knocked out and the World Cup winners soundly beaten. On the other hand, man seems to admire the big instinctively: the tall man is often esteemed without regard to his capabilities, the tall building attracts our admiration, and the large animals—the elephants, whales and giraffes—our benevolence. We both love and hate large size, depending on whether or not it constitutes a threat to our survival. If we are confused, it is because the choice between loving and hating is not subject to absolute rules, but is purely a value judgment. I believe our attitude towards legendary monsters is equally ambivalent. We laugh at them and we fear them, we love them and we hate them, but overall, in a curious way, we respect them simply for being monstrously big.

Finally, monsters must be 'undiscovered'. Discovery seems to ruin their piquancy. The case of the gorilla is a good example. It has been said that if someone hadn't found the gorilla, mankind would have had to invent it.[4] Actually, of course, the gorilla was invented long before it was discovered; it is the prototype of all man-like monsters. First seen by a white man in the nineteenth century (though reports of its existence had been circulating for two hundred years before that), it was endowed with the traditional monster image: horrendous, aggressive and sexually rapacious. The most recent and famous contributions to the gorilla myth are of course the Tarzan books of Edgar Rice Burroughs and the classic movie of the 'thirties, *King Kong*. In the former, as Vernon Reynolds[5] points out, the malevolence and exaggerated sexuality of the male gorilla provide a counterpoint to the reason, altruism and self-control of man. In the latter, there are signs of the dawning realization that the gap between man and the gorilla, man's closest zoological kin, is not absolute: King Kong was shown to possess a modicum of pure love and altruism.

Then the myth was exposed to scientific investigation, and the whole edifice crumbled. The infinitely less titillating reality is that the gorilla is a mild-mannered, man-fearing vegetarian that snoozes away the daylight hours and lives in peaceful coexistence with its neighbours of the African rain forest. George Schaller, an American zoologist, spent nine months observing the gorilla first hand in the wild; his book[6] swept away the last of our myth-oriented illusions. And as if to test the legend of the gorilla to its limits, a young Californian scientist, Dian Fossey, recently spent two years living in the closest intimacy with mountain gorillas in the area of the Virunga Volcanoes in East Africa.

Wildernesses are the legendary milieu of monsters, but they have to be a special kind of wilderness in order to qualify. The essential ingredient is mountains, but as most mountains are forested on their lower slopes and foothills, forests too have a prominent place in the legend. Lowland forests constitute a milieu in their own right, although they are relatively impoverished in monster fauna. The monsters of lowland forests are less monstrous, more human than the montane forms. Perhaps the best known of the lowland forests legends is that of the mischievous, gremlin-like Orang-Pendek of Borneo and Sumatra, often called the Sedapa. Sedapas are small, man-like, bipedal creatures between 2 ft. 6 in. and 5 ft. in height. It is said that their skin is pinkish-brown, that their bodies are covered with dark hair and that the head-hair is thick and long, providing a sort of mane which trails down the back. Sedapas are supposed to walk with their feet reversed, with the toes pointing backwards and with their narrow pointed heels directed forwards. The back-to-front foot is a classical myth-motif that occurs time and time again in both wild-men and monster legends. The trait of reversed feet occurs in the Yeti and Sasquatch stories, in the tales of hairy red men of the West African Ivory Coast and, as Kirtley[7] points out, in Irish and Swiss folklore and in the tales of the forest spirits of the Philippines and of the Tupi Forests of the Brazilian littoral. Narrow heels, also a familiar theme, are almost a guarantee that the inscriber of the footprints was not human, because if there is one universal character of the human bipedal foot it is that the heel is broad.

Unidentifiable footprints undoubtedly *are* to be seen in Bornean forests. John MacKinnon, an Oxford University graduate student of primate ethology studying the orang-utan in its natural habitat, has described to me footprints he has seen on several occasions. They are small (6 in. or so in length), broad and with relatively narrow heels. The footprints are too large for any local bear and too small for any local human resident. Whatever they are, they are there, and they require an explanation.

In contrast to the man-like forms of the lowland forests of Sumatra, which are small and innocent, we have the attestation of Lord Medway, a tropical zoologist, that larger and less cosy creatures are reputed to exist in the mountains of central Borneo. While climbing the Keling Kang Mountains on the Sarawak-Kalimantan boundary, Medway heard reports from many native sources of the existence of a bipedal primate having characteristics similar to those of the alleged Yeti of the Himalayas, including its 'gallon-sized' footprints. Medway, with his tongue firmly in his cheek, asked the editor of *The Times*, in whose columns the report appeared in 1960, whether the creature 'could be conspecific with Yeti in view of the fact that high mountain tops in Borneo frequently harbour the relict forms of Himalayan affinity'. Be that as it may, the point is well taken that according to the Alice-in-Wonderland rules of myth and legend, montane monsters differ zoologically from their lowland forest counterparts.

An apparent exception to this generalization is the Orang-Dalam of Malaysia, whose footprints have recently been photographed near the head-waters of the Endau river in southern Malaysia, an area of dense tropical rain forest.[8] The dimensions of the prints are stated to have been 16 in. by 8 in. Native accounts describe this jungle monster as being between 6 ft. and 10 ft. high, having a hairy body and bloodshot eyes, and as giving off an offensive smell. The size and general characteristics of the Orang-Dalam seem to tally with the mountain-living Yeti and the Sasquatch rather than with the Sedapa of the Sumatran and Bornean forests. The Orang-Dalam has certain claims to monster-status, but there is still very little information to go on. Other Malaysian reports of 'wild men of the woods' are of quite a different calibre and concern sightings of medium-sized and essentially human creatures, which could possibly be representatives of some of the primitive tribes of the Malay Peninsula described by Skeat and Blagden.[9]

Less well known 'wild men of the woods' are the Agogues of East Africa, which are human-like, pigmy forms with longish arms, shortish legs and hairy red-brown bodies. They seem to be of a mischievous rather than a menacing nature, and akin to the legendary sprites of temperate and boreal forests such as leprechauns, goblins, brownies, elves and fairies. The Duendi of the Colombian Andes, who 'like that very Mab' plait the manes of horses in the night, belong to the same school.[10] First-hand experience with the Duendi is related in a long-forgotten epic, *Tschiffley's Ride*, written in the early 'thirties by an English schoolmaster. However, as my purpose in this book is to concentrate on monsters rather than on 'wild men', I don't propose to consider these creatures in detail.

Forest monsters with one or two exceptions, it seems, are essentially little men who may have certain sinister connotations but lack the ogreish, nightmare-like, killer qualities of the hominoid monsters of the mountain wildernesses. Remoteness as a myth criterion becomes less necessary as the subjects themselves become smaller in stature and thus less obtrusive. The Sedapa, the Duendi and the Agogue are the modern counterparts of the wild men of the woods, whose existence was accepted by science up to three hundred years ago. Linnaeus (1707-78), the great Swedish naturalist and father of modern classificatory zoology, placed 'wild men', along with true men, with the apes and monkeys. Since monster buffs claim that Linnaeus knew what he was talking about ('They don't make scientists like *that* nowadays'), it is worth digging a little more deeply into the background of Linnaeus's classification.

In a book published in 1613 called *Purchas, his Pilgrimage*, Purchas recounts the adventures of one Andrew Battell of Leigh in Essex, who lived for many years in the Kingdom of Congo (now Gabon) and was familiar with 'a kinde of Great Apes, if they might be so termed, of the height of a man but twice as bigge in features of their limmes with strength proportionable, hairie all over, otherwise altogether like men and women in the whole bodily shape'.

We recognize this as a well-observed description of a gorilla, not exaggerated in any respect. But to readers who had never heard of the gorilla (it was not officially discovered until two hundred years later) this account must have struck a note of sheer fantasy. Had people been familiar even with the much smaller chimpanzee, Andrew Battell's account might have been the more believable, but the chimpanzee was unknown in England until 1699.

It is not hard for us to imagine the controversy that must have surrounded the report of huge, hairy, man-like forms of Herculean strength living in the wildernesses of Africa, because we are familiar with the same reports issued in slightly different form today. In its apparently 'outrageous' exaggeration of the facts, Andrew Battell's account of the African gorilla recalls the eyewitness reports of Himalayan Yeti and North American Sasquatch. Are these creatures fact or folklore? A few people were, no doubt, asking this question three hundred years ago, but the great majority—scientists along with the rest—were still under the influence of the commonplace acceptance in medieval times of 'wild men of the woods'. As Bernheimer[11] put it, 'medieval literature is shot through with the mythology of the wild men', and they frequently appear in the art of the period. These creatures were essentially men, though not necessarily human beings; they were curiously compounded of human and animal traits ' ... *without sinking to the level of an ape*' (my italics). In this comment, I believe, is to be found the real difference between monsters and 'wild men'; the former may take a variety of bestial shapes but the latter remain essentially man-like. The three characteristics of medieval 'wild men' were that they were excessively hairy, they carried a heavy club and their genitals were concealed by a twisted wreath of foliage (a characteristic, incidentally, of the present-day wild men of Malaysia, who are reputed to wear a loincloth of bark). Seen in the light of contemporary thought, Linnaeus was simply expressing the then-current belief in the existence of these twilight forms.

We can draw an analogy between Linnaeus's position and that of contemporary scientists. The great American zoologist George Gaylord Simpson in 1945 included the treeshrews in his classification of the primates. At that time Simpson was persuaded by anatomical evidence that this reflected the zoological truth. More recent studies of treeshrews have cast doubt on Simpson's designation and, in the view of many experts today, treeshrews are *not* primates. The evidence is still equivocal, but in a hundred years' time when, for the sake of argument, the case for the non-primate nature of treeshrews is proven beyond a shadow of doubt, Simpson and those like myself who followed his lead might be looked upon as extremely naive and credulous taxonomists.

The point is that scientists must base their conclusions on what is currently known; they are no better than their sources of information. And those who claim that Linnaeus was a visionary who knew a good monster when he saw one are merely underwriting ignorance for their own ends. Linnaeus had never seen an ape (with the possible exception of a dissected chimpanzee), let alone a mythical 'wild man'. His mention of *Homo troglodytes* (synonymous with *Homo nocturnus* and *Homo sylvestris*) does not, as has been suggested, confirm the existence of these creatures, it only underlines the paucity of information available to him at the time. Bigfoot devotees are forever quoting ancient Eastern

manuscripts, and triumphantly waving primitive woodcuts purporting to provide evidence that Bigfoot exists today. Why
should one imagine that writers and artists of the distant past
were any less imaginative than their counterparts today? Will
H. G. Wells's dreams of interplanetary travel be taken, in the
future, as evidence of their reality in the early twentieth century?
And will the paintings of Salvador Dali be paraded as proof that
even in those far-off days the ancients knew how to make flexible
watches?

The scientific confusion in the early days between the real and
the mythical is epitomized in the term 'satyr-apes', coined by
Edward Topsell in 1607 to describe a certain unidentified but
lascivious breed of monkeys with human bodies and long curved
penises in a state of permanent erection. Zoology as a science is
now relatively free of such hotch-potches. A similar confusion
between the real and the imaginary is found in the ancient
Chinese manuscripts dating back to the Chou Dynasty in 200 B.C.,
when the *Erh-ya*—an early form of dictionary—was composed.
This work appeared in illustrated form in A.D. 1200, and was re-
published in 1801 and, in 1929, in Japan. Five primates are listed
in the *Erh-ya*: Ch'u-fu, Hsing-hsing, Fei-fei, Wei and Nao-yuan.
The last two animals, according to Van Gulik,[12] are easily identifi-
able as the snub-nosed langur of Szechwan (*Rhinopithecus*) and the
gibbon (*Hylobates*) respectively. The descriptions of the first
three primates, however, have an incredibly familiar ring about
them. What is more, they are montane forms—mountain
monsters, as Van Gulik calls them—our kind of monster, in fact.

The Ch'u-fu has many features of the macaque monkey,
including a quadrupedal gait and a short tail. In the 1885 edition
of the *Pen-ts'ao-Kang-mu*, the great Chinese *Materia Medica*, the
following embellishments appear: the Ch'u-fu live in independent male and female groups which waylay humans (male or
female, as the case may be) and mate with them. They live in the
Ch'ung-wu mountains, are ape-like, with long arms, and they
throw things. The Hsing-hsing are small, and their call is like the
cry of a child; they are said to have a human face and the body of

a pig, and are capable of speech. Furthermore—and this is where the mythological links of the past and present reveal themselves— the Hsing-hsing is very fond of wine. The following is a quotation from Van Gulik's translation of a passage in the *Pen-ts'ao-Kang-mu*:

> The aborigines of Feng-hsi put wine and straw sandals by the roadside. When the Hsing-hsing see these, they will first call the names of the ancestors of the people who place the things there, then all of them will drink the wine in a group, and put on the sandals. In this manner they can be caught, and they can be kept in a cage.

This ancient device is a current motif of Nepalese mythology (see chapter 2), and according to Kirtley crops up all over the world.

The *Erh-ya* describes the Fei-fei as resembling both man and the orang-utan. It has a human face, long hair hanging down its back, it runs swiftly and it devours people. The *Erh-ya* emphasizes the creature's 'long lips', which Van Gulik interprets as a reference to the protrusile lips of the orang-utan. As we shall see in later chapters, this interpretation is not without interest. The Fei-fei beautifully demonstrates the confusion between fantasy and reality that is so typical of early descriptions of monkeys and apes. Apart from the characteristics already referred to, this giddy creature was said to be ten foot tall and—mark this —*to have feet that were directed backwards*. This last item is as I have said a classic of folklore, and can be traced back to its first mention in A.D. 863. Its most recent expression was in 1915, when Dr H. J. Elwes presented a paper at the Zoological Society of London on behalf of a forestry officer in Sikkim, J. R. P. Gent, who solemnly reported this explanation for some elongated tracks that his men had seen.

Mythical creatures *have* turned up in real life: the unicorn (the Arabian oryx?) and the dragon (the Komodo lizard?) for example. The gorilla, as we have seen, is the folk-figure come to life, but as myth and reality merged, the classic myth-motifs were shown up for what they were: romantic embellishments. The story of the gorilla is the very essence of myth—except for one thing: it happens to exist. It is perhaps with this model in mind that we should approach the problem of Bigfoot.

The devotees of the Bigfoot legend (and there are no more dedicated buffs, except possibly for the followers of U.F.O.s) are always reminding us that yesterday's myths are today's scientific discoveries. The pigmy hippotamus, the okapi and the mountain gorilla, the Komodo lizard, the giant panda, Gee's golden langur, *Rhinopithecus*, the snub-nosed langur of China, and *Pan paniscus*, the pigmy chimpanzee of Africa, are examples of mammals discovered in the last one hundred and fifty years. But of these only Gee's langur and the pigmy chimpanzee are discoveries of the last fifty years, and only one—Gee's langur—has been officially recognized as a new species in the last quarter of a century. The list of newly discovered mammals declines in diminishing progression as time marches on. So the idea that the patterns of past discovery can be adduced to explain the reality of present zoological enigmas is not really on. Inevitably, the world is shrinking as more people travel to more and more outlandish places. Certainly, wilderness, the traditional home of monsters, will continue to exist in the guise of National Parks. They may remain unspoiled, in the sense that litter baskets are outlawed, but they will not be untravelled. As every year passes and the net closes, it becomes harder to understand why no monsters have been captured, in spite of the numerous expeditions set up for this specific purpose; why evidence of skulls and bones is so singularly absent; and why Exhibit A—be it a mound of dung, a mummified hand, a switch of hair, or even a Yeti scalp—when sent to the laboratories for expert analysis turns out to be something quite different. These are the questions that intelligent people ask. Yetis and Sasquatches are not small creatures; far from it. They cannot simply duck under the nearest rock or fallen log to escape detection. The plethora of tracks that they leave behind them does not argue that they are either an intelligent or a cunning quarry, nor for that matter that they are a very shy one.

Time is running out for unknown animals as civilization closes in. We must find them soon or otherwise there won't be anywhere left to look: 'As the last unclimbed mountains are scaled, the homes of the Gods disappear.'[13]

2. *Bigfoot in Asia*

Thanks to military and Indian Civil Service pioneers in the last century, and the high mountaineers in this, the eastern Himalayas are better known than most of the other mountain ranges where monster myths are prevalent. It seems incredible that one can include in this generalization the mountains of British Columbia and the north-western seaboard of the United States, but I believe it to be true. Lacking the high mountains to be climbed and the grand variety of fauna to be exterminated, the coastal ranges of the North American continent in the boreal and temperate latitudes offer few incentives for exploration. Hunting is poor and the trapping difficult. There are few access roads, and owing to the dense and non-nutritious nature of the forests, the mountains provide no great challenge in terms of rare fauna. Finally, there are no pilgrims: there is little spiritual credit to be gained from trekking from Eureka, California, to Butte, Montana, to Vancouver or to Fort St John. In the later years of the nineteenth century there were many who did so, in the search not for a Mecca but for an Eldorado, but their sights were set on minerals, not mammals. The only citizens who have reason to enter these unknown areas today are the roadmakers and the loggers. Where there are no rivers, the only economic way of making a logging concession pay is to build a road, or at least a dirt track, to haul out the timber. But loggers are not David Thompsons or Lewises and Clarks. The track carved out by their bulldozers usually defines the limits of their territorial inquisitiveness. (It would seem that Sasquatch is more inquisitive than *Homo sapiens*, for the saga of the Bigfoot of the American north-west is peppered with tales of footprints discovered in the neighbourhood of road-building and logging encampments.)

But Tibetans, Sherpas, Hindu pilgrims, mountaineers, and that

34

most ubiquitous of all explorers, now extinct, the British big-game hunter, travelled extensively in the Himalayas. In the late nineteenth and the early twentieth century the Indian Civil Service and the British Army seem to have been exceptionally generous in granting leave to their senior employees, who were forever taking off on protracted hunting trips to the Himalayas and the Karakorams. One account of such a trip in the eighteen nineties by S. J. Stone, a Deputy Inspector-General of Police in the North-West Territories, reveals that even on holiday the British Raj was imbued with a stern sense of duty and an implacable belief in the virtues of corporal punishment: 'The birching I had given the coolies a few hours previously had put so much life in them that they had gone straight ahead without a halt.'[1]

Our knowledge of the geography and ecology of these areas owes much to these men, who underwent considerable hardship in the process of finding out. Stone describes one incident with classic British understatement: benighted at 14,000 feet, he settled down on a rocky ledge, tucked under his blankets and covered with a waterproof sheet. He had not been asleep for long when ' ... I was brought back to a sense of my awkward position by snowflakes falling on my face. My faithful umbrella that usually formed part of my pillow, saved my head ... While I was speculating on the probable depth [of snow] that would cover me by morning I fell asleep again ... fear lest my good umbrella should vanish in an extra strong gust prevented sound sleep.' Umbrellas, as well as a stern sense of duty, were clearly essential to such excursions, which today would not be undertaken without the most expensive of down-filled sleeping-bags and the best of nylon tents, to say nothing of oxygen-cylinders close to hand.

It is worthy of note that the big-game hunters of the early years of this century, such as Major C. H. Stockley, Colonel G. Burrard and Colonel A. E. Ward, never saw anything resembling a Yeti. All three wrote books about their adventures and reported faunal sightings in minutest detail; they recounted the shooting of a great variety of known and unknown Himalayan mammals; but never once in their accounts did they give a hint of a Yeti—a suspicious track or an ominous footprint. This negative evidence is important, for these men were expert big-game hunters and were accompanied by experienced *shikaris* and would assuredly have been keeping a sharp look-out for strange animals or an unusual spoor. Perhaps they were travelling in the wrong areas; perhaps their peregrinations were at too low an altitude; perhaps, being soldiers and government officials and anxious to preserve the respect of their colleagues back in the plains, they saw but said nothing. Or, again, perhaps there was nothing to see.

My chronological survey of Bigfoot in the Himalayas starts with the first mention of the Yeti myth in Western literature. It occurs in an article by B. H. Hodgson published in 1832.[2] Hodgson, who was the British Resident at the court of Nepal from 1820 to 1843, reports that his native hunters who were collecting specimens in the northern province of Nepal were frightened by a wild man which they called a *rakshas*, which is a Sanskrit word for a demon. Hodgson was somewhat scornful that his hunters had run away in terror from the creature instead of standing their ground and shooting it dead like a true British sportsman. Had they done so perhaps this book would never have needed to be written! The creature that Hodgson's porters saw walked erect, was tailless and covered in long dark hair. Hodgson considered that his porters had seen an orang-utan.

In 1889 in north-eastern Sikkim Major L. A. Waddell came across large footprints in the snow at 17,000 feet. He was the first European to see and report on the presence of mysterious footprints in the Himalayan snows.[3] Of course, he did not see the Yeti make the tracks; he was simply told by his porters that *what he was looking at were the tracks of the Yeti*. The willingness of the Sherpas to assure travellers that tracks of *any* description discovered in the snow are those of the Yeti is a recurrent theme in the literature of the subject. Such conning appears to be quite without malice aforethought and probably reflects the extreme politeness of the Sherpas, who regard it as excessively bad-mannered to disappoint anyone. In addition, as many authorities report, the Sherpas possess an element of mischievousness and love a good story.[4] There is no denying that the tracks Waddell saw *could* have been those of the Yeti, but without any evidence of the nature of the tracks his sighting must be registered as a 'possible' and not a 'probable'. His place in the annals of Bigfoot rests solely on his courage in espousing what was then, in the eyes of most people, simply a heathen myth.

As a matter of fact, Waddell, a major in the Indian Army Medical Corps, a Doctor of Law and a Fellow of the Linnaean Society, though often quoted in Bigfoot literature as if he was pro-Yeti, was profoundly sceptical of the tales of the hairy men of the snows, as he makes clear in his book *Among the Himalayas*:

> The belief in these creatures is universal among Tibetans, none however of the many Tibetans I have interrogated on the subject could ever give me an authentic case. On the most superficial investigation it always resolved into something that somebody had heard tell of. These so-called hairy wild men are evidently the great yellow snow-bears (*Ursus isabellinus*) which [are] highly carnivorous and often [kill] yaks. (p. 223)

Some twenty-five years after Waddell's experience, J. R. P. Gent, another Briton, a forestry officer working in Sikkim, brought some extraordinary tracks to the attention of the scientific world: 'The peculiar feature is that its tracks are about 18 in.–24 in. long and the toes point in the opposite direction to that in which the animal is moving.' The width of the track was 6 in. Gent went on to say, 'I take it that he walks on his knees and shins instead of on the sole of his foot. He is known as the Jungli-admi or Sogpa.'

Three points about this seemingly fantastic Yeti story are worthy of note. First, of course, Gent did not see the tracks himself but was merely reporting them second-hand from a native informant. Secondly, backward-pointing feet is a wide-spread myth-motif, quoted all over the world in respect of giants and hairy wild-men. And thirdly, the term *Jungli-admi*, or 'wild men of the woods', seems to remove this report altogether from the realms of Yeti folktales. The Jungli-admi were undoubtedly humans. Colonel Stockley in *Stalking in the Himalayas and Northern India* (1936) refers to his casual coolie labour as Jungli. Major-General Macintyre in his book *Hindu-Koh* (1889) tells of a primitive, much persecuted group inhabiting the forests and foothills of northern Kashmir and Nepal called the Jungli-admi, well-known to the British authorities.

The next major event in the saga of the Himalayan Bigfoot was the arrival of the high mountaineers. This was when things really started to perk up. Not so much because the mountaineers were particularly interested in the Yeti, but because mountaineering exploits, however trivial, have always been highly newsworthy. Lieutenant-Colonel C. K. Howard-Bury, leader of the first Everest Reconnaissance Expedition in 1921, saw human-like foot-prints on Lhakpa-La at between 20,000 and 21,000 feet. Here again the uninitiated might gather from reading some of the newspaper accounts of the sightings of the Yeti or its footprints that reputable European explorers are entirely credulous. But let Howard-Bury's own words put his view in its proper perspective:

Even at these heights [between 20,000 and 21,000 feet] we came across tracks in the snow. We were able to pick out tracks of hares and foxes, but one that at first looked like a human foot puzzled us considerably. Our coolies at once jumped to the conclusion that this must be 'The Wild Man of the Snows', to which they gave the name of Metoh-kangmi, the Abominable Snowman who interested the newspapers so much. On my return to civilized countries I read with interest delightful accounts of the ways and customs of this wild man whom we were supposed to have met. These tracks, which caused so much comment, were probably caused by a large 'loping' grey wolf, which in the soft snow formed double tracks rather like those of a barefooted man. Tibet, however, is not the only country where there exists a bogey man. In Tibet he takes the form of a hairy man who lives in the snows, and little Tibetan children who are naughty and disobedient are frightened by the wonderful fairy tales that are told about him. To escape from him they must run down the hill, as then his long hair falls over his eyes and he is unable to see them. Many other such tales have they with which to strike terror into the hearts of bad boys and girls.[5]

The report that really got the whole thing moving was the account published in 1925 by N. A. Tombazi, a British photographer of impeccable reputation and a Fellow of the Royal Geographical Society, no less.[6] Tombazi's sighting in the region of the Zemu Glacier at an altitude of 15,000 feet and at 300 yards' distance is worth recording in some detail:

The intense glare and brightness of the snow prevented me from seeing anything for the first few seconds; but I soon spotted the 'object' referred to, about two to three hundred yards away down the valley to the east of our camp. Unquestionably, the figure in outline was exactly like a human being, walking upright and stopping occasionally to uproot or pull at some dwarf rhododendron bushes. It showed up dark against the snow and, as far as I could make out, wore no clothes. Within the next minute or so it had moved into some thick scrub and was lost to view.

Such a fleeting glimpse, unfortunately, did not allow me to set the telephoto-camera, or even to fix the object carefully with the binoculars; but a couple of hours later, during the descent, I purposely made a detour so as to pass the place where the 'man' or 'beast' had been seen. I examined the footprints which were clearly visible on the surface of the snow. They were similar in shape to those of a man, but only six to seven inches long by four inches wide at the broadest part of the foot. The marks of five distinct toes and of the instep were perfectly clear, but the trace of the heel was indistinct, and the little that could be seen of it appeared to narrow down to a point. I counted fifteen such footprints at regular intervals ranging from one-and-a-half to two feet. The prints were undoubtedly of a biped, the order of the spoor having no characteristics whatever of any imaginable quadruped. Dense rhododendron scrub prevented any further investigations as to the direction of the footprints, and threatening weather compelled me to resume the march. From enquiries I made a few days later at Yoksun, on my return journey, I gathered that no man had gone in the direction of Jongri since the beginning of the year.

Tombazi's sighting and footprint possibly referred to a bear. The dimensions and the indistinct *narrow* heel-print suggest as much.

The 'thirties produced a handful of footprints and one alleged sighting. The personalities involved in the footprints are enough to make any keen student of mountaineering face the east and bow three times. Names like Eric Shipton, F. S. Smythe, H. W. Tilman, Sir Edmund Hillary and John (now Lord) Hunt and, finally, the noted anthropologist Prince Peter of Greece and Denmark, added weight to the meagreness of the evidence. Prince Peter's contribution was, in fact, neither a sighting nor a track, but a folktale. He recounts an incident, only too familiar to students of mythology, where a Yeti was captured by the villagers of the Jalap-La Valley in north Sikkim by the simple expedient of placing a bucket of fermented liquor, or *chang*, in its path. After drinking, the creature passed out, and was easily captured and tied up. Needless to say, he had escaped before morning. A similar tale crops up at least twice more in Yeti folklore and parallels the familiar themes of European and Chinese legend; the same tale is also found in classical Greco-Roman mythology.

The alleged sighting was an extraordinary event. Said to have taken place in 1938 or thereabouts, it was 're-issued' in 1959,[7] and concerned a Captain d'Auvergne, the curator of the Victoria Memorial, the unforgettable piece of Victoriana on the Maidan, bordering Chowringhee in Calcutta. According to the story, this gentleman travelling in the Himalayas, apparently alone, had injured himself and was in danger of succumbing from exposure and snowblindness when he was rescued by an 8 ft.–9 ft. Yeti, carried many miles to the creature's cave, and fed and nursed to complete recovery. He was then released and returned to civilization where, *inter alia*, he wrote an article for a research society journal[8] indicating that his saviour was a human, a survivor from prehistoric ages, a descendant of an oppressed minority group called A-o-re who had taken to the mountains and gone to seed, acquiring gigantic proportions and a number of bestial adaptations in the process. This fabulous tale has certain points of interest. First the A-o-re people of d'Auvergne's account recall the race of Tibetan ascetics described by Pater Franz Eichinger, a German doctor and missionary, as inhabitants of many remote areas in Tibet living in caves at altitudes between 10,000 and 20,000 feet, and capable of enduring intense cold. Eichinger's report and its implications for the Yeti myth are discussed in more detail in a later chapter. The second point of interest in d'Auvergne's story is that his 'rescue' has some parallels with the tale of Albert Ostman's 'abduction' by a Sasquatch discussed in chapter 3.

Perhaps the most sensational report to come out of the Himalayas, of an incident that took place in February 1942, is unfortunately the most dubious of all. It appears in *The Long Walk*, by Slavomir Rawicz. The report is suspect because Rawicz's account of his escape with six friends from a Siberian prisoner of war camp, and of his eventual crossing of the Himalayas to freedom in India, is regarded by many experts as a work of fiction. Both Blakeney and Shipton raised serious doubts and misgivings about the veracity of the book in their separate reviews.[9] Taking a few of their objections in a geographically systematic fashion, we can formulate a series of questions:

1. How is it possible for human beings in an already prison-weakened condition to cross the Gobi Desert under a scorching sun for eight days with a little food but without water; to be

followed after a brief respite at an oasis by a twelve-day slog without either water *or* food?

2. Is it conceivable that a group of men, after months of privation and complete divorcement from the contacts of civilization, should cross a highway (Umruchi to Lanchow) busy with traffic, and neither mention it nor, if they came upon it, await a passing truck which would have solved their problems? According to both reviewers, Rawicz and his men *must* have crossed this road.

3. How does one account for the discrepancies in the journey from the River Tsangpo (upper reaches of the Bramaputra) to the main Himalayan range? Shipton estimates that this journey, based on Rawicz's estimate of the speed of their march, should have taken a mere matter of five days; yet, according to Rawicz's account, the journey lasted for two months.

4. Is it conceivable that between the River Tsangpo and the main east–west Himalayan mountain axis, Rawicz and his friends neither saw nor heard human beings? This area is not a total wilderness, but is fairly well endowed with villages.

5. Once over the Tibet–Nepal or Bhutan frontier (the narrative does not specify which), a few days' march would have brought the escapees, providing they were following caravan tracks, to a number of villages where they could have obtained food. If they were *not* following defined routes, then they were probably wallowing along through steep-cliffed gorges filled with luxuriant tropical vegetation which would surely have elicited a comment from men escaping from the snowfields and tundras of Siberia; but not a word of such an environment appears in the book.

What is one to believe about Rawicz's book? It is a superbly told story of human endurance. But its weakness lies in the popular misconception that Tibet and Nepal are total wildernesses where one may wander for months without making human contact. The population of Nepal is nine million, and that of Tibet, one and a half million.

This is the backdrop against which the following extract from

The Long Walk must be viewed. Rawicz and his companions were in the process of crossing the Himalayas somewhere between Bhutan and Sikkim when they were held up for two hours or so by the sight of two creatures blocking their path:

The contours of the mountain temporarily hid them from view as we approached nearer, but when we halted on the edge of a bluff we found they were still there, twelve feet or so below us and about 100 yards away. Two points struck me immediately. They were enormous and they walked on their hind legs. The picture is clear in my mind, fixed there indelibly by a solid two hours of observation. We just could not believe what we saw at first, so we stayed to watch ... I set myself to estimate their height on the basis of my military training for artillery observations. They could not have been much less than *eight feet tall*. One was a few inches taller than the other, in the relation of the average man to the average woman. They were *shuffling* quietly round on a flattish shelf which formed part of the obvious route for us to continue our descent. We thought that if we waited long enough they would go away and leave the way clear for us. It was obvious they had seen us, and it was equally apparent they had no fear of us. The American said that eventually he was sure we would see them drop on all fours like bears. But they never did. Their faces I could not see in detail, but the heads were squarish and the ears must lie close to the skull because there was no projection from the silhouette against the snow. The shoulders sloped sharply down to a *powerful chest. The arms were long* and the wrists reached the level of the knees. Seen in profile, the back of the head was a *straight line from the crown into the shoulders*, 'like a damned Prussian', as P. put it. We decided unanimously that we were examining a type of creature of which we had no previous experience in the wild, in zoos or in literature. It would have been easy to have seen them *waddle* off at a distance and dismissed them as either bear or big ape of the orang-outang species. At close range they defied facile description. There was *something both of the bear and the ape* about their general shape, but they could not be mistaken for either. The colour was a *rusty kind of brown.* They appeared to be covered by two distinct kinds of hair — the reddish hair which gave them their characteristic colour forming a tight, close fur against the body, mingling with which were long, loose, straight hairs, hanging downwards, which had a slight greyish tinge as the light caught them ... They were doing nothing but move around slowly together, occasionally stopping to look around them like people admiring a view. Their heads turned towards us now and again, but their interest in us seemed to be of the slightest ... I looked back and the pair were standing still, arms swinging slightly, as though listening intently. What were they? For years they remained a mystery to me, but since recently I have read of scientific expeditions to discover the Abominable Snowman of the Himalayas and studied descriptions of the creature given by native hillmen, I believe that on that day we may have encountered two of the animals. I do insist, however, that recent estimates of their height as about 5 feet must be wrong. The minimum height of a well-grown specimen must be around seven feet (pp. 228–30).[10] [Italics mine.]

In a letter to Dr W. C. Osman Hill, Rawicz added several points to the above description: he remarks on the presence of buttocks, short legs and, rather surprisingly, a 'rounded' chin and a rather conically shaped head. It is difficult to understand how four such salient points should have been omitted from the original description. Unfortunately they complicate the issue even further, because two of them (buttocks and a chin) are human characters, while a conical head and short legs are ape-like. Rawicz also mentions how the creatures stamped and swayed when moving about, a description which evokes the locomotor patterns of neither man nor ape.

At first reading, the published description has a ring of truth about it, but collectively the individual statements do not stand up to critical analysis. The heavy, thick neck, the powerful shoulders and chest and the long arms are the physical features of the African gorilla, as is also the short, plushy fur. Rawicz refers to the gait twice in this extract; once he states that his creatures 'shuffled' and once that they 'waddled'; never, apparently, did they just walk. So far so good, because animals with a super-structure such as Rawicz describes would have a centre of gravity placed high in the body, well above the middle of the pelvis where it lies in modern man. Human walking is a complex business; without discussing it in detail at this juncture it is enough to say that man could neither walk nor stride unless his centre of gravity lay in close horizontal proximity to his hip joints. The inconsistency of Rawicz's story lies in the fact that while creatures with the build that he describes could waddle and shuffle, inevitably they would have had to go down on all fours sooner or later, which is precisely what he states that they *never* did during his two hours' observation. Gorillas and chim-panzees are known to 'knuckle-walk'.[11] Their habitual locomotion on the ground is a form of quadrupedalism in which the weight of the fore part of the body is taken not on the flats of the hands, as in monkeys and most quadrupedal mammals, but on the backs of the fingers, which are bent in the form of a hook. Waddling and shuffling could never conceivably be the habitual gait of a Yeti, even in the Goblin Universe. Such a gait would be totally uneconomic and incompatible with the Yeti's survival in the demanding physical conditions of high altitudes. Furthermore, the prominent buttocks mentioned in Rawicz's letter to Dr Osman Hill are out of place in a creature that shuffles, waddles, stamps and sways.

Whether *The Long Walk* is fact or fiction, or a combination of both, is really immaterial. Rawicz's report is unacceptable on functional grounds. The account would still lack conviction even supposing that what Rawicz saw were two bears. No bear is habitually bipedal; no bear, unless it is a mother with her cubs, is anything but solitary and no bear would be aware of the presence of humans—as these creatures clearly were—and not take to their inadequate heels. It is ironic that the most graphic account of a Yeti yet published should be under suspicion as a work of imagination.

The two other incidents in which Europeans were involved during the 1940s have apparently little to do with the Yeti of the popular folktale. They are interesting, however, because both stories involve langur monkeys, primates that could conceivably have inspired some of the Yeti stories. Langurs, which form part of a subfamily of Old World monkeys widespread in Asia, are called the Colobinae or leaf-eating monkeys. The commonest langur species found in India, Nepal, Sikkim and Bhutan is *Presbytis entellus*, or the Hanuman langur, the true sacred monkey of India. The Hanuman langur, a less aggressive, less predatory and less ubiquitous species than the other common monkey of India, the rhesus monkey, is represented in the Himalayan region by three races: *P. entellus schistaceus*, *P. entellus ajax* and *P. entellus achilles*. All three types are large monkeys weighing up to 46 pounds or more and, like all monkeys and apes, are capable of standing on two legs and even (unlike apes and most monkeys) hopping in this posture for brief periods.

Three army officers *en route* for the Kolahoi Glacier in Kashmir had reached the snowline, some 13,000 feet above sea-level, when they were surprised to see a large animal bounding towards them. It had a tail, a fringe around its face and a hairy coat which was long and reddish-brown in colour. Could they, they asked the editor of *Country Life*, have seen a Yeti? The editor very properly put their minds at rest and told them they had seen a langur (*Presbytis entellus ajax*), and there is no doubt from their description that this is exactly what they had seen. A point of interest here is that 13,000 feet is the greatest altitude yet recorded for langurs (table 4, p. 214), so even if this sighting does not add much to the resolution of the Yeti myth, at least it places langurs firmly on the list of 'possibles'.

The second event involving langurs was said to have taken place in 1948, though it was not reported until 1952. The aptly-named Thorberg and Frostis, Scandinavian prospectors working for the

Indian government, saw strange footprints round their camp which they were able to follow in the direction of the high pass on the border between Nepal and Sikkim called the Zemu-La. Finally, at 19,000 feet, Thorberg and Frostis caught up with a pair of langurs, one of which attacked Frostis and injured him quite severely, necessitating a hasty return to Darjeeling where Frostis was hospitalized. To some experts[12] Thorberg's story has a bogus ring. There are certainly some odd inconsistencies, not least of which is the altitude at which the langurs were seen. There has been no previous record of langurs above 13,000 feet. This fact alone would not be adequate to condemn Thorberg's story, as our knowledge of the altitudinal range of Himalayan mammals is altogether very vague. What is suspicious, however, is the size of the footprints, said to have been 12 in. by 6 in. No langur could produce a single hand- or footprint of these dimensions, so one can only assume that if this tale is true the footprints were composite in nature, consisting of the impressions of fore- and hindfeet superimposed. Even so, the width is unacceptable, for the langur footprint is no more than 2 in. wide, discounting the sideways-displaced big toe. However, it is common knowledge that footprints in snow can become misleadingly large as a result of melting.

Corrado Gini[13] claimed that on the basis of his research the story was a hoax, and Odette Tchernine[14] reports that there are no records that Frostis was ever admitted as a patient in any hospital in Darjeeling. All in all, I think it best that Thorberg's account be placed in the 'pending' tray, along with Rawicz's data, until further evidence of its veracity turns up.

The 1950s were the Golden Age for the Himalayan Bigfoot legend. This was when the folktale took hold of the public imagination in the West and when, I suspect, folklore started to deteriorate into fakelore. Michel Peissel, the archaeologist and explorer,[15] pointed out in 1961 that it was during this period that special licences (at £400 per Yeti) were introduced by the government of Nepal for Yeti hunters. Whether this was a device to coin a fast rupee or to provide an emergency fund for rescue operations is not clear, but nevertheless it indicates that Yeti-hunting was becoming commercialized and a source of national revenue. Official tourist brochures of the period proclaimed that Nepal was 'the land of Mount Everest and the Yeti'.

But it is from the mountaineers and explorers that we get the most lucid accounts of Yeti footprints. Ronald Kaulback is inclined to the theory that the so-called Yeti tracks might have been made by the snow leopard (see table 1, p. 208). Smythe's tracks in the Garwhal Himalaya were studied by R. I. Pocock, F.R.S., and diagnosed as being red bear (*Ursus arctos isabellinus*). Hunt saw his tracks at 19,000 feet while climbing the Zemu Gap. He stated in an interview with Ralph Izzard in 1955 that initially he assumed that the two parallel sets of tracks he had observed belonged to a German climbing team who were in the region at the time; one supposes therefore that they must have looked like *booted* tracks. Later, Hunt found that the Germans had not climbed the pass. His afterthoughts on the matter were that the tracks could not have been man-made, because it is normal practice in deep snow for following humans to walk in the tracks of the leader, in which case the track would have been single. Shipton's, Hunt's and Tilman's tracks were neither photographed nor measured, so there is little useful information to be gained from their accounts except in terms of location. If they saw tracks, there were tracks, and they must have been the tracks of something.

What I believe is the most important piece of evidence in the whole Yeti story came to light in November 1951. The central human figures were Eric Shipton and Michael Ward. The evidence was a giant footprint impressed in snow. Shipton and Ward, returning from the 1951 Everest Reconnaissance Expedition, were exploring the saddle at the head of the Menlung Glacier at 20,000 feet, close to the border between Nepal and Tibet. After negotiating an icefall they crossed the saddle and reached the glacier beyond at four o'clock in the afternoon at an altitude of some 18,000 feet. It was at this point that Shipton and Ward came across a set of fresh tracks in deep snow which they followed for about a mile along the edge of the glacier. As they

1. The giant footprint (13 in. × 18 in.) photographed by Eric Shipton on the Menlung Glacier in 1951 that still remains a complete mystery

2. (*left*) A previously unpublished 'Yeti' track photographed by E. S. Williams in 1956 and probably made by a red bear. (*below*) A track made by a human with a deep sense of scientific dedication. The 'angle of gait' is unusually well marked in this individual

descended the depth of snow diminished, and on the edge of the snowline the prints were seen at their clearest, as the snow covering the glacier ice at this height was little more than one inch deep. Shipton selected what he considered was the sharpest and clearest footprint of the series and took two photographs, one with Ward's booted foot as a scale and another with Ward's ice-axe serving the same function. The photographs were spectacular, and so were the results of their publication. Shipton's photographs, sharply in focus and perfectly exposed, are taken directly above the footprint. The photograph is unique, for it is the only item of evidence of the Yeti saga that offers the opportunity for critical analysis; ironically, however, it is also quite the most enigmatic. The many problems of interpretation of the Shipton print are discussed in chapter 5.

An interesting fact which clears up an eighteen-year-old mystery emerged from a discussion I had with Michael Ward a few years ago. A photograph of a trail of footprints leading across a sloping, rocky, snow-covered surface towards a moraine in the middle distance has appeared in many books written on the Yeti since 1952[16] and has prompted a considerable amount of speculation concerning the nature of the Yeti's gait, the length of the stride and so on. The truth of the matter, according to Michael Ward, and later confirmed by Eric Shipton, is that *the trail has nothing whatever to do with the footprint.* The photograph was taken earlier on the same day and in roughly the same area and was probably the track of a mountain goat; it was certainly not a view of the Yeti track discovered later in the afternoon. The negatives of the trail and the footprint were filed together in the archives of the Mount Everest Foundation and, presumably, this is how the mistake arose.

There is no doubt, too, that the footprint on the Menlung Glacier gave the whole business of the Himalayan Bigfoot an air of scientific respectability. Even the British Museum (Natural History) was stimulated to put on a special exhibit purporting to 'explain' the footprints. Unfortunately, the authorities were ill-advised, and the 'explanation' they provided — that these were the footprints of a langur (*Presbytis entellus achilles*) – caused a great deal of ribaldry. In view of what is known of the altitudinal range of the Himalayan langur, and the impossibility of equating the enormous Shipton footprint (13 in. by 8 in.) with the hands and feet of a monkey whose maximum foot dimensions are 8 in. by 2 in., almost any explanation would have been better than this.[17]

It was around this time that a simple explanation for the appearance of giant tracks in snow began to appear in the literature. It was being said that the melting effect of the hot sun would magnify prints of normal proportions to gigantic dimensions. In general terms, this is a perfectly reasonable suggestion: prints *do* melt and *do* enlarge under the effects of a hot sun, but in such a way that it is quite plain that their size is due to melting (see chapter 5).

A Mr A. Ahad was one of the first to raise the issue of the effect of melting on the size of footprints in snow. In a letter to the Secretary of the Royal Geographical Society (December 20th, 1951) Mr Ahad, a surveyor employed by the Pakistan government, stated that on two occasions he had come across footprints in the snow precisely similar to those of a human being, once on the Thipa Pass and once near the Zemu Glacier. The footprints were 8 in. long and were typical of a biped. They were arranged in a straight line, showing no 'angle of gait' (see plate 2), and they followed one another closely with not more than a few inches in between the heel of one print and the toes of its successor. Some fifteen to twenty days later, when Mr Ahad returned to the area of the second sighting, he found that the prints had melted and joined up together to give the appearance of 'giant' footprints. Norman Hardie[18] describes how giant-sized footprints can be formed by the collapse of the melting snow round the nucleus of the normal-sized print. Pater Franz Eichinger was reported by George Vine in a leading article in the *News Chronicle* (January 21st, 1959) to have expressed similar views.

Eric Shipton has described another form of snow artefact which he calls 'young elephant tracks'. The 'elephant' effect, as I have been able to demonstrate to my own satisfaction by experiment (see chapter 5), tends to occur in freshly fallen loose-packed snow, particularly in the early morning when the surface layers are frozen. As the foot is impressed on the crust, large triangular sections of snow on either side crack and fall inwards, leaving a roughly rhomboidal outline. With subsequent melting, these impressions end up as large holes in the snow which by virtue of their size and circularity might indeed have been made by a young elephant (see plate 5).

Among the dozen or so footprints reported during the 1950s, two are worthy of note if only because photographs of both are available. The Abbé Bordet, a geologist attached to the French Himalayan Expedition of 1955, reported in a scientific journal[19] the discovery of footprints in the Dudh Kosi Valley of Nepal at 12,350 feet. Bordet was on the return trip from Mount Makalu, and the footprints, which were reasonably fresh, comprised a single track and traversed a 30-degree slope. Bordet stated that they were 'similar' to Shipton's. On the face of it this claim lacks conviction.

Bordet's	Shipton's
1. Length 8 in.	1. Length 13 in.
2. Four toes	2. Five toes
3. Inner toe the largest	3. Inner two toes larger than remainder
4. Smaller toes widely separated	4. Smaller toes held together
5. Heel rather narrow	5. Heel exceptionally broad

This comparative table does not tell the whole story. Bordet published a second photograph demonstrating, as he claimed, that the creature had slipped and had thus redoubled and blurred the footprint.

The second footprint discovery, which has not previously been published, was made in the Karakorams by Professor E. S. Williams, now of the Middlesex Hospital Medical School in London. Williams was on one of the tributaries of Biafo Glacier, the Sim Gang, eight miles from the confluence with the Biafo, in early September 1956. The footprints he came across, which were remarkably similar to those discovered by Mr A. Ahad, crossed the glacier in a straight line. Unfortunately light conditions were extremely poor, and Williams's photographs do little more than show the outline of the foot and the broad pattern of a track (see plate 2).

A third incident reported in the 1950s had a very marginal bearing on the central problem, but it is worth quoting as an example of the sort of tantalizing report that, for all one's efforts, simply remains a tantalizing report. The *Daily Telegraph* (November 16th, 1953) published a story that a Mr Parekli, an Indian mountaineer, had stated that a live Yeti was to be seen in the zoo at Shigatse, a town in Tibet. According to Parekli's description, the captive was a stunted creature with a conical head and reddish-brown hair. Mr Parekli later saw a so-called Yeti scalp 'at Thyangboche' [*sic*] which 'partly confirmed' the report. If the zoo exhibit was as artificial as the scalp, which probably came from the monastery at Khumjung a few miles from Thyangboche, then it must have been a sight to see. Conceivably, of course, the stunted creature may simply have been an orang-utan whose colour is reddish-brown and whose head, though not exactly conical, is certainly tall. According to Charles Stonor,[20] the creature was in fact a gibbon.

The 1950s saw the inauguration of several Yeti expeditions. The *Daily Mail* Expedition set off in 1954, and 1957 saw the first of the three expeditions sponsored by the late Tom Slick, a wealthy, philanthropic, liberal-minded oil-millionaire from Texas. The *Daily Mail* Expedition produced two admirable books[21] and some equivocal footprints, but not much else in a material sense, except a Yeti 'scalp' or two.

The Slick-Johnson Expedition in 1957 produced similarly negative, but less widely publicized, results. The goodies brought back by the expedition — the mummified paw of a snow leopard, a mummified human hand and a footprint or two — add up to nothing at all. No single item contributed one jot or tittle of proof to the Himalayan Bigfoot legend. One cannot help but note that with all the aids, resources and scientific expertise at their disposal, the four expeditions set up *for the sole purpose of tracking down and capturing the Yeti* could produce no scrap of real evidence that would persuade the average zoologist or anthropologist to give the matter a second thought.

However, one sighting by a Sherpa called Da Temba is of considerable interest in view of the proposed expeditions to the Arun Valley in 1972. Dyrenfurth[22] reports that Da Temba saw a creature wading in a stream, the Chhoyang Khola. The sighting was at night; the creature was 4 ft. 6 in. tall and it fled when a flashlight was aimed at its face. Gerald Russell, a member of the expedition, found tracks at the site next morning. Dyrenfurth remarks that the presence of at least two kinds of Yeti is established, one that lives in the snows, and another that lives in high altitude rain forests. Dyrenfurth's conclusions are presumptive but, nevertheless, the sighting adds a little backbone to the belief that a small-sized Yeti, the Teh-lma of Sanderson's Proto-pigmy group (see p. 21), exist in the tropical valleys of the Nepal Himalayas.

So far in this chronological survey of Bigfoot in the Himalayas, emphasis has been laid on the sightings and reports by Europeans. This is because sightings by Sherpas, which are apparently almost daily events in some areas, have a timeless, non-specific quality that makes them useless as data. In addition, the narratives are so clearly garnished with traditional folklore themes that the mind tends to reject them out of hand. Possibly this is a case of throwing the baby out with the bathwater.

Norman Hardie quotes a Sherpa telling him, 'we followed the tracks of the two Yeti, they were both females – their breasts were so large they have to throw them over their shoulders before they bend down'. In the same vein, it is a contention among the Sherpas that normally, if chased by a Yeti, a human being can escape by running at top speed *down* a slope. The Yeti are hampered when they try to follow by their long hair which falls over their eyes and blinds them. These tales, and others like the *chang* incident reported by Prince Peter of Greece, and like J. R. P.

Gent's account of backward-pointing feet, are the bathwater. Can one exclude the possibility that there might be a very small infant, embryonic perhaps, mixed up with the soapsuds?

Before I am accused of all sorts of prejudices, let me hasten to quote one sighting by no less a personage than the Abbot of Thyangboche Monastery. It is a modest account, although it was presented, according to John (now Lord) Hunt, in an uninhibited manner. In Hunt's words:

> Seated with Charles Wylie and Tensing [Norgay] beside our host, a rotund figure robed in faded red, I questioned him about the Yeti—better known to us as the Abominable Snowman. The old dignitary at once warmed to this subject. Peering out of the window on to the meadow where our tents were pitched, he gave a most graphic description of how a Yeti had appeared from the surrounding thickets, a few years back in the winter when the snow lay on the ground. This beast, loping along sometimes on his hind legs and sometimes on all fours, stood about five feet high and was covered with grey hair, a description which we have heard from other eyewitnesses. Oblivious of his guests, the Abbot was reliving a sight imprinted on his memory as he stared across at the scene of this event. The Yeti had stopped to scratch—the old monk gave a good imitation, but went on longer than he need have done to make his point—had picked up snow, played with it and made a few grunts—again he gave us a convincing rendering. The inhabitants of the Monastery had meanwhile worked themselves into a great state of excitement, and instructions were given to drive off the unwelcome visitor. Conch shells were blown and the long traditional horns sounded. The Yeti had ambled away into the bush.[23]

This is an *ex cathedra* statement if ever there was one, but, on the other hand, it is a low-key description which could easily fit some other animal—a bear, for instance. The hyperbole that usually colours the tales of the Sherpas is totally lacking. Yet if it was a bear why didn't the Abbot say so? Perhaps it was totally unimportant to him *what* the creature was. What *was* important was the story and its telling. This incident perhaps exposes the very machinery of myth-making.

Incidentally, the traditional Western belief that Sherpas are terrified of Yetis and hold them in religious awe does not appear to be wholly true; the reports are conflicting. Lord Hunt recalls that in 1937, when he and his party came across footprints near the Zemu Gap, the Sherpas were terrified, and in the same year Smythe reported that his porters were 'very frightened'. Again, in 1955, the Abbé Bordet commented on the 'religious fears of his porters'. But according to other accounts the Sherpas have an almost flippant attitude towards the Yeti—reminiscent of the relaxed attitude of residents of Inverness-shire to the Loch Ness Monster. Neither indigene sleep uneasily because of the monsters at the bottom of their gardens. One might expect that it would be a different matter if one were alone on a remote glacier or in a small boat bobbing about in the middle of the loch: indeed, several witnesses in F. W. Holiday's book on the Loch Ness Monster[24] specifically stated their fears on this latter point. However, Professor von Fürer-Haimendorf, who is a noted anthropologist, and an expert on the religious and social customs of the Tibetans, the Sherpas of Nepal and the little-known groups of north-west Indians like the Nagas, found no evidence of fear of Yetis amongst the Sherpas. He told me that Nepalese children of eleven or so spend many days on end in the mountains, quite alone, tending goats or yaks on the high pastures. He expressed the opinion that the Yeti has no religious significance, in our sense, for the Nepalese. The Abbot of Thyangboche's matter-of-fact description of the Yeti he saw recalls G. S. Kirk's discussion of the association of myth and religion.[25] Kirk denies that myth is necessarily associated with the special ecstasy or intensity of feeling that is an essential property of religion. The intensity apparent in the re-telling of myths is inherent in the excitement of the subject matter itself and/or in the histrionic leanings of the teller. The Abbot, Lord Hunt reported, was excited by the telling but showed no particular symptoms of religious fervour for the content.

So-called Yeti scalps have a ritualistic function in the Sherpa dance-dramas, it is true, but this doesn't necessarily make them sacred objects in themselves. This will perhaps surprise those who remember that Sir Edmund Hillary persuaded the elders of the village of Khumjung to allow their 'sacred' Yeti scalp to be removed for study by Western experts. The truth of the matter is that it is highly likely that a 'Yeti' scalp, or any object of interest to the community, whether of religious significance or not, will be kept in a monastery or a temple because these are probably the only public edifices in the village. Thus, by absorption as it were, the scalps acquire a semi-sacred status.

This conflict of opinion over attitudes to the Yeti probably arises out of the very different ideas held by Westerners and the Nepalese as to what constitutes religious significance. Lawrence Swan, the American biologist and experienced Himalayan traveller, has expressed the view that the Sherpa has extreme difficulty in dissociating the 'real' of everyday life from the unreal 'real' of his religious beliefs. One Sherpa, after helping Swan and Marlin Perkins to create a 'sacred Yeti scalp' from goat-skin, seemed to revere the artefact as if it was indeed a holy relic.

The Abbot of Thyangboche provided further evidence that the Yeti is by no means universally regarded with religious awe. According to Michel Peissel he pooh-poohed the Yeti: 'It is a sort of bogeyman that mothers talk about when children misbehave.' Sherpa Tensing Norgay, the conquerer of Everest with Hillary, said in an interview in 1955: 'As Sherpas we are used to hearing from our childhood of stories about Yeti from our older people, and even to this day you will find a naughty child hushed to silence when his mother says to him, "Hish, hish, here comes the Yeti." ' These two rather low-key quotations suggest that the Yeti holds a familiar but relatively unmenacing place in Nepalese and Tibetan folklore, resembling the role of the traditional bugbear of the West.

Now to return to the major sightings by Europeans. The

Hillary Expedition of 1960–61, supported principally by the World Book Encyclopaedia, was conceived primarily as a physiological exercise. Its main purpose was to study the adaptation of climbers to high altitudes; its secondary targets were mountaineering, meteorology, glaciology and Yeti-hunting. Included in the expedition were the physiologists James Milledge and Griffith Pugh, and the zoologists Lawrence Swan and Marlin Perkins (a mammalogist at the St Louis Zoo, Missouri). The climbers included Michael Ward, who was on the 1951 Shipton Reconnaissance Expedition, and Norman Hardie. The journalists were Barry C. Bishop[26] and Desmond Doig.

There are two ways of looking at the results of the Hillary Expedition, depending on which side of the fence one is sitting in the first place. It is possible to see the expedition as a wholly destructive affair, in the course of which giant footprints were shrugged off as the melted remains of a fox's pugmarks, Yeti-skins were unmasked and shown simply to be bear-skins, sacred scalps of the Khumjung and Pangboche Monasteries were debunked as crude artefacts made from the skin of a goat-antelope, and the native folklore of the Sherpas was demonstrated to be nothing more than the ignorant superstition of a backward people. On the other hand, one can see the expedition as a splendid exercise in ghost-laying, in which the presence of giant footprints in snow was shown to be simply the result of the sun melting the superimposed tracks of small quadrupeds, and in which the probability that Yetis were only bears after all was amply demonstrated.

Of course if, like me, you happen to be sitting *on* the fence rather than on one or other side of it, then the Hillary Expedition brought to light a number of very interesting facts:

1. Large footprints can be produced by the melting and blending of smaller footprints lying close together. *Comment:* The signs of melting are so obvious that no one with any experience would confuse a melted footprint with a fresh one. Not all the prints seen over the years by reputable observers can be explained away in these terms; there must be other explanations for footprints,

including, of course, the possibility that they were made by an animal unknown to science.

2. A so-called Yeti-skin was in fact the skin of a blue bear. *Comment:* Although the Sherpas assured Hillary and his team that the bear-skin (a specimen of the rather rare Tibetan blue bear, *Ursus arctos pruinosus*) found in a villager's house close by the monastery at Beding was that of a Yeti, this does not mean that all the sightings of Yeti are of blue bear. According to a number of authorities, the Nepalese recognize two sorts of Yeti: the Dzu-teh and the Meh-teh. The Dzu-teh is a large hairy creature, 8 feet or more in height, that preys on cattle and is aggressive towards human beings. The Meh-teh is a smaller, carnivorous creature with an ape-like appearance that lives in the rocky regions between the treeline and the permanent snow. The Meh-teh walks on two legs and has a high-pitched mewing-yelping call frequently heard by villagers. A third variety, which is not often mentioned, and is outside my present mandate, is the Teh-lma, a pigmy which lives in the forests at the foothills of the Himalayas and is as mischievous as a goblin or a gremlin. All are flesh-and-blood animals and not spirits or demons. The Indian philologist Sri Swami Pranavanandra[27] asserts that the suffix *teh*, *tre* or *dred* means 'bear' in Tibetan, a contention supported by the Tibetan-English dictionary in which the word *dred* is translated as 'the yellow bear'. *Mi* (or *Me*) means 'man', so Meh-teh could mean 'Man-bear'. A different interpretation has been given for the meaning of teh by a philologist Yonah N. Ibn Aharon,[28] who asserts authoritatively that it does not mean 'bear' but 'thing'. Thus Dzu-teh means 'Big thing' and Meh-teh means 'Man-like thing'·

3. The Khumjung scalp flown to London via New York was a curious conical affair, completely covered with dark, coarse, bristly hair and characterized by a hairy keel or skin ridge (plate 7). Reputed to be two hundred and forty years old, and holding an apparently semi-sacred place in the annual dance festival of Mani-Rimdu, the Khumjung scalp was pronounced by scientists from three countries to be fabricated from the skin of a rather rare goat-antelope of the Himalayas called the serow.

Marlin Perkins and Lawrence Swan, the two zoologists of Hillary's expedition, fabricated a 'Yeti' skull-cap from serow-skin for themselves. *Comment:* It is only fair to point out however that while the Khumjung scalp and the one from Pangboche are fabrications, this does not necessarily mean that there was not an original model. A 'real' scalp is said to exist in the monastery at Rongbuk in Tibet, now unfortunately closed to the scalp-hunters of Britain and America.

The Sherpas' reiterative and tedious insistence that all tracks seen and all skins and scalps discovered are those of a Yeti should not be regarded simply as the result of ignorance. On the contrary, it may be a matter of extreme sophistication. After all, if the elders of the village of Khumjung can reach a deal with Sir Edmund Hillary whereby a cap of serow-skin is permitted to be exhibited with great reverence and at enormous cost in the three major capitals of the world in exchange for the renovation of the monastery and the building of a new school at Khumjung, then who can say who are the wise men? It would be less than fair if I did not add that the scalp incident, far from indicating Hillary's naivete, was, it seems to me, the action of a wise and compassionate man who knew the value of a *quid pro quo* for assuaging the feelings of a proud and generous race of people. Hillary had his scalp, they had their school, honour was satisfied and charity was kept at bay. Since 1961, Hillary has built schools in Thami, Pangboche, Thyangboche, Chaunrikharka and Junbesi, and teachers and schoolbooks have been supplied at no cost to the Sherpas.

The Hillary Expedition of 1960–61 had the effect of dampening the enthusiasm of all but the staunchest of Yeti supporters. Scientists smiled knowingly, mountaineers lost interest, and journalists found other fish to fry. Only Bhutan, a country which has never really had its fair share of Yeti publicity, soldiered on: in 1966, with a brilliant stroke of Bigfootmanship, the Bhutanese Post Office brought out a set of triangular-shaped Snowman stamps.

In the summer of 1970 the Yeti at last came back into the news with a classic sighting – classic in the sense that its observer was a mountaineer of high repute. Don Whillans, the deputy leader of the British expedition that conquered the south face of Annapurna, accompanied by Dougal Haston, found and photographed a trail of footprints at 13,000 feet in Nepal in March of that year (plate 3). That night in the bright moonlight he saw at some considerable distance from his tent a creature moving across the crest of the ridge. It was 'bounding along on all fours', and to Don Whillans it seemed to resemble an ape or an ape-like creature.[29] He didn't see it again. An excerpt from Don Whillans's account of the affair, quoted in Chris Bonnington's recent book,[30] demonstrates that the attitude of some of the Sherpas towards the Yeti is one of wariness rather than fear.

> The following morning I went up to make a full reconaissance to the permanent Base Camp site and I took the two Sherpas along. I thought I'd see their reaction at the point where I'd photographed the tracks the day before. The tracks were so obvious that it was impossible not to make any comment, but they walked straight past and didn't indicate that they had seen them. I had already mentioned that I had seen the Yeti, not knowing exactly what it was, but they pretended they didn't understand and ignored what I said. I am convinced that they believe the Yeti does exist, that it is some kind of sacred animal which is best left alone; that if you don't bother it, it won't bother you (p. 59).

The photograph of the trail itself is not very easy to interpret owing to the depth of the snow, the oblique perspective and the lack of scale. It must be remembered, too, that there is no evidence that the animal Whillans saw in the moonlight and the prints that he had photographed earlier in the day were in any way connected with each other, but as both unexplained tracks and unidentified animals are rare at this altitude, it is reasonable to associate them. Whillans's observation has another claim to fame: it is the first European sighting to have taken place *at night*. Nocturnal meetings with Yetis are common enough in Sherpa tales; in fact the Yeti is classically described as a nocturnal animal.

In this chapter I have reviewed chronologically the gradual development of the Yeti saga, from B. H. Hodgson's second-hand sighting in 1832 to the sighting by Whillans in 1970. There were of course a number of other observations by Europeans during this period. Certain reports stretch one's credulity too far to merit consideration in this chapter; for instance, Jean Marques-Rivière quotes the story of an unnamed Hindu pilgrim who saw ten giant ape-men, 10 ft.–12 ft. in height, gathered in a ring, one of them beating on a tom-tom made out of a hollow log.[31] Rawicz's account, on the other hand, which on the face of it is a fairly reasonable and sober one (though inconsistent in a number of physical details), is included in spite of the suspicion that Rawicz's book *The Long Walk* is a work of fiction.

What emerges from this account of sightings of one sort and another is that, Rawicz apart, *only two Europeans* have ever seen what might conceivably be a Yeti. The first was N. A. Tombazi in 1925 and the second was Don Whillans in 1970. Even if we can accept Thorberg and Frostis's account, it does not really constitute a third sighting because Thorberg's description points un-equivocally to a known animal, the Himalayan langur. The con-ditions under which Whillans saw his 'Yeti' were not ideal, and it is impossible for us to draw any firm conclusion from the report or the footprints.

We are thus left with only one sighting by a European. Let us consider it again. Tombazi saw something fleetingly 'two to three hundred yards away' which was 'exactly like a human, walking upright'. 'It showed dark against the snow and ... wore no clothes.' The footprints which he examined later were 'similar in shape to those of a man', but only 6 in.–7 in. long and 4 in. wide at the broadest part. These are not the proportions of a human foot but they *are* characteristic of a bear's hind paw. Tombazi goes on to say that what little could be seen of the heel narrowed to a point. Posterior narrowing of the heel is also a bear-like characteristic, and decidedly not a human one; in man the heel takes the major part of the weight in walking and standing, and it is broad and rounded.

There is little in Tombazi's report that constitutes firm evidence one way or another. The prints suggest a bear, but the body and the gait of Tombazi's apparition were apparently human. Do bears look human when seen at a distance? Do they walk like men? Bears when standing are excellent bipeds, but when essaying something totally unnatural—like walking—they are clumsy and grotesque. The bear's anatomy is consistent only with bipedal standing, not with bipedal walking. At a distance a bear might be mistaken for a man when standing still, but it is almost inconceivable to imagine anyone, however scientifically naive, mistaking a bear's walk for a human walk. Tombazi was reputedly a highly intelligent man, an experienced and much-travelled Englishman who would not mistake a walking bear for a walking man. So what are we left with? Simply this: Tombazi either saw something that science does not know anything about—a man-like creature with a bear's foot—or his memory of a creature *walking upright* was at fault. We must note, however, that in his own words his sight of the creature was 'fleeting'.

All in all, the European sightings of the Yeti, *The Long Walk* excluded, don't provide us with any detailed idea of what the Yeti might look like. We have to turn to Sherpa accounts for that. I suggested earlier that Sherpa accounts do not constitute scientific data because of their vagueness as to time and place, the obvious garnish of common folklore themes, and motivation derived from the animistic philosophy of Tibetan Buddhism. As I have said, Lawrence Swan emphasizes the difficulty of distinguishing between the two kinds of reality that exist in the Sherpa mind: 'there are so many devils and miracles and other "realities" in their religion that what we consider "real" on the substantial basis of evidence is not clearly separated in their minds from the "realities" of their religious beliefs. Sherpas can move from "real" animals in a physical sense to "real" things in a religious sense rather easily.'[32] Added to these philosophic considerations, the suspicion that a benign and innocent form of commercialism is operating must make the Sherpa accounts suspect as material for critical analysis; but when all is said and done it is only through the Sherpas that we can build up an image of what it is that we ought to be looking for.

The following is a sort of Identikit profile of the Yeti based on eighteen separate Sherpa reports gathered from the literature. This of course represents a very small sample of the total. It is probable that some of them are composite, and refer to the two principal types of Yeti that the Sherpas recognize, the large Dzu-teh and the smaller Meh-teh. This might, for instance, account for the wide range of variation in size. In many cases the reports themselves are 'group opinions', being derived from a group of Sherpas or villagers collectively. In a number of instances, individually named Sherpas have told their stories to authors, but it is not always clear whether the incident happened to the Sherpa in question or to someone else. Professor von Fürer-Haimendorf is sceptical about Sherpa stories. In spite of the fact that he has worked and travelled in the Himalayan region for many years, he tells me he has never met a Sherpa who has *actually seen a Yeti*; the Sherpa's son, or his father or his cousin had seen a Yeti, not he himself. Sons, fathers or cousins were always strangely unavailable to tell the story for themselves.[33]

The profile of the Yeti, based on the features most frequently given in Sherpa tales, goes like this: height varies between 4 ft. 6 in. and 16 ft. The head hair is long and sometimes falls forward over the eyes. The face is partially naked, often white-skinned, with features reminiscent of an ape or a monkey. Hair, predominantly reddish-brown to dark brown or black in colour but lighter on the chest, covers the whole body. Shoulders are heavy and hunched, arms are long and extend to the knees or thereabouts. The posture is roughly man-like though slightly stooped. The walk is partly bipedal and partly quadrupedal.

It is particularly interesting that there is such a great variation in size in these accounts. Just over half the reports state that the creature is over 6 ft. in height; rather less than half the reports state that it is under 6 ft. The height most frequently given is between 5 ft. and 6 ft., and the commonest analogy is that it is about the size and build of a youth. The appearance of a *conical-shaped skull*, one of the most constant features in reconstructions of the Yeti, is only mentioned in six out of the eighteen reports. Perhaps the strangest fact of all is that nearly three-quarters of the reports describe the Yeti as *partly bipedal and partly quadrupedal*; only four reports state unequivocally that it is bipedal. This is of special interest in view of the emphasis on two-footedness in the literature. One facet of the anatomy of the Yeti that is clearly mythical is that its feet point backwards. As I have already said, this is a classical myth-motif. No individual Sherpa eyewitness account mentions this phenomenon, but it turns up regularly in the description given by groups of porters or villagers.

When we turn from Yeti structure to Yeti habits and habitats, we are at a loss for hard evidence. All we can do is to list the characteristics that most often crop up in Sherpa tales. (An asterisk indicates a monster myth-motif well known to folklorists in many parts of the world.)

ECOLOGY

1. *Habitat*. The Yeti live in caves high in the mountains* between 14,000 and 20,000 feet. Or they live in the impenetrable thickets of the montane forests at about 10,000 feet (the former belief is by far the more widespread).
2. *Activity Rhythm*. Nocturnal.*
3. *Diet*. Carnivorous. The Yeti preys on yaks as well as on smaller mammals such as the pika (Himalayan mouse-hare), which is found at a maximum altitude of 20,000 feet or thereabouts. Characteristically, they discard the intestines before eating these creatures. When hungry the Yeti may raid villages and carry off human beings.*

HABITS

1. *Vocalization*. The repertoire of the Yeti calls includes loud roars, noisy yelps, loud mews, and, most characteristically, a high-pitched whistling call.
2. *Body odour*. Yetis have a vile, pungent smell.*
3. *Physical behaviour*. Yetis have tremendous physical strength and

3. Another supposed Yeti track discovered near Machapuchare, Nepal, in 1970 by Don Whillans. Probably the track of a quadruped

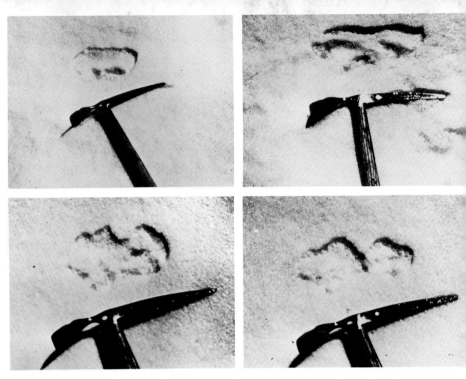

4. Tracks of a canid (fox or grey wolf) to show the marked variations that can occur from print to print. These photographs are taken from a sequence of ten impressions

5. (*below*) 'Elephant-track', showing the subsidence of the edges of the track to give a rhomboidal shape. The result of subsequent melting will be to give the footprint (human in this instance) a roughly circular outline

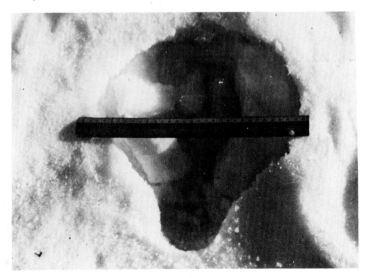

can uproot trees and lift and hurl boulders over vast distances.★ The breasts of the females are so large they have to throw them over their shoulders when running or when bending down.★ In both sexes these creatures are impeded when running down slopes by their long head-hair, which falls over their eyes and thus blinds them.★ Yetis are inordinately fond of alcohol (e.g. *chang*) which can be used as a bait to trap a Yeti after it has become intoxicated.★

4. *Social behaviour*. Unrecorded. Yetis are usually observed as isolates.

Straightaway it is apparent that whereas much of the physical description, and even the ecology, lies within the bounds of possibility, the Yeti's behaviour owes much to the imagination. The reason is easy to understand. One must accept that many of the reported Sherpa sightings are based on fact. Whether the creatures the Sherpas saw were known or unknown to science is in a sense beside the point. They saw *something*. Thus the record of actual sightings is bound to have a more down-to-earth ring about it than the accounts of the ecology and habits, which cannot be so easily observed at a chance encounter. The behaviour and ecology of wild animals are only determined by long and arduous field studies followed by months of careful statistical analysis, and not by isolated encounters by untrained observers.

As far as I am aware there is no record of an individual Sherpa providing a first-hand account of a female Yeti throwing its breasts over its shoulders or stumbling down the mountainside with its hair over its eyes. However, the latter motif, which crops up frequently, may well be founded on fact and subsequently have become tacked on to the Yeti tales. J. D. Hooker, the renowned naturalist, spent two years in Sikkim, 1848–9. He tells how on one occasion after a fresh fall of snow his Lepcha porters loosened their pigtails and *combed their long hair over the eyes* to protect them from the glare.

It is usually assumed that people who live in the country know more about the natural history of animals than those who live in towns. In general terms I suppose this is true, but it is a popular delusion to imagine that country folk are universally and automatically experts on the animals that live on their doorsteps, any more than they are experts at forecasting the weather. It seems reasonable to assume that expert knowledge of local animals is a fall-out of the necessity to hunt them for food. In this context it must be remembered that in Buddhist societies killing animals is taboo. Norman Hardie was not over-impressed with the Sherpas' knowledge of the animals on their doorstep. He comments that their expertise is restricted to the yak, which, as Hilaire Belloc recounts,[34] is a different matter altogether:

> As a friend of the children, commend me the yak —
> You will find it exactly the thing:
> It will carry and fetch, you can ride on its back
> Or lead it about with a string.
> The Tartar who dwells on the plains of Tibet,
> A desolate region of snow,
> Has for centuries made it a nursery pet,
> And surely the Tartar should know.

Sherpas never hunt leopards, bears, goats or antelopes, so they have no reason to know about the ecology and habits of these creatures. The widely held view that the Sherpas would not mistake a bear, a monkey or anything else for a Yeti may be without foundation.

*   *   *

The Himalayas, the Karakorams and North America are not the only habitats of monster myth, and before we remove ourselves to America's North Pacific coast to examine the Sasquatch, less well-known creatures deserve some consideration. Monster stories emanating from the Caucasus, the Pamirs, the Tien Shan mountains, the Altai range and the mountainous fringes of the Gobi Desert seem to indicate that there are three quite recognizable types: the Almas and Kaptar (or Ksi-Kiik), man-like, man-sized forms; the Golub-Yavan and the Tok, Yeti types; the Dzu-teh (or Gin-sung), a giant, man-like monster of the American Sasquatch type.

Odette Tchernine, an English writer and journalist and an authority on the Russian side of the problem, uses the common Mongolian name Almas to describe all the strange human and near-human-like creatures reported from almost every remote region of mountain or cold desert between the Caucasus and the Urals in the west, and the coastal ranges of Siberia, bordering the Sea of Okhotsk, in the east. Tchernine's restrained attitude towards the nomenclature of Russian monsters is wholly admirable, and I intend to follow her lead by referring to the wild men of Central Asia as Almas irrespective of the many regional synonyms.

Strictly speaking, Almas are outside the category of Bigfoot; they have few ape-like characteristics, and come into the class of 'wild men' rather than 'monsters'. The tales of Almas lack most of the mythological overtones of the Yeti and the Sasquatch and thus have a ring of reasonableness about them. Their attribution by Sanderson and many Russian scientists as surviving members of the ancient Neanderthal race of *Homo sapiens* is startling but not wholly outrageous. This possibility is discussed in more detail in chapter 7.

Information on Russian wild men is difficult to obtain. Wildman research in the U.S.S.R. has had its ups and downs, and for many years was not officially recognized, with the result that the normal channels of communication, such as newspaper reports, magazine articles and popular books, are unavailable. There has been some improvement in the official attitude since 1958, and at least one field expedition to the Caucasus, led by Professor Jeanne Kofman, has received official blessing. According to Odette Tchernine, research is also going on in the Chatkal Range north of the Pamirs and to the east of Tashkent.

In 1958–9 four booklets on the subject of Russian monsters were published in the U.S.S.R. by a special commission set up by the Academy of Sciences to study the problem, but the main source of information comes from individuals with long-term interests in the phenomenon. The leading authority in the Soviet Union at present is Professor Boris Porshnev, a historian and scientific expert who headed the special commission. In Ulan Bator, capital of the Republic of Mongolia, lives a Professor Rinchen, now of an advanced age, who for many years has collected data from the area of the Gobi Desert and the desert enclaves of Dzungaria and the Tarim Basin. It is from these two men that most of the information, wholly in the form of traditional folktales and eyewitness reports, has come. Both Odette Tchernine and Ivan T. Sanderson maintain a close correspondence with Porshnev and Rinchen, and the information that they have been able to extract is fully documented in their books. Unlike the Himalayas, British Columbia and Northern California, the Russian information provides little in the way of material evidence such as footprints, skeletal material, photographs or film. A skull found in the Altai Mountains in 1953 is said to be of an Almas. The skull is illustrated in Odette Tchernine's book *The Yeti*, and from all appearances it is of a young adult of the species *Homo sapiens sapiens*, or modern man, of a mongoloid type; there is nothing mysterious about it.

This is not necessarily to imply that no evidence exists, but it does mean that the problem of making sense out of the reports becomes more of a job for a folklorist than an anthropologist or a zoologist. Most of the incidents quoted independently by Tchernine and Sanderson have the non-specific, timeless quality of myth and legend. One more solid incident, which was reported fairly widely in newspapers outside the Iron Curtain, was the experience of A. G. Pronin, a hydrologist from Leningrad University. In 1957 Pronin was on a technical mission to the Pamirs. While selecting a site for his camp on the edge of the Fedchenko Glacier he saw, on a cliff-top across the ravine a quarter of a mile away, a man-like figure, with hunched shoulders and long arms, covered all over with reddish-grey hair. Although it is not precisely stated in the report,[35] the indication is that the creature was bipedal. Pronin reported that it walked with its legs far apart. A few days later Pronin caught a second glimpse of this creature, which is apparently well-known to the Kirghiz herds-men and villagers as the *Guli-avan* (or *Golub-yavan*), a name which, according to Gordon Creighton,[36] simply means 'wild man'. The *Guardian* of February 4th, 1960, carried an article by Victor Zorza mentioning an expedition to the Pamirs in 1959 led by a Professor Stanyukovich. The expedition found nothing to substantiate Pronin's observations, but it *did* find evidence of Neolithic human occupation in the shape of artefacts, cave drawings and the evidence of the domestic use of fire.

The Almas race has, seemingly, a tremendously wide east–west distribution. From the Pamirs in the west it extends to the central Chinese escarpment in the east, a distance of about 1,800 miles. Both Sanderson and Tchernine report that wild-men stories continue right up into the mountain ranges bordering the Sea of Okhotsk in eastern Siberia, an easy zoogeographical jump one might think – in terms of the logic of the Goblin Universe – to the Aleutians and thus to the historic land bridge of the Bering Straits. The Bering Straits are the traditional pathway for migrating animals from Asia to North America and vice versa. With this one-time land link, the problem of the zoological affinities of the Asian and the North American man-like monsters apparently solves itself. Unfortunately, the further to the north-east of Asia we go the slimmer becomes the evidence, even the evidence of folklore. Almas *may* be talked of in these regions but we have yet to see any real evidence for it except in terms of the vaguest of generalizations (though admittedly this is probably due to lack of communication).

N. M. Przewalski, the discoverer in 1881 of the Mongolian wild horse, known universally as Przewalski's Horse, was one of the first scientists in the world to suspect the existence of wild men in Mongolia. He returned to Russia at the end of his travels with a skeleton and a skin of the new horse, but only the evidence of folktales for the existence of wild men.[37] Not surprisingly, the Russian government applauded the first and kept quiet about the second. In the early years of the present century the same fate was accorded the reports of subsequent explorers – the St Petersburg orientalist and the zoologist Baradiyn and, later, the zoologist Khaklov. Khaklov travelled widely in the regions of Dzungaria, between the Altai Mountains to the north and the Tien Shan range to the south. From Kazakh herdsmen he patiently collected stories of wild men of this region, carefully checking one witness's story against another. One Kazakh that Khaklov interviewed recalled that the previous year he had been in the Iren'-Kabyrga Mountains when he and another herdsman on horseback captured a wild man. The description of the creature is as follows:

> A male of less than average human height covered with brown to reddish hair, long arms reaching below his knees. Shoulders which are stooped with a narrow, hollow chest. His brow sloped backwards from the bony crest projecting over his eyes. His lower jaw was massive, and he was chinless. The nose was small and the nostrils wide and flared. The skin on his forehead, forearms and knees was horny and calloused. His legs bent and bowed at the knees. His feet resembled human feet and were one and a half to twice as broad. The toes were widely splayed and the big toe was shorter than in man and set apart from the others. The hands had long fingers and were similar to a man's hand. At the back of his neck was a protuberance, 'a hairy rise', similar to that seen in some hound dogs.[38]

A female specimen was described by another witness. Physically the description matches that of the male. Presumably, because this Almas was observed while in captivity, some aspects of her behaviour were recounted to Khaklov:

> The creature was usually quite silent and bared her teeth on being approached. She had a peculiar way of lying down; she squatted on her knees and elbows resting her forehead on the ground and her hands were folded over the back of her head. She would eat only raw meat, some vegetables and gravy and sometimes insects which she caught. When drinking water

she would lap or sometimes dip her arm into the water and lick her fur.

The description of the male specimen is of rather special interest for a peculiar reason which will become apparent in chapter 4 when the case of the Minnesota Iceman is considered. Could this description be in fact the 'model' (or one of the models) from which the Iceman might have been fabricated?

Two particular features of Almas stories are worth noting. The first is that on a number of occasions Almas have voluntarily associated themselves with human beings. For example, an Almas was discovered breast-feeding a human infant, and on another occasion a group of Almas invaded a camp, briefly left unattended, and on the return of the herdsmen were found warming themselves around the fire. This tale is particularly interesting because it suggests a peculiarly human attitude, an awareness of the benefit of fire. Most wild creatures are frightened of fire, so this behavioural characteristic of the Almas provides supporting, if circumstantial, evidence for their humanity. The final example of the kinship of Almas with man concerns a much-revered lama at the monastery of Lamyn-Hegen, who was reported to be the offspring of a Mongolian man and an Almas woman.

The second point, which serves as a corollary to the first, is that Almas stories noticeably lack the mythical overtones of the Yeti tales. It is clear that whereas the Tibetans and the Nepalese regard the Yeti of the high snows as a beast, and look upon it with a measure of superstitious awe, the Kirgiz, Kazakh and Mongol herdsmen regard wild men as familiar and harmless eccentrics in need of a certain amount of care and protection. It is true that in some areas to meet an Almas is to court bad luck, and to shoot one is liable to have unpleasant repercussions in the form of bad weather or drought. But this superstition is not inconsistent with the human status of Almas, for human beings with physical peculiarities such as albinism, a cast in the eye or even left-handedness are credited with similar evil powers by unenlightened races. The overall impression is that the inhabitants of Central Asia regard

Almas as human beings – if somewhat degraded ones – and not as monsters in any sense of the word. It is tempting (and at the present time there is no evidence to justify taking a harder line) to believe that Almas are human beings, perhaps the remnants of a primitive, culturally archaic population that has survived in the empty mountain regions of Central Asia for many thousands of years. Whether their history extends back to Palaeolithic times, and whether they could conceivably be descendants of Neanderthal populations of the Würm (or Wisconsin) glaciation is even more speculative. The fossil evidence of Neanderthal Man in Asia is rather suggestive. Well-known fossil sites of Neanderthal Man are found in the Crimea (Kiik-Koba and Staroselj'e); and one site at Teshik-Tash is located in the mountains that form part of the Pamir range in Uzbekistan. It seems fairly certain that during the last interglacial period, some fifty thousand years ago, humans of the Neanderthal race were living in the general area in which Almas are now reported to exist. What is missing is any evidence linking the two populations.

Professor Rinchen believes that because of the build-up of military activity in this area, and in the resulting construction of railway lines and roads in the last few decades, Almas have been disappearing from Mongolia and the Gobi Desert. He emphasizes that this trend has affected all animal populations, such as those of the wild horse and the wild camel which are on the fringe, if not over the edge, of extinction.

Professor Jeanne Kofman, whose field work in the Caucasus mountains has been going on for some years, may be gathering information from the last stronghold of the Almas. Certainly her research, using modern opinion-poll techniques, has been rewarding and has resulted in the accumulation of over three hundred reports and other items of 'evidence', none of which unfortunately proves very much by itself. Perhaps the application of modern computer techniques leading to an Identikit likeness of an Almas may convince the scientific establishment of the U.S.S.R. that a continent which has produced the wild horse and the wild camel might conceivably be harbouring a wild man as well.

3. *Bigfoot in America*

The United States is a country of big things – Texas, the Empire State Building, the giant sequoias, the Palomar telescope and foot-long hot-dogs – so it is fitting that the monster in its own back-yard should be universally known as Bigfoot. Footprints, which are about the only material evidence for the existence of an American monster, are unquestionably *big*. A length of 16 in.– 17 in. is average, and 22 in. is not unheard of. Translated into terms of stature, the owners of such feet must stand between 9 ft. and 12 ft. high; higher, one would think, than some of the trees and shrubs among which they seem so neatly to disappear when sighted.

Stories of the Sasquatch have been part of American Indian tradition for centuries, and as Sanderson[1] and Kirtley[2] have pointed out, they are also part of the folklore of Central and South America. Although in the last twenty years there has been a tremendous revival of public interest since these creatures have come to the attention of the 'white settlers', it is a reasonable assumption, from what we know of early written records that, like Peyton Place, the story of Sasquatch has been continuing for a great many years.

A catalogue of names, events and dates makes dull reading, therefore I have condensed the principal sightings of the North American Bigfoot over the past fifty years into a compact table which summarizes the basic facts (table 2, p. 210). Authors like Ivan T. Sanderson and John Green, and investigators like Rene Dahinden, the Swiss-Canadian Sasquatch-hunter, have made a far better job of recording the major events of the Sasquatch saga than I could ever hope to do, simply because they have looked into many of the incidents at first hand. Dahinden and Green have literally gone over the ground studying the scene of the crime,

73

interviewing witnesses and forming opinions based on their own assessment of the terrain and the personalities involved. I have heard many of Rene Dahinden's library of taped interviews with all sorts of people, including oil company prospectors, highway superintendents and deputy-sheriffs of police. My role is to analyse some of this data and comment upon the possibilities and probabilities that emerge in the context of zoology, ecology, human anatomy and human evolution.

The term Bigfoot has been in colloquial use since the early 1920s and in the first instance was a brain-child of the press. As I have said, strictly speaking 'Bigfoot' refers only to the legendary creatures of Northern California but has now spread to Oregon and Washington. Across the 49th Parallel in British Columbia, the colloquialism is the Sasquatch, a name derived from that used by the Salish Indians of south-west British Columbia, meaning 'wild man of the woods'. The traditional name for Bigfoot used by the Huppa tribe of the Klamath mountains of Northern California is *Oh-mah-'ah* (often shortened to *Omah*), and in the Cascade range further north similar creatures are (or were) known as the Seeahtiks, traditionally supposed to emanate from the heart of Vancouver Island.

The earliest record of large mysterious footprints in North America dates back to 1811 when a well-known explorer and trader, David Thompson, was attempting to reach the mouth of the Columbia River by crossing the Rockies at the site of what is now Jasper, Alberta. Climbing in deep snow, Thompson came across a track 14 in. by 8 in. showing four toes, a deep impression of the ball of the foot, short claw marks and an indistinct heel. He believed it to be the track of a grizzly bear, but his companion would have none of it. Neither will John Green, in whose book[3] the story is retold. The description itself is an inadequate basis for any far-reaching conclusions, but Green's objections that it could not have been a bear because bears have five toes not four and because the toes were too long, are not altogether convincing. Brown bears sometimes appear to be four-toed because the little inner toe (equivalent in position to the human big toe) frequently leaves no mark in mud or on the ground: furthermore, the occasional absence of an inner toe on the hindfoot is well known.[4] Green's second point, that the toes were too long (4 in., according to Thompson), is not valid because the author gives no indication of whether this measurement represented the length of the pads; if it was the latter, then 4 in. would not be excessive for a large grizzly bear with a 14 in. foot. However, it must be said that a foot of 14 in. overall length is pretty gigantic, although 16 in. has been recorded for an Alaskan brown bear.

The first and only well-documented account of the capture of an alleged Sasquatch appeared in the *Daily Colonist* of Friday, July 4th, 1884, published in Victoria, British Columbia. The incident took place near the township of Yale on the Fraser river, the centre of many subsequent sightings and incidents. Jacko, as the creature was called, was captured by the crew of a train winding its way along the Fraser river from Lytton to Yale in the shadow of the bluffs of the Cascade mountains. The description of Jacko given by the *Colonist* is paraphrased as follows: Jacko is of the gorilla-type standing about 4 ft. 7 in. in height and weighing 127 lb. He has long, black, coarse hair (on his head?) and except for the short glossy hair all over his body he resembles a man. His forearm is much longer than a man's and he possesses extraordinary strength being able to take a fresh branch and tear it in two as no man could do.

On the face of it, the description would fit an adult chimpanzee or even a juvenile male or adult female gorilla, but unless it was an escapee from a circus it is difficult to imagine what an African ape was doing swanning about in the middle of British Columbia. At that time chimpanzees were still fairly rare creatures in captivity. The alternative inference that has been made is that Jacko was a young Sasquatch. His subsequent fate is quite unknown, although Jim McClarin tells me that it is believed that he was later exhibited in Barnum and Bailey's Circus. The story, though historically interesting, gets us nowhere. Subsequent reports in 1901, 1907 and 1915 centred round Vancouver Island and the Fraser river area. But in 1910 a gruesome event in the

Nahanni Valley area of the Northwest Territories extended the northern range of the modern version of the myth. The Nahanni Valley, sometimes known as Headless Valley, near the Great Slave Lake, is a notorious 'lost world', and has a somewhat evil reputation for permanently absorbing prospectors who visit it. In 1910 two brothers named MacLeod were found dead in the valley with their heads chopped off. Inevitably the Sasquatch was by some lumbered with the crime in spite of the fact that homicide does not rank high in the annals of Bigfoot anywhere in the world.

In 1918 a story appeared in the *Seattle Times* of July 16th concerning the 'mountain devils' who attacked a prospector's shack at Mount St Lawrence, near Kelso, Washington State. These creatures were supposed to be members of the Seeahtik tribe. They were half-human, half-monster, were 7 ft.–8 ft. tall and possessed the gifts of hypnotism and ventriloquism and the ability to make themselves invisible (a folktale characteristic). The Seeahtiks have been known to other tribes, such as the Clallam and Quinault Indians, for centuries, and were thought by them to be a by-blow in the story of the creation of man from animals. Seeahtiks were creatures which had stopped off at an intermediate stage.

Canadian reports occur sporadically through the 'twenties, 'thirties and 'forties, but it is only in the middle and late 'fifties that Bigfoot affairs began to develop thick and fast. One of the classics of Bigfootery occurred in 1924 but, strangely, remained unrevealed until 1957 when John Green, the present editor of the *Agassiz-Harrison Advance* and a dedicated investigator into Canadian and American Bigfoot problems, researched the story following a lead given him by a reporter on the *Vancouver Daily Province*.[5] The gist of what is known as the Ostman Story is as follows:

In 1924 Albert Ostman, a lumberman of Scandinavian origin, now retired, decided on a vacation with a bit of prospecting on the side. He made arrangements to visit an area at the head of the Toba Inlet, opposite Vancouver Island, where, reputedly, gold had once been mined and the claim subsequently abandoned. He set out well equipped with rifle, dried and canned food and simple utensils. After a week of camping and rugged travelling he came to a delectable camp site under some cypress trees with a handy freshwater spring. On his second night at this spot he awoke to find himself on the move. He was being carried, like a sack of potatoes, inside his sleeping bag which was partially closed at the top by an enormous hand. He estimates that he travelled twenty-five miles, very uncomfortably, in this manner. Finally, dumped on the ground, he crawled out of his cloth prison to find himself in a cliff-enclosed valley and in the presence of a family of four Sasquatches: a father, an eight-foot giant, mother, a good, strapping seven-footer, a teenage son of the same height and a younger, immature daughter. Ostman remained in this strange community for six days or more, during which time he was neither attacked nor even menaced. On the contrary, he appears to have provided rare entertainment for the family, who were spellbound by his equipment and food supplies which had been kidnapped with him.

Albert Ostman was able to give a convincing account of the Sasquatch family which does not ring false in any particular. His description indicates that these creatures were *human*, except for their hairiness and their technological simplicity; clearly, tool-use had no place in their economy. Ostman emphasized the powerfulness of the big toe, which he described as *longer* than the remaining toes and well separated from them. He described the feet as being padded like a dog's, presumably a reference to prominent cornified pads or callosities on the sole of the foot. Of some importance, in view of William Roe's account, which appears below, is Ostman's description of the adult female. In his own words, 'she had very wide hips and a goose-like walk'. Taken overall, Ostman's description hangs together and seems to describe giant, hairy members of our own species. To cut a longish story short, Albert Ostman eventually escaped from the clutches of the Sasquatches and returned to civilization. In 1957 he told his story, thirty-three years after the event. Why did he keep quiet so long? The reason he gives has become a cliché of the whole Sasquatch saga. He did not think anybody would believe him.

What are we to think of Albert Ostman's story? It is wholly circumstantial, and the only assurances of veracity are Ostman's declaration before a Justice of the Peace on August 20th, 1957, at Fort Langley, B.C., and the favourable reports of his sincerity from persons like John Green and Rene Dahinden who have interviewed him. The anatomical peculiarities of the Sasquatch family are expressed in very reasonable terms, and his observations on behaviour, if unimaginative, are without obvious inconsistencies. One aspect of his story however does not ring quite true. On the basis of the height and weight estimates, his Sasquatch family must have weighed collectively over 2,000 lb. This is equivalent to the weight of five male gorillas, or twelve male chimpanzees, or fourteen average-sized human beings. Ostman saw no evidence of meat-eating so, on negative grounds, his captors must be regarded as vegetarians. Yet in Ostman's tale no great emphasis is laid on food-getting behaviour; he mentions grasses with sweet roots, spruce and hemlock tips and tubers which the mother and son collected and brought back to the 'camp', but the adult male is not credited with any food-getting activities, unless of course Ostman himself represented the old man's contribution to the family larder. Grasses and spruce tips, rich though they may be in protein, hardly seem an adequate diet for a biomass of close on 18 cwt. It might be expected that massive creatures of vegetarian habits would require vast quantities of low-energy foods, the collection of which would occupy each individual's entire waking hours; yet from Ostman's story this type of food-gathering does not seem to have been taking place.

The type of vegetation involved in the Ostman story could, broadly speaking, be classed as coniferous forest. However, on the extreme west coast of North America from Alaska to San Francisco the forest is of rather a special type called coastal evergreen forest.[6] Colloquially it has been called coniferous rain forest, reflecting the high level of rainfall and high humidity which prevail there. One of the effects of this forest type has been to produce a great variety of trees, including Douglas fir, western hemlock, western red cedar, Sitka spruce and, further south,

California redwood. Mixed in with these conifers are deciduous species like maples, oaks, alder, birch, willow and poplar. The coniferous trees may reach an enormous size including redwoods up to 350 ft. in height and 20 ft. in diameter.

Frank L. Beebe of the British Columbia Provincial Museum in a report in 1967 to Mr W. K. Kiernan, the Minister for Recreation and Conservation of British Columbia, emphasizes the density of the forest growth, and that the quantity of food (fruits and berries) produced by the deciduous understorey is sadly impoverished. As for the general food supply in coniferous forest, Beebe states: ' ... this type of vegetation produces the very poorest quality of low-energy food and the least quantity of high-energy food of any forest type on the planet.'[7]

Further south, in Northern California, this forest type produces a somewhat richer understorey with plenty of berries in later summer and early autumn.

Ostman's story relates to the mountainous area inland of the Toba Inlet in British Columbia, a region of coastal evergreen forest, where low-energy foods are 'of the very poorest quality'. Gorillas, whose size and dietary requirements could be regarded as comparable to a Sasquatch's, live in tropical (as opposed to temperate) montane forest, where the understorey is bounteously endowed *all the year round* with the staple food of the mountain gorilla. The mountain gorilla's diet includes celery, bedstraw, nettles, bark, bamboo and a wide variety of understorey plants. Albert Ostman's story fails to convince me primarily on the grounds of the limited food resources available.

Two other stories, those of William Roe and the Chapman family, were investigated by John Green and recorded some years after the respective events. Both were the subject of sworn testimonies. William Roe's story has several points of interest. Roe, a roadbuilder and an experienced hunter and woodsman, was exploring in the area of Mica Mountain near a little town called Tete Jaune Cache in eastern British Columbia in 1955. He spotted what he thought was a grizzly bear but, on longer inspection, he realized it was something quite different. Roe's description can be summarized as follows: the creature was 6 ft. tall and 3 ft. wide (across the trunk) weighing approximately 300 lb. It was fully covered with dark-brown, silver-tipped hair and heavy breasts indicated that it was a female and yet, I quote, ' ... its torso was not curved like a female's. Its broad frame was straight from shoulder to hip'. Its arms were moderately long reaching almost to the knee, and its feet were broader than a man's. When it walked, according to William Roe's account, it placed its heel down first. (This observation is of considerable relevance because the 'heel-strike', as it is called, is a characteristic of human walking or striding. See chapter 5.) The head was higher at the back than the front, the nose was flat, the lips protruding; the ears were man-like but the eyes were small and dark 'like a bear's'. A feature which particularly struck Roe was the neck, which was ' ... un-human, thicker and shorter than any man's I had ever seen'. The creature finally spotted Roe and walked rapidly away, watching him over its shoulder as it went.

The special point of interest in this story is first, the proportions of the female's body. According to Ostman's story, the hips of the female were very broad with the result that she could only manage a waddling gait; a logical enough extrapolation from structure to function. Roe, on the other hand, makes a strong point of the absence of prominent hips in his female and of her human-like stride. One feels that they cannot both be right unless Roe's girl was really immature, which the prominence of the breasts seems to deny. The second point concerns the alleged female Sasquatch filmed by Roger Patterson and Bob Gimlin in 1967. This important event in the Californian Bigfoot Story is con-sidered in some detail below.

The Chapman story, emanating from a simple Amerindian farm family, recorded twenty years after the event, has less to tell us. It is interesting to note that in contrast to the sophisticated detail of the Roe and Ostman affairs, *The Ruby Creek Incident*, as it has been called, is a simple tale simply told. The remote Chap-man farm was visited one day in 1940 by an eight-foot high male creature which emerged from the woods and approached the farmstead. Mrs Chapman grabbed the children and sensibly fled, but not before she had seen enough to convince herself that this was no bear, an animal with which she was quite familiar. On return to the house it was found that a heavy barrel of salted fish had been overturned and its contents scattered, and that gigantic footprints encircled the house. Measurements of 16 in. length and 8 in. maximum width and with a step of 4 ft. are said to have been recorded. As John Green, who followed up this incident, says, there are inconsistencies in Mrs Chapman's story when compared with the original contemporary press accounts. The fish-barrel incident, of course, is the stuff that myths are made of and has its analogues in Bigfoot tales from Tibet to California.

These are the best-known incidents, but by now there must be two or three hundreds of sightings of Bigfoot, a few of which are listed in table 2, p. 210. One of the most striking things in my own analysis of the Canadian Sasquatch incidents, compared with the Californian ones, is the predominance of sightings of the creature itself as opposed to the mere discovery of its footprints: in California you find the footprints but in British Columbia you see the feet. An identical conclusion has been reached, quite independently, by Frank Beebe in the report to the Minister already referred to.

In 1958, seventy-four years after the Jacko incident, and with an uncharacteristic lack of enterprise, the United States discovered the Sasquatch. Their dilatoriness is even more incomprehensible when one recalls the story of Ape Canyon in Mount St Helen's range in Washington State, seventy-five miles north of Portland, Oregon. In 1924, miners in this area pursued a running battle with Sasquatches lasting several days, culminating in an attack in strength by the Bigfoot hordes which drove the miners out, never to return. This sounds like a movie script, and perhaps it was, but the story of the Siege of Ape Canyon has been authenticated by a survivor of those perilous days when there was trouble at the mine. Fred Beck told his story to John Green and to Rene Dahinden:

One day they saw a big ape-like creature peering out from behind a tree. One man fired and apparently hit it in the head, but it ran off. Next Fred Beck met one of the apes at the canyon rim and shot it in the back three times. It fell down a cliff into the canyon, but they never found a body.

At night the apes counter attacked, opening the assault by knocking a heavy strip of wood out from between two logs of the miners' cabin. After that there were assorted poundings on the walls, door and roof, but the building was designed to withstand heavy mountain snows and the apes failed to break in.

There is a general impression that a large group of apes hurled big rocks at the cabin. Mr Beck does not altogether confirm this. There was indeed the sound of rocks hitting the roof and rolling off, and they did brace the heavy door from inside. They heard creatures thumping around on top of the cabin as well as battering the walls, and they fired shots through the walls and roof without driving them away. The noises went on from shortly after dark until nearly dawn, perhaps five hours altogether.

The cabin had no windows and of course no one opened the door, so in fact the men inside did not see what was causing the commotion outside. Nor could Mr Beck say for sure, when I questioned him about it, that there were more than two creatures outside. There were that many because there had been one on the roof and one pounding the wall simultaneously.

However many there were, it was enough for the miners, who packed up and abandoned their mine the next day.[8]

The anchor-man of California Bigfootery was, and I quote, 'a hard-eyed catskinner'.[9] In case you feel this is a case for the R.S.P.C.A., let me hasten to add that a catskinner is one who bulldozes logging roads for a living. One day in October in 1958, Jerry Crew, the catskinner, came upon some tracks in the mud. They were very big tracks deeply impressed in the soil and had the look of human footprints. They measured all of 16 in. long and 7 in. wide and they were all over the place. They went up hill and down dale and continued into situations that seemed to defy the ingenuity of a hoaxer with a footprint machine. Mr Crew and his team had observed tracks like these for several weeks, but on this occasion Jerry Crew made a plaster cast of one of the prints. His photograph holding the cast, which stretches from his collar to his belt, was widely publicized and immediately elicited stories of previous footprint discoveries and earlier Sasquatch encounters.

The Crew footprints were seen in the neighbourhood of Bluff Creek Valley and this region has since become the centre of Sasquatch activity; other localities where footprints have been discovered are in the Onion Mountain and the Blue Creek Mountain areas which, together with Bluff Creek, form a wooded mountainous region of forty square miles covered with dense coniferous vegetation with a heavy understorey of manzanita. Apart from a few dirt access roads to logging sites, the region is entirely wild. Hunting and trapping in such densely wooded and mountainous country is not rewarding and there is little reason for people whose business does not involve road-making or logging to enter the area. There are vast tracts of this sort of country in the Pacific north-west. Washington, Oregon and Northern California contain about 54,000 square miles of mountainous territory, much of which is forested and can truly be called wilderness areas. Flying from San Francisco International Airport to Portland, Oregon, as I have done on several occasions, effectively drives away any preconception one might have of a sophisticated, sun-drenched and over-populated Pacific Coast thick with orange groves and expensive country clubs. For five hundred miles, a few miles inland from the sea, a bird's-eye view reveals nothing more than ridge upon ridge of coniferous mountain forest. There is no *a priori* reason why quite a sizeable population of Sasquatch should not hide itself in these mountains and remain undiscovered; no reason, that is, if they were a species that could survive without eating. It is the pure logistics of food-supply in an area which is impoverished in this respect, even in summer let alone winter, that is one of the principal stumbling-blocks to acceptance.

In his book on the Yeti of the Sherpa-lands of Nepal,[10] Charles Stonor argues the ecological reasonableness of the Yeti's existence: 'Here is this vast terrain, with a minimum of natural enemies for the Yeti, possibly indeed none at all, and sparsely inhabited *by a race of men who are not hostile or curious, and above all are without weapons.*' The italics are mine, and are there to emphasize the essential difference between the Bigfoot situation in Nepal and in north-west America. The first half of the sentence is valid for either area, but the second half most assuredly is not.

Table 2, p. 210, setting out Sasquatch sightings, does scant justice to the richness of the circumstantial evidence for the existence of Bigfoot in North America. In 1969 alone, sixty separate Sasquatch incidents were reported. Yet one cannot help reminding oneself that for all the hundreds of sightings of the creature itself and the tens of thousands of footprints that have been seen, *no Sasquatch has ever been captured.* Movie films have been taken on three occasions, of which more later, and still photographs more than once, but never a live creature (the enigmatic Jacko of Yale, B.C., excepted), a dead body, a skeleton or even a single bone has come to official notice.

Tom Slick, whom we have already met in the context of the Yeti, did not in his enthusiasm overlook the Bigfoot in his own backyard. For three years from 1960 to 1962 he had personnel in the field searching for evidence. It has proved difficult to find out exactly what the Tom Slick Expedition *did* find. The benefactor himself died in 1963 in a mid-air disaster in his private plane, and his executors are remarkably taciturn. My requests for factual information concerning the dates and the personnel involved in the Bigfoot expeditions in Asia and North America have met with no success.

Other 'research organizations' have been in the field, sponsored by Roger Patterson, head of the Northwest Research Foundation and the first man to film a creature said to be a female Sasquatch, and Robert Morgan of Miami, Florida, whose 1970 expedition was reported in *National Wildlife*.[11] The results of this latter expedition were inconclusive. Some tracks were discovered, also some 'strange fecal matter', and some hairs. Both of these items of evidence were submitted for study to the Smithsonian Institution, Washington, D.C., whose provisional report indicates that the faecal matter closely resembled that of bears and the hair was also, possibly, from a bear. Other less-qualified entrepreneurs have mounted expeditions to trek into the unknown, equipped with the ultimate in sophisticated recording equipment. I am not aware that any of these jaunts have had the slightest success. In fact at this juncture one might make a general observation that the casual observer (for instance, the motorist driving home late at night) has a considerably greater chance of *seeing* a Sasquatch than any professional or semi-professional searcher. The obvious explanation is that there are more 'casual' than 'professional' observers, but one would have thought that the professionalism of the few would easily outweigh the chance factors operating in the case of the amateurs. Apart from Roger Patterson and Ivan Marx (see below), I have not heard of a single professional who has so much as glimpsed the hide or hair of a Sasquatch.

From the forty-three detailed sighting records available to me the following description of the Sasquatch emerges. The Sasquatch is upright-walking and, although some reports describe its gait as a shuffle and others as a slow, rocking walk, the consensus is that it just 'walks', from which one might reasonably infer the qualification 'just like man does'. The Sasquatch is covered in reddish-brown or auburn hair; the head hair is often said to be as long as 5 in.–7 in., falling over the forehead in a 'bang' or a Japanese-doll fringe. The breasts of the female are described as hairy except in the region of the nipples (as in Patterson's film, see below). In several reports the hair below the knee is described as black. A change of hair colour below the knee has also been mentioned in Yeti reports. Although auburn is the commonest overall colour mentioned, black crops up, also beige, white and silvery-white. Genitalia are seldom remarked upon except that is for the breasts. Albert Ostman in a taped interview with Rene Dahinden commented that the penis of the adult male was small, no more than 2 in. in length. Most observers, however, are pretty reticent on the subject.

All reports emphasize the dissimilarity of the Sasquatch and a bear, particularly in terms of bodily proportions. Sasquatches have human-like legs, hands and feet. The prominence of the big toe is frequently commented upon; it has been said to be 'bulbous' and 'twice the size of a chicken's egg'. Universally commented upon are the breadth of the shoulders and the depth of the chest; estimates of shoulder width range up to 4 ft. It is often stated that the broad shoulders, the hunched appearance due to an apparent absence of a neck, remind the observer of an American football player.

The face is described as monkey- or ape-like, with a backwardly sloping forehead, a flattened nose and a slit-like, lipless mouth. A cone-shaped head has also been remarked upon.

A frequent comment is that when observed, the creature stands and stares, immobile and expressionless, with its arms hanging by its sides. In no single instance of which I am aware has the Sasquatch shown aggressive behaviour in gesture or physical action.

An analysis of the sighting and footprint data known to me, summarized in table 2 and based on the reports of seventy-two incidents from British Columbia, Alberta, Washington, Oregon and Northern California, reveals some interesting points:

1. *Stature.* Estimated stature of the Sasquatch ranges between 6 ft. and 11 ft. The commonest height quoted is 7 ft.–8 ft. (17 estimates out of 29 possibles).

2. *Length of footprint.* Footprints range in size from 12 in.–22 in. In 66 per cent of 33 reports the commonest quoted range is 14 in.–18 in., with a mode of 16 in.

3. *Width of footprint.* Relatively few records are available, but the most frequently reported width is 7 in.

4. *Peak viewing season.* Records show that the Sasquatch or its footprints have been observed in every month of the year. High

seasons are June–July and October–November, and the low
season is December–April. It is probably relevant to note that
June–July corresponds to the holiday season and October–
November to the hunting season.

5. *Daily periodicity*. Sightings at night are rather more common
than during the day (22 at night, 17 by day). John Green however
reports that in his records daylight sightings outnumber nocturnal
ones in the proportion of 3 :1.

6. *Sex*. Males are more commonly observed than females in the
ratio of slightly greater than 5:1.

My data are far from complete. Over three hundred eyewitness
reports are known to exist. I believe that my personal collection
constitutes a random sample; it represents the incidents that have
come to my notice from various 'unsolicited' sources. The data,
in a number of cases, are based on tape-recordings of interviews
with eyewitnesses made available to me by Rene Dahinden.

Some regional differences are apparent from table 2, p. 210.
Sightings of the Sasquatch itself are more common in British
Columbia than in Northern California, while quite the opposite
is true of footprint observations. This fact was abundantly evident
up to the beginning of 1969. Then in that year a rash of sightings
of the creature itself took place in Northern California, somewhat
redressing the notable regional difference. Up to the end of 1968,
footprints predominated at the odds of 10:1. By the end of 1969
the odds on seeing a Sasquatch, and not simply a footprint, had
shortened to 5:3. The odds in British Columbia shortened only
very slightly in 1969, so the likelihood still remains that if you
want to see a Sasquatch you should visit B.C., but if it is footprints
you are after, Northern California is your best bet.

It is interesting to speculate why such an outbreak of sightings
occurred in Northern California in 1969. Does it reflect an increase
in the population numbers of Sasquatch? Or a growing brashness
and devil-may-care attitude among the surviving Sasquatch
population? Is it that more people are on the look-out for the Sasquatch because of the publicity it has received and, for the same

reason, are less shy of risking ridicule by telling their stories? Or, on the other hand, have the citizens and the holiday visitors been over-stimulated by the increasingly frequent press reports and magazine articles so that they observe what they have been told to watch out for?

One of the problems, perhaps the greatest problem, in investigating Sasquatch sightings is the suspicion with which people who claim to have seen a Sasquatch are treated by their neighbours and employers. To admit such an experience is, in some areas, to risk personal reputation, social status and professional credibility. I know of one investigator whose marriage broke up because of a neighbourhood whispering campaign. I also know of a deputy-sheriff who lost his job because he talked to the press. There is also the case of a highly qualified oil company geologist who told his story but insisted that his name should not be mentioned for fear of dismissal by his company on the grounds of 'diminished responsibility', or some such charge. This man's factual report is all the more convincing as a result of his obvious distaste for personal publicity.

It would be fascinating to investigate the psychology and sociology of such archaic attitudes that are more redolent of Salem in the eighteenth century than of the United States of America in the twentieth. I have no doubt that the attitudes of the righteous citizens of the Pacific north-west states are identical with those of Salem, a notorious crucible of witchcraft. Sasquatches are the devil's business. In the realms of the Yeti no such prejudices appear to exist. Even the Abbot of Thyangboche (see chapter 2) can see no threat to his immortal soul by underwriting the reality of the Bigfoot of the Himalayas.

The Sasquatch, so it is claimed, has been filmed three times. First, in California in 1957 — though it was not announced to the press until late November 1970 — by Ray Wallace from Toledo, Washington. Wallace's Sasquatch is said to be gorilla-like except for 'ivory-looking claws' which were $1\frac{1}{2}$ in. long and $\frac{1}{4}$ in. thick. Other dimensions were: stature, 10 ft.; weight, approximately 1,000 lb; fingers, 8 in. long; and wrists, 8 in. thick. Mr Wallace adds, for good measure, that the Sasquatch has been seen to pick up fifty-gallon drums full of grease and throw them 150 feet (a classical myth-motif which only reinforces the somewhat fabulous ring to the whole affair). Mr Wallace is said to have 15,000 feet of colour film of the Sasquatch. I do not feel impressed with Mr Wallace's story.

In early November 1970, one Ivan Marx of Colville, Washington State, talked to a reporter of the *Vancouver Daily Province* about the occasion the previous October when he had filmed a seventy-foot sequence of a crippled Sasquatch 9 ft. high and weighing 800 lb. The authenticity of Marx's film has still to be confirmed.

The best item of the Californian Bigfoot saga I have kept to the last – the Roger Patterson film. In theory this should have wrapped up the whole thing. One can hardly quarrel with a movie taken at a range of approximately 100 feet showing a continuous sequence 20 feet long of 16 mm. colour film of a Sasquatch head on, in profile and in rear-view; but of course it all depends on the movie – and the star.

It is difficult to do justice to Patterson's film in mere words, but as few of you who read this book will have seen the film, I must do my best to re-create the essentials.[12] First of all, here is the background. Roger Patterson, a very attractive and sincere well-spoken man of about forty, has had a varied career around the fringes of show business; for some time he worked in rodeo. At the time the film was taken, Patterson was living in Yakima, Washington. His professional curiosity in the Sasquatch had been aroused some years earlier. With his colleague Bob Gimlin, who let it be said is somewhat of a 'third man' character in this affair, Patterson was trekking on horseback high up the Bluff Creek Valley in Northern California in the autumn of 1967 in search of the Sasquatch when he chanced upon a female of the species. The first few frames of the movie are all over the place, just as if they had been filmed by a man on the run which is precisely what Patterson says he was doing – running towards the Sasquatch and shooting as he went, his horse having thrown him at the first sight of the creature. When the film settles down, the Sasquatch is seen in profile to begin with, striding easily, arms freely swinging, walking from left to right along the far side of a dried and silted-up stream-bed. During this brief sequence, which is in reasonably good focus, the Sasquatch turns towards the camera. She does not turn her head, she pivots at the hips as if her upper body were rigid; just, in fact, as one might turn with a stiff neck. The physical and psychological attitudes of the creature appear totally relaxed almost to the degree of nonchalance. The final sequences pick up the creature as with her back to the camera she disappears with the same unhurried pace into the forest to vanish finally amongst the vine-maples and rhododendrons of the understorey, for all the world like a classic Charlie Chaplin fade-out. I say 'her' because this is what she is said to be, but see below.

Physically the creature was heavily built, particularly around the chest and shoulders; the trunk was chunky with hardly a change in width from shoulders to hips. The whole body was covered in short, almost plushy, dark reddish-brown hair. The top of the head was somewhat conical and flowed into the trunk without the interruption of a neck. The face was bare and, as far as could be seen, dark in colour. The palms of the hands were hairless, and so were the soles of the feet, which seemed to be light in colour. The legs were hefty and powerfully muscled. A prominent pair of buttocks stuck out from behind, mimicking a not quite so prominent pair of furry breasts in front.

My own impressions, recorded immediately after seeing this film at least half-a-dozen times at a private preview set up in Washington, D.C. on December 2nd, 1967, can be summarized as follows:

1. The walk was consistent in general terms with the bipedal striding gait of modern man, *Homo sapiens*.

2. The cadence of the walk, the general fluidity of body movements and the swing of the arms were to my mind grossly exaggerated. At the time I annotated this statement with the comment that the walk was 'self-conscious'.

3. In spite of the heavy, pendulous breasts visible as the creature turned towards the camera, the style of walking was essentially that of a human male.

4. The appearance of a somewhat cone-shaped top to the skull is definitely non-human, but occurs consistently in adult male gorillas and in male orang-utans. The function of the bony crest, which provides the anatomical basis for this appearance, is to give supplementary attachment areas for heavy jaw muscles necessitated by massive jaws and teeth. Essentially it is a male characteristic, only very occasionally seen, to an insignificant extent, in females.

5. The physical build of the creature with its heavy neck, shoulders and chest strongly suggests that the centre of gravity of the body would lie at a higher level in the Sasquatch than it does in man; this in turn would alter the characteristics of the walk, which reduced to its mechanical baseline is a problem of moving the centre of gravity through space. The assumption therefore is made that in spite of the anatomical appearance that argues to the contrary—the centre of gravity of the subject is precisely as it is in modern man.

6. The presence of buttocks, a human hallmark, is at total variance with the ape-like nature of the superstructure. Buttocks, however, are *consistent* with the pattern of the walk and, thus, with the inferred position of the centre of gravity of the body. The upper half of the body bears some resemblance to an ape and the lower half is typically human. It is almost impossible to conceive that such structural hybrids could exist in nature. One half of the animal must be artificial. In view of the walk, it can only be the upper half.

Subsequently, I have seen and studied the film, frame by frame, a dozen times or more and I have no reason to change the opinions expressed above, only to add to them an important deduction which only came to me some time after the initial viewing. I was puzzled by the extraordinary exaggeration of the walk: it seemed to me to be an overstatement of the normal pattern, a bad actor's interpretation of a classical human walking gait. If I should put myself in the position of a hypothetical joker I would ask myself why spoil the ship for a ha'porth of tar? Why ruin a good hoax by ordering my actor to walk in this artificial way? This proved unanswerable for several months until the solution dawned upon me when seeing a colleague at the Smithsonian Institution pace out the dimensions of a museum gallery that was to be turned into offices and store rooms. Being a man of small stature he was walking in an abnormal, exaggerated manner, determined that each of his steps should represent a linear yard. It suddenly occurred to me that perhaps this was what our purported Sasquatch was doing. He (in spite of the breasts) was making sure that every step, every footprint in the sandbar, told a tale. The footprints of the Bluff Creek Sasquatch female of Patterson's film attested to a foot length of 14 in.–15 in., which indicates a stature of between 7 ft. 8 in. and 8 ft. 3 in. (not of 6 ft. 9 in. as suggested in John Green's reconstruction). The length of the step[13] of Patterson's creature was stated to be a mere 41 in. This is inconsistent with its height estimated from footprint size; the step of an 8 ft. man would be approximately 56 in. A 56 in. step would be impossible for a man of average height (5 ft. 8 in.) although one of 41 in. would be within his capacity providing he 'strode out'. Stature, foot size and step length in man, other things being equal, form a closely-linked structural-functional complex. All three factors should be consistent with each other. Could it be that the 'exaggerated' walk of Bigfoot was designed to magnify the normal step length, an effect which, in the event, failed miserably?

Other criticisms were levelled at the creature's appearance by scientists invited to view the film. William Montagna, the distinguished director of the Regional Primate Research Center at Beaverton, Oregon, an expert on primates and, in particular, the skin, pointed out that human female breasts do not bear hairs however hirsute the rest of the body. Frank Beebe of the British Columbia Provincial Museum, who concluded quite independently that the bodily form of Patterson's Bigfoot was male in spite of its female appendages, also made an extremely pertinent observation. Why, he asks, does a creature with a tall bony crest on its skull, as Patterson's creature clearly had, have a non-protuberant abdomen? To understand this apparent irrelevance one must appreciate the biological meaning of the bony crest which forms such a prominent feature of male gorilla and orang-utan skull anatomy. The crest is an adaptive device to provide supplementary attachment for muscles operating the jaws. Gorillas and orangs have big massive jaws and teeth, which demand very large muscles to operate them during chewing. Heavy jaws are necessitated by a diet of large quantities of roughage, low-energy food which demands powerful mastication. This type of diet results in a heavily loaded stomach and intestine and, consequently, a pot-bellied appearance. This configuration is also seen in many leaf-eating monkeys such as Ateles, the spider monkey of South America.

This is how matters stood in 1968. It was not until the end of 1971 that any further progress was made with Patterson's film. Rene Dahinden, tired of the brush-off attitudes of North-American scientists who refused to take the matter seriously, decided to come to Britain and Europe at his own expense in order to stir up interest among the scientific community. He brought with him samples of all the evidence: tape-recordings of eye-witness accounts, casts and photographs of footprints—and the Patterson film. His travels through Europe, and his reception—particularly in the U.S.S.R.—are another story, but in Britain the response was swift and, as it turns out, very revealing. I was able to introduce Rene Dahinden to a colleague of mine, Dr Don Grieve, an anatomist who specializes in the human gait. A copy of Patterson's film was handed to Grieve who analysed it, frame by frame, and produced the report which appears as an appendix.

The gist of Grieve's analysis is as follows: the creature has a stature of no more than 6 ft. 5 in., which brings it well within the range of human variability. Its walk is human in type and, possibly, identical with that of modern man. Let's take Grieve's observations slowly and one at a time and see what conclusions we can draw from them.

A stature of 6 ft. 5 in. is fine; there is no reason to exclude the Sasquatch on these grounds. *But* the footprints associated with this creature are totally at variance with its calculated height. The footprints are said to have been between 14 in. and 15 in. in length. On the basis of the coefficient given on p. 119 this should equate with a stature of 7 ft. 8 in.–8 ft. 3 in. The space (the step) between one footprint and the next is given as 41 in. A creature 6 ft. 5 in. in height should have a step of 45 in., particularly, as it is seen in the film, when striding out; in fact in view of the exaggerated nature of the walk, the step might be expected to be somewhat longer than the normal, say 50 in. The conclusion is inevitable. The footprints must be fakes or the film is. Of course, both film and footprints could be faked but one thing is certain; they cannot both be true-bill.

Grieve's second point is not nearly so easy to draw conclusions from. Surprising as it may seem to anyone unfamiliar with Bigfoot affairs, the frame speed at which Patterson took his film is unknown. Was it 16 f.p.s. or 24 f.p.s.? Patterson states that he cannot recollect; his camera was equipped to run at either speed. The sort of situation where human or mechanical faults, unaccountably, come between the photographer and world renown is another of these clichés so characteristic of life in the Goblin Universe. How many U.F.O.s and Loch Ness Monsters would now be immortalized if the camera hadn't been left in the car?

Grieve's point is that if the movie sequence was filmed at 24 f.p.s. then the creature's walk cannot be distinguished from a normal human walk. If, on the other hand, it was filmed at 16 or 18 f.p.s., there are a number of important respects in which it is quite unlike man's gait. One cannot help thinking it likely that Patterson (though no movie camera specialist) would have used 24 f.p.s. if only because he must have been aware that this speed is best suited to T.V. transmission. After all, it was never his intention, as his subsequent actions showed, to restrict the showing of the film to the family circle; the film has in fact been widely shown to paying audiences in Canada and the U.S.A. However, this is entirely speculative, and the truth is that we don't know, nor apparently is there any way of telling from examining the film, the frame speed at which it was taken.

Grieve's analysis gives little support to Patterson's claim that his creature was a real live Sasquatch; on the other hand – on the grounds of the estimated stature alone – it does much to discredit it.

There is little doubt that the scientific evidence taken collectively points to a hoax of some kind. The creature shown in the film does not stand up well to functional analysis. There are too many inconsistencies; yet no scientist to whom I have spoken and who has seen the film, has any direct evidence to prove that the episode was anything but what it purported to be. My own comment quoted in an article in *Argosy* magazine (February 1968) was that there was nothing in the film which would prove conclusively that this was a hoax. In effect, what I meant was that I could not see the zipper; and I still can't.

There I think we must leave the matter. Perhaps it was a man dressed up in a monkey-skin; if so it was a brilliantly executed hoax and the unknown perpetrator will take his place with the great hoaxers of the world. Perhaps it was the first film of a new type of hominid, quite unknown to science, in which case Roger Patterson deserves to rank with Dubois, the discoverer of *Pithecanthropus erectus* or Java man; or with Raymond Dart of Johannesburg, the man who introduced the world to its immediate pre-human ancestor, *Australopithecus africanus*.[14]

The year 1969 produced two new centres of Sasquatch activity besides California: Bossburg, in the eastern part of Washington State just south of the Canadian border, and Oroville, also in Washington State. The relevant data is tabulated in table 2. The Bossburg tracks have rather a special claim to fame (see chapter 5). One cannot help noticing how Sasquatch data escalate as year succeeds year and the publicity grows. John Green's records of sightings for 1961–9 read as follows: 7 – 9 – 12 – 11 – 12 – 29 – 21 – 27 – 42. For 1970 we can confidently expect that the 1969 figure will have been exceeded.

Lest you should imagine that the Sasquatch is a parochial

phenomenon restricted to the western seaboard of the U.S.A. and Canada, let me put the record straight. According to Ivan Sanderson's files, which he has been kind enough to let me quote, twenty-nine incidents involving humanoid monsters (including twenty-five sightings) took place between June 1964 and December 1970 in the states of Michigan, Illinois, Wisconsin, Ohio, West Virginia, Pennsylvania, Georgia, Alabama, Tennessee, Arkansas, Arizona, Texas, Oklahoma and Missouri.

One incident that took place in the Deltox Marsh, near Fremont, Wisconsin, in November 1966, was personally investigated by Ivan Sanderson.[15] Six young men were taking part in a deer drive, but instead of deer they flushed a large, powerfully built creature covered with shortish dark hair that walked on two legs. It was barrel-chested with a thick, short neck, a heavy body tapering to the hips, and exceptionally long arms. The behaviour of the creature was leisurely and unafraid; its attitude towards the hunters was inquisitive rather than aggressive. Its gait was man-like, and it walked slightly stooped, with a swinging motion of the arms. As no doubt you will have already remarked, the young men's consensus description is highly reminiscent of Roger Patterson's furry starlet of Bluff Creek.

The North American Bigfoot or Sasquatch has a lot going for it. It is impossible on the evidence presented in this chapter to say that it does not exist. Too many people claim to have seen it or at least to have seen footprints to dismiss its reality out of hand. To suggest that hundreds of people at worst are lying or, at best, deluding themselves is neither proper nor realistic. There are some, no doubt, who are guilty of pure inventiveness for one reason or another; there are some whose imaginations are over-active; there are some who are drawing on information they already possess; and there are some whose mammal identification is sadly at fault. But — on the grounds of probability alone — there must be *some* observers who are honest, detached and well-informed, and it is these people, if we knew who they were, that should be harkened to. But this attitude is essentially a subjective one; there is no way of proving that such observers exist, affidavits,

6. Sherpa Kunjo Chumbi proudly demonstrating the 'Yeti' scalp at a viewing of the supposed relic at the British Museum (Natural History), London

7. A close-up of the 'Yeti' scalp, which turned out to be simply a man-made piece of fakelore

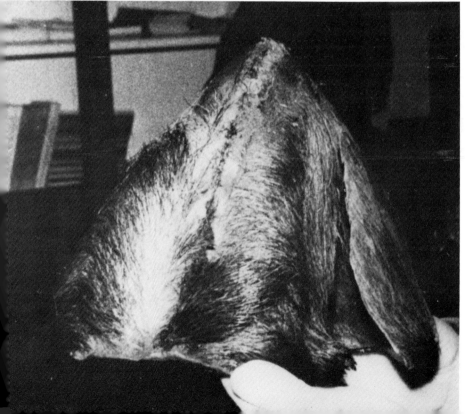

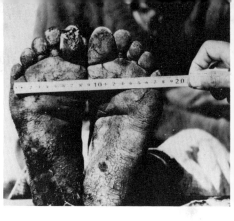

8. A sadhu demonstrating his immunity to cold at 18,000 feet. The footprints of these ascetics may have contributed to the myth of the Himalayan Bigfoot. (*top left*) The same man was able to crunch up and swallow glass-tubing without any apparent ill effect

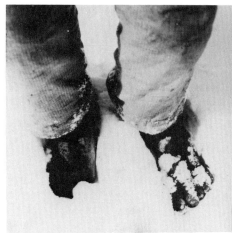

impeccable reputations and apparent sincerity notwithstanding.

Eschewing subjectivity, what is there left to go on? The answer is evidence, the indirect evidence of footprints, and the deductions derived from ecology, anatomy and evolution. These are factors which we will be looking at critically in later chapters.

In Skamania County, Washington State, the Sasquatch is protected. There is a $10,000 fine, an unprecedented amount, for anyone breaking the by-law by killing a Bigfoot. A county ordinance of this sort might be interpreted either as a vote of confidence in Bigfoot by its responsible citizens, or an exercise in self-promotion. Who knows?

4. *Tales from the Minnesota Woods*

This chapter is all about the Iceman. Let me say at this stage that my role in the curious affair was distinctly that of 'voices off'. The central figures, the real heroes of the investigation, were Ivan T. Sanderson and Bernard Heuvelmans, who uncovered the mystery. From a journalistic point of view the Iceman was a great story while it lasted, but I believe it has only served further to degrade the Bigfoot legend. The Iceman affair in fact can be regarded as a logical culmination of a trend that started when the name of Bigfoot was first attached to a commercial enterprise. Perhaps it was a hamburger stand, a motel or a supermarket; whatever it was, it started a chain reaction. In the interests of non-partisanship it should be noted that this phenomenon is ubiquitous. Not even the Himalayan states are wholly free from the taint of commercialism. Witness Nepal's reported four-hundred-pound levy on Yeti hunters. Witness, too, the recent issue of stamps from Bhutan. Flushed with the financial success of their 1966 Abominable Snowman stamps, they repeated the theme in 1970 with an even more astonishing 3-D set. This issue is all the more remarkable because it purports to represent the animals of Bhutan, and includes not only a classic ape-like Yeti figure but an African elephant and a suspiciously African-looking rhinoceros.

The story of the Minnesota Iceman is a tortuous affair, principally as a result of the manoeuvres of the 'owner' of the Iceman exhibit, Frank D. Hansen. The quotes surrounding the word owner are meant to underscore a critical component of the whole puzzling story, for according to Hansen's declaration to the press and other responsible persons who have interviewed him, the *real* owner is a well-known multi-millionaire living on the West Coast of U.S.A. and connected with the movie business. The *Sunday Times* quoted Hansen as stating that the owner was a very wealthy man whose pleasure 'is to have something rare, something that other people don't have'.

The bare facts of the story in chronological sequence are as follows. On December 17th, 1968, Ivan T. Sanderson and Bernard Heuvelmans, a Belgian zoologist and the author of several very excellent books on unknown animals, inspected a creature frozen in a block of ice and enclosed in an insulated coffin maintained by refrigeration. Their visit to Frank D. Hansen's farm in a remote area of Minnesota near the township of Winona was the result of a tip-off to Sanderson that a strange hominoid creature was being wintered there after a two-year, moderately successful, tour of the carnival grounds of the United States. Hansen received Sanderson and Heuvelmans in a friendly manner and gave them unrestricted access to the Iceman immured in his chilly tomb. They spent two days studying the creature in the restricted confines of the trailer in which the coffin was housed. Space problems made it difficult to photograph the Iceman *in extenso* or even to make really reliable drawings. Sanderson describes how he was forced to lie on the plate glass lid of the coffin, face to face with the monster, in order to make his detailed sketches (plate 17). What the two investigators saw, drew and photographed will be described later. The important point to make at this stage is that both men—both highly experienced and well-informed men—*accepted the creature on its face value*. Bernard Heuvelmans's conviction that what he saw through a sheathing of ice in a cold trailer in the yard of a snow-bound farmstead in a remote region was a true-bill unknown hominid is confirmed by the publication of an article in February 1969 in the *Bulletin of the Royal Institute of Natural Sciences of Belgium* entitled 'Notice on a specimen preserved in ice of an unknown form of living hominid: *Homo pongoides*'. In the eyes of zoologists Heuvelmans committed a grave scientific sin with this article. It would not have been so bad if he had merely contented himself with publishing the report, but by *naming* a creature whose existence in nature was uncertain, and at the time unprovable, he put himself in an untenable position. The procedure of giving a name to a new species of animal is a highly formalized affair in zoology and is bound by rules of protocol far more precise than those which govern the actions of the diplomatic corps. The reason for such exactitude is very right and proper. When naming a new species it is necessary to designate a certain specimen as the 'type' so that, for ever afterwards, the name and the particular animal so named are linked. Even if the Iceman turned out eventually to be a real creature, Dr Heuvelmans, who clearly believed it to be a form of Neanderthal man, would have to show that the creature was specifically different from *Homo sapiens* (a species of which Neanderthal man is generally regarded as a subspecies called *Homo sapiens neanderthalensis*) before the name *Homo pongoides* (indicating a *new* species of man) could be officially recognized. This procedure would not be an easy one even if it were possible, and so I think it highly unlikely that *Homo pongoides* will ever take its place nomenclatorially along with *Homo sapiens* and *Homo erectus*. In 1969 Sanderson published a somewhat more cautiously worded paper in the journal *Genus*.[1]

The essence of what Sanderson and Heuvelmans saw, albeit through plate glass and a thick layer of ice with the opacities and other imperfections of artificial freezing and refreezing, is briefly summarized from their respective papers as follows:

General appearance (plate 17). The body is lying on its back, the right arm across the lower abdomen and the left arm crooked above the head; the knees are slightly bent. The torso appears long and massive giving the impression of flowing into the thighs, an appearance which is due presumably to the absence of any outward swelling at the hips. The length of the creature is about six feet. The body apart from the face, palms of the hands and sides is covered with fairly long, dark-coloured, coarse hair, the roots of which are widely separated from each other. The hair shows an 'agouti' pattern (see below).

Face. The creature is somewhat pug-faced, the tip of the nose turning upwards revealing wide, flaring, thick-walled nostrils; on the septum between the nostrils is a narrow band of hair. The forehead is sloping but the top of the head is lost in the depth of the ice. The face is broad and the mouth is slit-like, lacking the everted lips of modern man. The eye-sockets are large and, according to Sanderson, empty, but Heuvelmans asserts that the left eyeball is dislocated and is lying on the left cheek. In Heuvelmans's opinion the creature had been shot by a high velocity bullet through the right eye, blowing out the back of the skull. It has been stated by Hansen, the lessee, that this area is badly smashed. The explosion dislocated the left eye from its socket. The condition of the left forearm would be consistent with such an injury supposing that the creature had raised its left arm to cover its face from frontal assault.

Arms and hands. The arms appear to be long and excessively hairy. The left forearm is apparently fractured about midway along its length and the flesh is seen to be gaping at the site of the wound. The hands are gross, disproportionately large with long, slender, tapering thumbs. On the palm of the left hand, the bare skin on the inner side (ulnar side) extends backwards on to the wrist to form a sort of 'heel' to the hand, precisely as one might find in the hand of a monkey but certainly not of an ape or a man.

Legs and feet. Compared with the arms the legs are rather short but very 'human' in appearance; they are also extremely hairy. The feet are tremendously broad and spatulate, the big toe is aligned alongside the second toe (a human characteristic) and the nails are blunt and straight-edged. The big toe is not excessively 'big' relative to the small toes.

The genitalia. The penis is long, slender and tapering, and the scrotum rather small: when erect the penis would certainly not have been particularly striking in its dimensions.

So much for the external appearances upon which both Sanderson and Heuvelmans agree, differing only in minor detail. We can take it, then, that the description of what they saw is accurate. Before plunging into a critical analysis of this *objet trouvé* from an anatomical viewpoint, I think we ought to give some consideration to the provenance of this remarkable exhibit.

Frank D. Hansen, the lessee of this property, stated in the early days of the Iceman affair that the creature had been found floating in a 6,000 lb block of natural ice, in the Sea of Okhotsk, an oceanic enclave between the Kamchatka peninsula and eastern Siberia. The fishers of this extraordinary catch were initially said to be Russian sealers and later Japanese whalers. After trials and tribulations with the Customs and various unspecified political agencies, the Iceman—still deep-frozen—turned up in Hong Kong in a Chinese dealer's emporium where it was purchased by someone, presumably an agent of the mysterious Mr X, the anonymous mogul of the West Coast, flown to the U.S.A. and rented to Mr Frank D. Hansen who then proceeded to exhibit the creature around the carnival circuits of the U.S. heartlands for a couple of years at thirty-five cents a peek. In 1969 the Iceman was on exhibit, billed as the 'Siberskoye Creature frozen and preserved forever in a coffin of ice'.[2] In 1970, Hansen with a double-bluff (or was it a double-double-bluff?) 'confessed' in the magazine *Saga* that he had shot the Iceman in the woods of Minnesota in 1960 and that his story about the Sea of Okhotsk was simply an example of the fairground showman's traditional spiel. In fact the provenance of the Iceman has been so thoroughly obfuscated that there is no consistent zoogeographical story to criticize. Its origins are as mysterious as the origins of Bigfoot itself. The possibility that its provenance in fact was some sort of monster-factory or wax-museum in Hollywood will develop as the story unfolds.

I first heard about the Iceman on February 3rd, 1969, from Ivan Sanderson, a few weeks after his visit to Hansen's ranch, and I studied his comprehensive report and scale diagrams. My first reaction, based on the creature's anatomy, was extreme dubiety;

the characteristics of the Iceman seemed to me then—as now—to combine the worst features of apes and man and none of the best features which make these two groups extremely successful primates in their respective environments. As described, the Iceman's foot was specifically adapted neither for climbing, as in a chimpanzee for example, nor for a two-footed walking gait on the flat as in man. The hands were typical of neither apes nor of humans but were a ridiculous compromise between the two.

Transitional forms passing from one evolutionary grade to another within a phylogenetic line do occur in nature. Perhaps the best example of this in the fossil record is provided by the horses (Equidae) whose evolutionary progression, dating from the Eocene some sixty million years ago, provides a continuous series of forms successively replacing one another in time. But it is of paramount importance to appreciate that however transitional a species may seem to have been in retrospect, it was in its time perfectly successful being wholly adapted towards its environment. This is mandatory, otherwise the transitional species would have been eliminated by natural selection and there would have been no successors.

Whatever the Iceman is, it is no fossil. If it is not made of latex rubber and expanded polystyrene it represents a living species; there are no alternatives. Therefore the questions one must ask are the usual ones when dealing with a new form: what kind of species is it? and for what type of environment is it adapted? Applying this type of reasoning to the Iceman does not prove very rewarding; the species is indeterminate on the present evidence, and its adaptiveness equivocal. Its zoological affinities are neither wholly human (hominid) nor wholly ape (pongid); on the face of it, the Iceman is some crazy sort of hybrid. We know that an ape-human cross is genetically impossible and therefore we must make the assumption that the creature is not a 'sport' but a representative of an existing population. The likelihood of such an aberrant population being a prehistoric survival is remote (the existence of such populations is discussed less tersely in chapter 7).

Using Sanderson's scale diagram (plate 18), which as he admits was drawn under considerable difficulties, but which was later matched and correlated with Heuvelmans's photographs, I have been able to measure the relative limb lengths of the Iceman. The relative proportions of the upper limb and lower limb can be expressed as a percentage, the so-called intermembral index. Modern man, whose arms are shorter than his legs, has an index varying between 67 and 72; apes, whose arms are longer than their legs, possess an index that, depending on species, lies between 103 and 150. The index of the Iceman is 87 indicating that the proportions are characteristic neither of apes nor men. There is a considerable amount of data on the hand index[3] in primates: this index reflects the relative length of the hand compared with the length of the arm as a whole. For the Iceman this index is 32·5. The range in *Homo sapiens* is 22·7–26·1, and for the apes from 23·1–31·0. Other indices, which reflect bodily proportions, consistently indicate that the Iceman's measurements are neither those of fish, fowl nor good red herring – nor man, nor ape for that matter. The Iceman, in fact, does not match up to the blueprint of any known primate or, indeed, any known animal. This does not mean that the Iceman cannot exist, it simply makes it just that much more improbable.

There are a certain number of very odd features about Sanderson's and Heuvelmans's descriptions. The hair, for instance. The pattern of hair distribution seems indisputable: present where it ought to be and absent in the expected places like the face, the palm of the hand and the sole of the foot. But Sanderson makes a very significant observation that goes unremarked in Heuvelmans's report. The hairs, Sanderson avers, are agouti. On the face of it this is not a particularly soul-shaking item of information. Agouti is a condition where the hairs are composed of alternating bands of dark and light and is probably familiar to most people as the fur pattern of a squirrel. The agouti pattern is regarded as a phylogenetically ancient character that has become lost in evolution in certain groups as a result of increasing specialization. The agouti pattern of hair coloration is also extremely common amongst the primates. It is seen in the monkeys of both the New and Old Worlds; but at the higher levels of primate evolution — amongst the apes and man — it is completely unknown. That the Iceman should possess agouti-patterned hairs is a zoological improbability of the highest order. If we can take this observation of Sanderson's as valid, and there is no reason why we should not, then the likelihood that the Iceman is an artefact — a man-made object — is high.

As a result of Sanderson's initial curiosity and his subsequent probing, assisted by the growing interest of the scientific establishment, the Iceman Saga entered a new and incredibly devious phase that, in the event, destroyed any semblance of open-mindedness that one might once have held.

I don't propose to do more than attempt a brief outline of the extraordinary complexities of the story, because they are largely irrelevant to the main theme of this book, which is to assess in *biological* terms the possibility of the existence of monsters. As the Minnesota Iceman story unfolds, it reveals itself as a problem for a detective agency rather than for a biologist.

Ivan Sanderson, whom I have known for many years, telephoned me soon after his discovery with the suggestion that I, as curator of the primate collections at the Smithsonian, was in a good position to interest the Institution in the affair. Sanderson held the view that the Smithsonian was the proper authority to investigate the matter scientifically. In those early days this seemed a very exciting prospect, and consequently I approached S. Dillon Ripley, Secretary of the Institution, who was most enthusiastic about the project and agreed that we should take an official interest. I drafted a rather pompous press release indicating that although the Institution was somewhat sceptical, it was open-minded enough to cooperate fully in the investigation. The first step obviously was to see and if possible to get hold of the specimen but this was not to be. A letter from Mr Ripley to Frank Hansen elicited the reply that the specimen was no longer in his hands but had been removed by its anonymous owner. A further paragraph implied that when the creature was exhibited in the coming (1969) summer season it would 'in many respects resemble' the original exhibit which, Mr Hansen believed, would probably never be shown to the public again. So it seemed that the 'original' had been replaced by a model, but there was of course no guarantee that the 'original' was 'real' in the first place. Mr Hansen was most careful not to commit himself in this respect, then or at any other time.

In February 1969, the article by Bernard Heuvelmans appeared in a Belgian scientific journal, a mere two and a half months after the event. In this article, as already stated, Heuvelmans expressed his opinion that the corpse was 'real' and represented an unknown species of man. Now that the missing 'original' had been publicly authenticated as human, the apparent bullet wounds took on a somewhat sinister meaning. There was only one thing to be done and that was to inform the law.[4] So Mr Ripley wrote to Mr J. Edgar Hoover, director of the Federal Bureau of Investigation, requesting the cooperation of the F.B.I. in tracing the original exhibit. Mr Hoover was not very helpful and simply pointed out that as no violation of a federal law had been proved the F.B.I. had no power to act.

In the meanwhile George Berklacy of the Public Relations Office of the Smithsonian and I had been doing a little digging on our own. Berklacy after an exhausting and dangerous mission on the telephone tracked down a commercial organization on the West Coast that claimed to have made the Iceman for Frank Hansen out of latex rubber and hair in April 1967 (the year it went out on the first tour of the circus midways). The name Pete Corrall was mentioned in connection with the model. Berklacy and I decided against releasing this name at the time, but since Hansen mentions Pete Corrall in the *Saga* Magazine article as the man who put the hairs into the Iceman model, there seems no special reason why it shouldn't be mentioned now. Of course there is no proof that the story that Berklacy was given was true—in fact Sanderson told me later that he has been in contact with at least two other organizations which claim the same honour, but at the time it seemed to confirm my steadily growing conviction that the Iceman was a model and always had been a model. On my advice, the Smithsonian Institution issued a press release withdrawing its interest in the Iceman, much, I think, to the relief of all concerned, who were understandably jittery at the prospect of press headlines proclaiming 'Smithsonian Scientists Fooled by Carnival Exhibit'. The official disclaimer by no means ended my personal interest in the affair but it seemed to me that in view of what we had learned, it was only proper that the Smithsonian should be taken off the hook before it was too late. Indeed, there was some danger that it was already too late since Hansen had by then opened his new season by displaying the Iceman in a shopping precinct in St Paul, Minnesota, and was attracting scientific customers from nearby universities. It is not without relevance with regard to Hansen's motivation that as a crowning touch he had by now added to his display boards bearing the title 'The Near-Man, the Siberskoye Creature', the words 'Investigated by the F.B.I.'.

The Smithsonian's 'withdrawal of interest' statement provided a spate of wild rumours, notably that the Smithsonian, and probably Ivan Sanderson as well since he was known to be working in close association with us, had somehow got their hands on the corpse and found it to be genuine. As the announcement of a missing link would be embarrassing for the established scientific view, the Smithsonian were suppressing the facts! Another rumour suggested that the Mafia, who were credited with having an unspecified interest in this matter, were bringing their considerable influence to bear to stop any further scientific investigations being carried out by myself on behalf of the Smithsonian. The cloak-and-dagger school, who see an iron hand in every velvet glove, were having a ball, and for a day or two I admit I went around Washington with eyes skinned and a firm grip on my British umbrella.

Prior to his opening at St Paul, Hansen held a press conference at his ranch near Winona at which the *Rochester Post-Bulletin* reporter Gordon Yeager was present. The gist of Hansen's statement, Yeager reports in the issue of April 21st, 1969, was that the Iceman was man-made, an illusion, and was not his property anyway. Yeager asked a number of penetrating questions, but he says that most of them were smoothly parried by Hansen whom he credits with being an 'excellent showman'. Herein I believe lies the secret of the Iceman – showmanship.

However, the saga is not yet quite done. After St Paul, the exhibit moved on to Grand Rapids, Michigan, where it was filmed by Time-Life Inc. This film, together with the colour pictures taken by Gordon Yeager at the press conference, make it quite clear that the creature in the ice is not identical with the one that Sanderson and Heuvelmans drew and photographed in December 1968. For example according to Bernard Heuvelmans the mouth was 'slightly open and one can see a yellowish tooth ... ' In Yeager's photographs the mouth is agape and at least four teeth can be clearly seen. Moreover the left big toe which was firmly apposed to the toes in the 'original' was now quite widely separated from them. Other minor differences were apparent to me. Ivan Sanderson claimed categorically that this exhibit was not the one that he and Heuvelmans had examined. On the face of it, therefore, there was a good case for believing that a 'model', a ringer, had been switched for the 'original' at some time; in fact Frank Hansen in his letter to the Smithsonian six weeks earlier stated as much. But there is still no certainty that the 'original' was any more 'real' than the substitute model. By June 1969 I had made up my mind, and nothing that has transpired since, including Hansen's 'confession' in *Saga*, has made me see any need to change it; the substance of a memorandum that I submitted at the time to Mr Ripley is paraphrased below. There comes a time when even an 'open' mind has to decide one way or the other! So here, chronologically, is my wholly speculative reconstruction of the Iceman Affair.

Frank Hansen, a clever showman of the Barnum school ('There is one born every minute') conceived the idea of a monster exhibit on – or rather in – ice. Ice is more dramatic than pickle as a preservative, and, what's more, ice gives the right degree of opacity and gloss to a model which serves both to heighten the illusion and prevent too close an inspection. Hansen decided on a classy exhibit and equipped himself with a model made by top experts in the field, a high-quality 'coffin' and an expensive trailer. At a guess, this equipage would have cost him not less than $50,000 (£20,000). At the beginning of the summer of 1967 he started touring the Iceman; he was moderately successful in 1967 and 1968 but, as he admitted to newsmen in 1969, his investment had not yet paid off. After the summer season of 1968 Hansen felt he must do something to drum up business and conceived a very subtle publicity campaign. Somehow he managed to leak information through a colleague that reached Ivan Sanderson. On Hansen's admission, he knew of Sanderson's books and of his overwhelming interest in unexplained phenomena in general and 'Abominable Snowmen' in particular. He was banking on a positive reaction from Sanderson, which, in the event, exceeded his wildest dreams. As it happened, quite by chance, Bernard Heuvelmans was staying with Sanderson at the time and Hansen, unbeknownst, had caught two fish with one fly – and two vociferous, well-informed, and determined fish at that.

Under somewhat Charles-Addams-like conditions – a remote farmhouse in the middle of a Minnesota winter – Sanderson and Heuvelmans were faced with a brilliantly executed model. Psychologically, anyone who had spent a lifetime in search of unknown animals as these two had was bound to be impressed by what he saw. Heuvelmans was so impressed that he plunged into print without further ado. Sanderson, equally impressed, was more cautious. The publicity that developed as a consequence of that December evening was both heartening and embarrassing for Frank Hansen. What started as a publicity stunt had become a global furore; papers all over the world carried the story. The unexpected had happened. *Science was taking the Iceman seriously!* This needed careful handling. Perhaps the letter that Secretary Ripley wrote to Hansen was the last straw. Now even the Nation's Capital was in on the act! However, providing that he, Hansen, made no statement that could be legally challenged, this bonus publicity could be turned into an advantage rather than a liability. It was essential that the 'original' had to disappear and a substitute substituted to deepen the mystery and keep the Iceman free of curious scientists who would, inevitably, come nosing around following Heuvelmans's report in the Belgian scientific press.

The only way that this could be done, short of having another expensive model made, was to defrost the existing model, make minor alterations that would support his statement to the Smithsonian in which he said his new exhibit would 'in many respects, resemble' the original and re-freeze it. (It is perhaps significant that Hansen went on vacation some time between March 25th and April 12th, during which time the changes could have been effected.)

Soon after his return with the refurbished model, he arranged for a press conference at his ranch when the Iceman was thrown open for inspection and photography. At this conference he emphasized the man-made nature of his substitute model and, at the same time, avoided giving any inkling of the nature of the original. The extravagant claim that the creature had been discovered floating in a block of natural ice in the Sea of Okhotsk was explained away as mere showman's patter to pull in the customers.

I take my hat off to Frank Hansen, not because he glorified the monster myth (in my opinion he helped to debase it) but because he showed supreme skill in his chosen profession. I don't believe he ever told a lie – he simply talked his way around every issue. He was always one step ahead of the rest of us, and if there is a Barnum Award, my vote would go to Frank D. Hansen. He never claimed anything for this exhibit other than that it was a mystery, which indeed it was – and still is.

Perhaps the real puzzle that arises from this theoretical reconstruction is how two experienced zoologists like Ivan T. Sanderson and Bernard Heuvelmans could have been misled. I have already indicated a possible explanation in terms of the psychological pressures that they experienced at the time. But is this enough? I fear it is the weakest link in my reconstruction. Both these scientists will undoubtedly refute both my analysis of the events and the imputation that they were the victims of brain-washing, and insist that what they saw was the real thing. They have already provided the reasons for their beliefs. I repeat that my reconstruction is purely speculative, inasmuch as I can offer no kind of proof for my suggestions, which are simply the result of intuitive reasoning. For three or four months I was steeped up to the eyebrows in this business. I spent many hours in conversation with Sanderson and Heuvelmans and others involved, I have studied the documents and press reports relating to the case, as well as films, photographs and drawings, over a period of several months. I know something about the anatomy and ecology of man and of his evolution. I am also reasonably conversant with the universal patterns and manifestations of the monster myth. One cannot involve oneself to this extent without developing a kind of sixth sense. Perhaps the story of the Iceman is more complicated than the simple peccadilloes of a fairground showman. Perhaps there are sinister overtones involving Customs irregularities, secret societies and rackets of one sort or another, but if so I don't recognize or care about them. Cloaks and daggers are not my *métier;* biology is, and it is on the biological probabilities that my case rests.

The aftermath of the Iceman, in a sense, is anticlimax but even anticlimax can be interesting. On June 30th, 1969, the *National Bulletin* carried the headline: I WAS RAPED BY THE ABOMIN- ABLE SNOWMAN. As a front-page banner this rates second only to such classics as 'Vicar accused of nude stable-girl slaying' and 'M.P. in Hyde Park bandstand scandal'. First of all it is interesting to see that just as 'nude' is regarded as more evocative than 'naked', the Abominable Snowman carries a bigger punch than either the Bigfoot or the Iceman. In fact, what the headline was all about was the Iceman.

Apparently the young woman concerned — Helen Westring — was on a solo hunting trip in the woods near Bemidji, Minnesota, when she met an Abominable Snowman [*sic*]. It had pink eyes ringed with white fur and was covered all over with brown hair; it had a short neck, huge hands (11 in. long and 7 in. wide) and long arms. This creature proceeded to rip off Helen's clothes 'like one would peel a banana'. It then looked at her intently, especially at 'the area between my legs', threw her down on the leaves and with much grunting and heaving achieved its purpose—but luckily Helen had fainted. Then, on recovering her wits, she shot it—through the right eye, just as Bernard Heuvelmans had deduced. And that was how the Iceman died, at the hands of a simple American girl avenging her honour in the woods of Minnesota.

But Frank Hansen has another story. It was *he* who shot the Iceman in the woods of Minnesota—same woods, different story. This rather surprising tailpiece appeared in *Saga* Magazine in 1970. Surprising, because it seems out of character for the urbane Hansen to descend to melodrama. In the article he describes how, while still in the Air Force, he went on a hunting trip to the woods of northern Minnesota with some fellow officers. Becoming separated from the rest of the party, he shot and wounded a doe and followed it into a swamp. When he finally came up with it he found three hairy creatures tearing the animal to pieces with their bare hands and drinking its blood. One of the creatures with a screech sprang at Hansen who fired his rifle, hitting it in the face and apparently killing it instantly. Hansen in an access of terror fled from the spot and after stumbling about for a time finally managed to rejoin his party. He had decided not to mention the event to anyone for fear of ridicule which might possibly endanger his last few years of service before discharge from the Air Force. But, according to his article, after many sleepless nights he made his way back to the scene. It was early December and by now snow had come to the Minnesota woods. Finally Hansen reached the spot where he had tangled with the Iceman. In the article he describes how he tripped over a snow-covered log which—horror upon horror—turned out to be the creature he had shot a month or two earlier—frozen stiff!! Hansen felt that it was too dangerous to leave the corpse where he

9. A remarkable photograph of an orang-utan from Sumatra. No wonder apes
are called anthropoid, or manlike

10. An enlarged section of a frame from Roger Patterson's film of a Sasquatch at Bluff Creek, Northern California

11. Rene Dahinden and Roger Patterson displaying casts of Sasquatch footprint

found it because it might be traced to him. So, naturally, he hauled it back to his married quarters at the Air Force camp and stuck it in his deep-freeze where of course no one could conceivably trace it to him. Mrs Hansen agreed to throw out all her carefully preserved produce and substitute the Iceman, suitably folded. Mr Hansen then told his wife 'let's not tell a single person about this. We'll just leave it there until Spring'. In the event, the Iceman spent the next seven years folded in a receptacle intended primarily for beef steaks and garden peas.

In 1967 Hansen had had a replica made in Hollywood. He stated that the hairs were inserted individually by a special technique by Pete and Betty Corrall (whose names had been given to George Berklacy, the Smithsonian Press Officer, when we were attempting to track down the provenance of the model). It was this model that during the 1967 season was displayed on the midways of the nation. In 1968 Hansen felt the time had come to switch to the 'original' (although *why* he should want to do so is obscure, supposing his *Saga* story were true, unless it was based on the assumption that the last place anybody would look for a real corpse would be in a carnival exhibit).

When, at the end of 1968, Sanderson and Heuvelmans saw the creature and reported on it, Hansen felt the wisest course for him, in order to avoid the inquisition of scientists, federal authorities and so on, was to switch the bodies again; so back into the show coffin went the model and the 'original' was spirited away to an unknown hiding place where, presumably, it lies to this day unseen, unmourned and probably—if real—smelling to high heaven.

This is Hansen's story, and it is one that has considerable parallels with my own reconstruction which was written over a year prior to the publication of Hansen's article. My reconstruction, let it be said, was an in-house memorandum and never published at the time, but I now have the Smithsonian Institution's permission to do so. The major difference of course is that in my interpretation there never was an 'original'. The discrepancy between my reconstruction and Hansen's story is not

8

so great as it might seem for, in his concluding paragraph, Hansen indicates that he expects many people to brand his account as pure romance. He adds, 'Possibly it is, I am not under oath and should the situation dictate, I will deny every word of it.' This statement and the article's subtitle – 'Fact or Fiction' – argues strongly against it being an article of faith. Why did Hansen write this transparently dubious account? Not for money, apparently, as he categorically states that he is not receiving a single penny from *Saga* Magazine. For purely altruistic reasons? Perhaps. It is conceivable that his conscience is the clearer for this quasi-confession, who knows? Personally, I don't believe a word of it, but I do think he should get the Barnum Award for the second year running.

5. *The Evidence of the Footprints*

This chapter is all about footprints: the footprints of man and his monsters. In a sense, it is the most critical chapter in the whole book because footprints are the only available form of evidence on which objective judgments can be made. The reality of Bigfoot, in theory at any rate, stands or falls on the impressions that in its passage it has left on the skin of the earth.

There have been plenty of famous footprints. Good King Wenceslas imprinted his in the snow, and Man Friday settled for a sandy beach. Innumerable dinosaurs left the marks of their passage in the mud and clay of Cretaceous lake beds. Movie stars of the 'thirties were honoured to make their marks in wet concrete outside Grauman's Chinese Theatre in Hollywood, while for Sherlock Holmes it was the peaty soil of Dartmoor that bore witness to the passage of an enormous hound.

Foolhardy it may be to reconstruct a life-form from its footprints, but when footprints are the only evidence available, they cannot be ignored. This is the sort of problem that palaeontologists constantly have to rationalize. The fossil evidence for the early pre-Australopithecine stages of human evolution, for instance, could be packed into a cigar box and still leave room for a few cigars, but this paucity does not inhibit scientists from drawing provisional and (inevitably) controversial conclusions; and it is right that they should do so. The only alternative is to place the suspect fossils in a drawer and forget about them until such a time as a larger series becomes available. The disadvantage of this procedure, admirable though it is in principle, is that when the drawer is closed on a new discovery, palaeontology dies a little: as a science, palaeontology thrives on controversy, and without it it would lose momentum. The virtue of an inexact science lies in the fervour of its acolytes.

HUMAN FOOTPRINTS

Man has a unique form of walking that distinguishes him quite clearly from his fellow primates. It might be imagined that what is special about man is his ability to walk on two legs and not on four, as I have discussed on many occasions elsewhere.[1] Man shares the ability to walk on two legs with many other primates, with some mammals like the bear, with a few living and many extinct reptiles and with all birds. The trend towards bipedal walking is well-established in primate evolution. Nearly all higher primates walk bipedally when this method of getting about facilitates some particular activity, such as the carriage of food or the use of the hands in offensive and defensive actions, but no primate other than man is *habitually* bipedal. As far as fossil hominids are concerned, it is probable that several different versions of two-footed walking evolved in species that have since become extinct. It is even within the bounds of reason that some of these creatures thought to be extinct could be alive today, living in Asia and America, and leaving their enigmatic spoor scattered over these continents for the sole purpose, it would seem, of shaking our faith in the established principles of human evolution.

Whatever the footprints found in the snowfields of the Himalayas or on the dirt roads of Northern California turn out to be, they are not the footprints of modern man, *Homo sapiens*. Size apart, some of them are certainly reminiscent of human prints, and could conceivably be the footprints of unknown members of the human family. If they are human, then the indication is that Bigfoot walks in quite a different manner from our own species. As my purpose is to demonstrate these distinctions, the first task is to provide a standard for comparison by describing the human style of walking.

Modern man walks with a stride, and it is this accomplishment that makes his gait unique. Human striding is a highly complex affair, and in order to simplify a bio-mechanical problem that affects all parts of the body, it is best to concentrate principally on the feet where, in a sense, it is all happening. Admittedly, to describe human striding in terms of the foot is rather like explaining television in terms of the final product seen on the box; it gives one little idea of the technical problems involved but, at least, the message is clear.

The human foot, which, after the brain, is the most specialized part of the body, is made up of a heel, a shank and a set of five toes. The foot is not simply a slab of flesh and bone, that carries the weight of the body like the pedestal of a lavatory pan, but a dynamic structure that varies its shape and dimensions in accordance with the demands of the substrate. Shoes reduce the potential plasticity of the foot, but by no means eradicate it. Surprisingly, the anatomy of the habitually shod foot differs insignificantly from that of the habitually naked one. The dynamics of the human foot are eloquently expressed in the prints that it leaves, and a 'walking' print is readily distinguishable from a 'static' print, a point of some importance in the interpretation of Sasquatch tracks, some of which appear distinctly static.

The process of striding starts when an individual, standing upright with his feet together, commences to move forward. The wish to advance activates, through a series of complex neurological linkages, the muscles of the legs and the hips, with the result that the body sways forward at the ankles until its centre of gravity extends beyond the area circumscribed by the supporting feet. Man, at this crucial phase, is all set to fall flat on his face. That he does not do so is a matter of reflex activity; he saves himself by swinging his leg in front of his body to act as a prop. By this action he has restored the *status quo* and is no longer in danger of falling. Having initiated this hazardous procedure of loss of balance followed by recovery, he continues the process. So, dicing with disaster, man progresses onwards by means of a series of smoothly integrated, alternating swings of right and left legs. Disaster is never very far away during human walking, and often enough it strikes without warning. The banana-skins of life are ready and waiting for the over-confident, the elderly and the drunk.

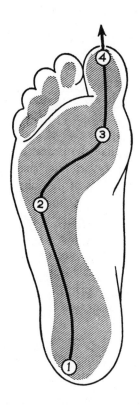

FIG. 1.

When the foot hits the ground, it hits heel first. This phase is known as the *heel-strike* (1 in figure 1). Normal individuals strike the ground first with the outside of the back of the heel (reference to the wear on one's shoe will readily confirm this). As the stride progresses and the body starts to catch up with the leg (as a punt catches up with a punt-pole), the point of contact of the foot with the ground moves forward along the outer border of the sole (2 in figure 1). By the time the body is immediately above the supporting foot, the main point of contact with the ground has shifted from the outer border to the inner border. Now the weight of the body is being supported largely by the ball of the foot behind the big toe (3 in figure 1), and the heel is lifted off the ground. The final phase of striding is a function of the big toe alone, hence the relative massiveness of its proportions. The line of weight-bearing shifts from the ball of the big toe to its extreme tip, an action which propels the body forwards towards the next step. This is known as the *toe-off* phase (4 in figure 1). The whole process is called *striding*. The function of the little toes in striding is quite different. They are not involved in *propulsion*. Their role is purely one of stabilization; they prevent the foot from sliding backwards.

During the toe-off phase, the big toe straightens out and the little toes bend up, thus accounting for the characteristic appearance of a walking footprint impressed on some unyielding surface such as the linoleum of the bathroom floor. It can be seen that while the big toe impression is continuous with the ball of the foot, the little toes appear to be separated from it. When the substrate is yielding, as in the case of soft sand, an interval between the little toes and foot is not apparent in a footprint because the sand squeezes up under the curl of the little toes, leaving a narrow ridge.

The 'waisted' appearance of the footprint is typical of a normally arched foot on an unyielding surface; the elevated parts of the arch do not leave an impression, although of course a foot that lacks a good arch leaves a much wider impression. But even a foot with a normal arch leaves a 'flat-foot' impression if the substrate is soft enough for the foot to sink into (plates 13 and 15).

Finally, an important point in analysing the man-like Sasquatch footprints is to reach some estimate of stature from the length of the foot. The following formula gives a reasonably accurate method of calculating the relationship in man:

$$\text{stature} = \text{greatest foot length} \times 6\cdot6$$

It has been assumed that this relationship would also hold good in a bipedal hominoid such as the Sasquatch. The statures deduced from footprints in table 3 have been derived from this formula.

I am very well aware that the last few pages have been hard going, but the problem of footprints and their interpretation is so critical for the understanding of the Bigfoot problem that I make no apology for inflicting some of the fundamentals of human walking and footprint-ery upon you.

Footprints in mud, sand and clay are considerably easier to understand than footprints in snow, so I propose to consider them first.

SASQUATCH FOOTPRINTS

The majority of the footprints attributed to the Sasquatch are found in mud, dust or river silt. A few prints in snow have been recorded in recent years (see table 2, p. 210), as a consequence of the growing popularity of snowmobiling and ski-ing which take more people than ever before into the mountainous regions during the winter. One might expect that in any natural population of animals a good deal of variation in size and shape occurs; so it is with Sasquatch tracks.

However, there seem to be two distinct types of Sasquatch track, and the differences between them appear to go beyond the range of normal variation expected within a single species of mammal. This in itself is bound to make one rather suspicious. The business of moving about is so basic to an animal's survival that locomotion is almost the last function of the body which one would expect to show major differences within a species. Hair colour, eye colour, ear length, stature etc. are the sort of characteristics which one might expect to vary because they have little or no effect on the survival of the individual; but differences in the fundamental anatomy of the foot occurring within a species are quite unacceptable. In any other animal group, such differences would indicate that the creatures concerned belonged to two different genera—if not to two different zoological families.

The evolutionary 'distance' implied by placing two species of Sasquatch in separate families would be as great as the evolutionary distance between apes and man, or cats and dogs. It is unthinkable that the Sasquatch of north-western America, if it exists at all, should consist of such two distinct families or even genera. The only alternative to such a travesty of evolutionary principles is that *one* of the two Sasquatch footprint types are man-made artefacts.

The two types of footprints are illustrated in plates 11 to 16. The first, which I call the 'hourglass' by reason of its waisted appearance, has been seen in the Bluff Creek–Blue Creek areas of Northern California. The second – the 'human' variety – has been seen and photographed in Washington State.

The hourglass type can be recognized by six distinctive characteristics:

1. The impressions of the five toes are separated from the ball of the foot by a substantial ridge of soil or sand.

2. The toe impressions and the ridge that separates them from the ball of the foot are arranged obliquely with a forward slant from the outer to the inner border of the foot.

3. The big toe is approximately the same size as the little toes (see big-toe width index in table 3, page 213).

4. A well-marked ridge divides the ball of the foot, the fleshy pad immediately behind the big toe, into two separate elements.

5. The shank of the foot is hourglass shaped.

6. The impression of the heel is deeper on the inner rather than the outer side (contrary to the human type which is deeper on the outer side).

The fundamental interpretation of these footprint characteristics is fairly straightforward. The well-marked ridge between the toes and the rest of the foot is a sure indication that the Sasquatch's toes (if this is indeed a *real* footprint and not a fake) are much longer, more ape-like, than in man. The prominence of the ridge, which extends behind the big toe as well as the small toes, is a clear indication that all the toes are sharply bent during walking. The obliquity of the ridge tells us exactly how the foot is moved during the final phase of striding. *Homo sapiens* takes off from the inner side of his foot, from the big toe in fact; the hourglass footprints indicate that the Sasquatch takes off from the outer side of his foot. The smallness of the big-toe impression of the hourglass tracks is further confirmation that the Sasquatch does not propel himself forward at the end of each step by the powerful leverage of the big toe. All in all, the hourglass footprints indicate a totally different style of bipedal walking to that used by *Homo sapiens*, modern man. The differences between the impression of the human foot and that of the Sasquatch are shown in figure 2.

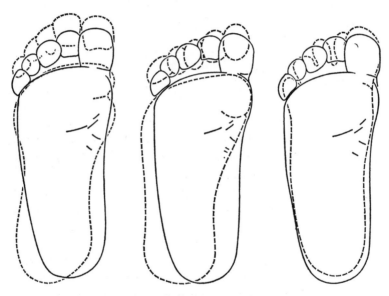

FIG. 2. A normal human print (solid line) superimposed on (left and middle) two variants of the hourglass-type (broken line) and (right) on the outline of the human-type (Bossburg). Not to scale.

The gait of the Sasquatch, judged on the basis of the hourglass footprints, is 'pigeon-toed'. Most human beings walk with their feet turned out—the so-called 'angle of gait'. The Sasquatch apparently walks with its feet turned in. There is a curious and persuasive consistency about the hourglass footprints. They present an aberrant but, nevertheless, uniform pattern. This is hard to reconcile with fakery. One might pose the question: who other than God or natural selection is sufficiently conversant with the subtleties of the human foot and the human walking style to 'design' an artificial foot which is so perfectly harmonious in terms of structure and function? These arguments can be equally well applied, and with greater force, to the 'human' print from Bossburg, as we shall see.

Another factor that might be adduced in favour of the hour-glass tracks is their variability. If they were all the same they could automatically be written off as a hoax, because precise uniformity within a species is not a characteristic of nature, whereas variety is.

The hourglass tracks sometimes show the five toes looking for all the world like peas in a pod (figure 2, middle), and sometimes the big toe is slightly larger than the others (figure 2, left), but never so large as in the human type of track, where the toes steadily increase in size from the outer to the inner border (plate 15). Another difference is that in the hourglass the ridge behind the toes is ruler-straight while in the human type the ridge is curved with its convexity directed forwards.

The human-type track from Bossburg, Washington State, was first seen in October 1969 by a butcher of the name of Joe Rhodes. The sighting was reported to Ivan Marx, whose interest in the Sasquatch was well known. Marx made casts of the foot-prints (plate 17). Subsequently in the same area Marx and Rene Dahinden discovered a set of tracks and followed them for half a mile. Rene Dahinden has told me that he counted 1,089 prints in all. The remarkable feature of the Bossburg tracks is the evidence that the Sasquatch concerned is a cripple.

The left foot appears normal, and in every respect is similar to a modern human foot – similar, that is, until one considers the matter of size. The Bossburg tracks, large even for a Sasquatch, measure 17½ in. by 7 in. Apart from satisfying the criteria established for modern human-type walking, the Bossburg prints have, to my way of thinking, an even greater claim to authenticity. The right foot of the Bossburg Sasquatch is a club-foot, a not uncommon abnormality that labours under the technical name of *talipes-equino-varus*. The forepart of the foot is twisted inwards, the third toe has been squeezed out of normal alignment, and possibly there has been a dislocation of the bones on the outer border (but this last feature may be due to an imperfection in the casting technique). Club-foot usually occurs as a congenital abnormality, but it may also develop as the result of severe injury, or of damage to the nerves controlling the muscles of the foot. To me, the deformity strongly suggests that injury during life was responsible. A true, untreated, congenital *talipes-equino-varus* usually results in a fixed flexion deformity of the ankle in which case only the forepart of the foot and toes touch the ground in normal standing. In these circumstances the heel impression would be absent or poorly defined; but in fact the heel indentation of the Sasquatch is strongly defined. I conclude that the deformity was the result of a crushing injury to the foot in early childhood.[2]

It is very difficult to conceive of a hoaxer so subtle, so knowledgeable—and so sick—who would deliberately fake a footprint of this nature. I suppose it is possible, but it is so unlikely that I am prepared to discount it.

Thus there are three alternatives in the interpretation of Sasquatch footprints. Either both types of footprints are fakes, both are real, or one is real and the other is faked. I have already discussed how unlikely it is that both are real. If both are fakes then we must be prepared to accept the existence of a conspiracy of Mafia-like ramifications with cells in practically every major township from San Francisco to Vancouver. Even if we accept the conspiracy angle there is still another hurdle to be jumped. How could footprints of such realism and functional consistency have been made? Rubber-latex moulds bonded to a boot or shoe might explain how the footprints are reproduced, but the mechanical problems would be immense, particularly when it is borne in mind that the hoaxer would have to walk considerable distances over difficult terrain wearing such unwieldy contraptions. There is also the problem that footprints are found in conditions where an ordinary man is too light to make any impression in the substrate. However, it is not impossible that some of the footprints were made in this way.

A footprint machine, a kind of mechanical stamp, has been suggested, but an apparatus capable of delivering a thrust of approximately 800 lb per square foot that can be manhandled over rough and mountainous country puts a strain on one's credulity. Nevertheless, once again, this is a possibility that should be borne in mind. There is no *a priori* reason why the footprints seen on the dirt roads of the Blue Creek Mountain area in Northern California could not have been faked in this way, although as Dr Maurice Tripp, a geologist, has pointed out, impact ridges, which would be expected from a mechanical stamp, are absent in the footprints he has studied.[3]

There is ample evidence that some footprints have been faked. While researching a B.B.C. T.V. programme in 1968, Ron Webster, the producer, met a roadmender who assured him categorically on this point in a filmed interview. A gentleman called Ray Pickens described to a reporter quite recently how he made a pair of 16 in. feet out of wood and nailed them to a pair of boots. He also claimed to have made a middle-sized pair and a small pair for his wife and child. Mr Pickens is a citizen of Colville, near Bossburg, prime Sasquatch country. I have on my files photographs of a further set of tracks which were clearly made by a hinged, wooden contraption which wouldn't fool the village idiot.[4]

Both the Blue Creek–Bluff Creek and the Bossburg footprints are, in different ways, biologically convincing. The hourglass type is intrinsically consistent but, I suspect, functionally inadequate. The 'human' tracks are convincing for different reasons. First because of the crippled right foot, which I find impossible to accept as a hoax; and, secondly, because of the normality in structural and functional terms of the left foot. I am sure that *some* Sasquatch tracks are fakes, but it is beyond reason to suppose that they all are. Indeed if there was only one real print among 99 fakes it would still be obligatory to explain the one.

In view of the real, biologically unacceptable, differences between the hourglass and the 'human' types, the conclusion is
inevitable: one must be real and the other must be a fake. But
which is which? Will the *real* Sasquatch please stand up! Of the
two challengers my money is on the Bossburg tracks, the
'human' type in my classification, for reasons already well aired
above.

There is one final consideration: the tracks found and photographed by Roger Patterson at Bluff Creek after he had seen and
filmed the so-called female Sasquatch. The footprints are a variant
of the hourglass type and as discussed on p. 94 are already under
suspicion for the reason that their dimensions are not in accord
with the stature estimated from the film.

YETI FOOTPRINTS

Although a number of authorities have stressed the effects of
melting or sublimation on footprints in snow, there is no real
experimental basis for the belief that single footprints can become
enlarged and still retain their shape, or that discrete prints can run
(or melt) together to form single large tracks.

In January 1961 I had the opportunity of carrying out some
preliminary experiments on melting of footprints while on holiday at Val d'Isère in the French Alps. Owing to the frequency
of snowstorms at that season of the year and the lack of sun,
the experiments were inevitably of rather short duration;
one experiment lasted for four and a half days, but this was
exceptional.

The method employed was as follows: a 'stamp' was designed
to provide a footprint in the snow of standard size and simple
outline. A fenced-in area facing south and some twenty-five feet
from the nearest building was chosen as the site for the experiments. Two footprints were impressed into the snow to the depth
of one inch; one was left exposed to the sun, the other (the control)
was covered with a cardboard hood. Measurements were taken
twice a day at 9.00 a.m. and 3.00 p.m. Three dimensions were
recorded—overall length, forefoot width and heel width. Records

of hours of sunlight, cloud cover, maximum and minimum ambient temperatures, snow conditions and snow temperature were kept.

Imperfect as they were for one reason or another, these experiments provide evidence of the minimum degree of enlargement that can be expected. Observed enlargement of 'footprints' ranged from 10 per cent to 22·5 per cent of the original dimensions. The factors responsible for producing a high rate of melt were hours of sunshine. In the absence of sunshine, high ambient temperatures and the freshness of snow were critical factors in the production of melting. In uncompressed snow, footprints melted more rapidly than when the snow was settled or artificially compacted. Enlargement of footprints therefore seems to be a very real factor in the production of giant tracks. One thing that melting cannot do (as it is often claimed) is to *increase* the length of the step, the distance between one footprint and another. Naturally, melting can only *diminish* it.

There is no difficulty in identifying a footprint that has become enlarged by melting. The outline becomes woolly and the details in the floor of the print become blurred. The pattern of melting in sun however differs from that in shade. On exposure to sunshine, the print becomes chamfered along the sharp edge furthest away from the slanting rays of the winter sun. In warm, cloudy conditions, melting produces a gradual attrition of both edges and both extremities so that the print loses its crisp, punched-out look and becomes woolly in outline and saucer-like in section.

Two other observations are of interest; the 'double' print formed by superimposition of one footprint on another, and the 'elephant-track' effect. I performed a series of experiments on overlap using the artificial stamp, the booted foot and the naked foot—my own, needless to say; can dedication go further? In fresh, deep snow, little or no evidence of overlapping was apparent, but in fresh, shallow snow (one inch on a concrete path) the separate outlines were easily discernible. The sharp edges of the artificial stamp left a much clearer record of a double print than the rounder contours of the naked foot, but melting rapidly obliterated the evidence. This observation is extremely important in the analysis of footprints in snow.

'Elephant-tracks' have been noted by Shipton and others. Low night temperatures leave the snow surface icy and crusted to a depth of 2 in.–3 in. or more, so icy in fact that it may easily bear the weight of a man without collapsing. Later in the day the icy crust gives way when weight is applied. At either side of such a footprint a roughly triangular area of snow caves in and the resulting outline is rhomboidal. If melting is now superimposed, gigantic, circular, elephant-like tracks result (plate 5).

In table 1, p. 208, the principal footprints seen by travellers and mountaineers in the Himalayas over the last sixty years have been listed. The facts in this table, condensed into a more digestible form, are as follows:

1. Footprints have been seen in most months of the year, the major 'closed' season being the summer monsoon (June–July–August).

2. Footprints have been seen at altitudes of between 12,000 and 22,000 feet; the majority occur at 15,000 feet or higher.

3. Fifteen of the sightings of footprints are from the eastern Himalayas, three from the western Himalayas (Karakorams) and three from an intermediate region (Kulti Valley, Lahoul and the Khandosanglam Pass).

4. Five toes are usually observed, but occasionally only four.

5. Typically the length of the step is short, usually 18 in.–24 in. The length of footprints is very variable and ranges from 6 in. to 24 in.; typically they are between 10 in. and 12 in. In width they vary between 4 in. and 12 in., but most commonly are 6 in.

6. In those instances where footprints were actually measured, it is possible to estimate their overall proportions in terms of the width-length index (greatest width × 100 divided by greatest length). These indices are much more typical of bears whose index range is 51–52 than they are of humans (34–40).

To end this chapter I propose to look at some of the better

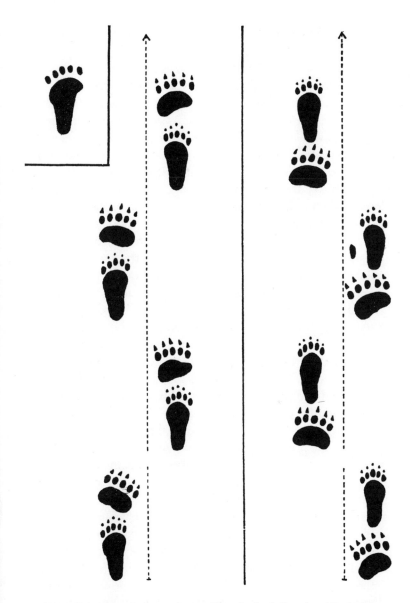

FIG. 3. Footprints of a brown bear walking slowly (left) and rapidly (right). Note the reversed position of the fore- and hindfeet at the two speeds. Inset is the theoretical intermediate. (After Coutourier).

known 'Yeti' footprints in the light of the experiments and observations on melting.

To begin with, it should be emphasized that no two 'Yeti' tracks recorded by various travellers are exactly alike.

The line of footprints photographed by Professor E. S. Williams on the Sim Gang tributary of the Biafo Glacier in the Karakorams in 1956 are shown in plate 2. An unclear photograph of a single footprint is also available, and provides the basis for the reconstruction shown in figure 4. At first sight the single footprint looks very like the outline of a human right foot. However, on closer inspection it is apparent that the outline of the foot is distinctly non-human; what should be the inner border of the footprint, if it were human, is clearly the outer border. Such an appearance could have been produced by the track of a bear walking quadrupedally so that its left hindfoot overlapped and was superimposed upon its left forefoot (figure 4). As Bernard Heuvelmans rightly points out, the bear's foot is a sort of mirror-image of the human foot; the fifth toe of the bear is somewhat larger than the first.[5] The angle that the forepart of Williams's print makes with the hindpart corresponds with the relative alignment of the fore- and hindfeet of bears. The forefoot turns inwards and the hindfoot is directed straight ahead or slightly outwards (figure 3). The lack of detail in Williams's photographs, and the evidence from the irregular outline, suggests that some melting of the print and distortion by wind erosion had occurred by the time the photograph was taken. Williams suggests that the track was not more than twenty-four hours old. Melting might account for the absence of any marks of pads or claws, or any evidence for the superimposition of two separate impressions. That this is a bear's track accords very well with both the zoo-geographical evidence of the habitat range of Himalayan bears and the composite size of the overlapping prints ($10\frac{1}{2}$ in.). It is impossible to state categorically that Williams's prints are those of a bear and not of a Yeti, but in the spirit of Bishop Ockham it seems more reasonable to explain a phenomenon in terms of the known than the unknown.

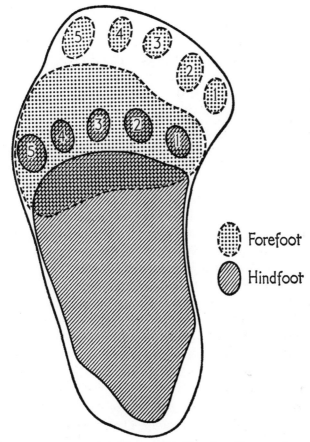

Forefoot

Hindfoot

FIG. 4. Reconstruction of a left fore- and hindfoot of a red bear superimposed.

The prints and track photographed in the Dudh Kosi Valley by the Abbé Bordet were discussed in chapter 2. The depth, and the absence of 'elephant-track' subsidence, indicates that they were probably made during the day in soft snow. Again, these tracks do not suggest that the perpetrator was either a human or a nonhuman primate. Bears usually have five toes on each foot, but as the hindfoot print quite frequently shows only four the tracks which show only four toes could have been those of a bear. From their size (8 in. in length), the locality and the altitude, the Asiatic black bear (*Selenarctos thibetanus*) is the most likely suspect.

In June 1955, Squadron-Leader L. W. Davies, now Warden of the Outward Bound School at Ullswater, was in the Kulti Valley, Lahoul, where he took a number of excellent photographs of footprints bordering a glacial stream. Davies avers that the prints were no more than twenty-four hours old and although he is adamant that the spoor was Yeti and not a bear, his photographs tend to confirm their bear-like nature. Davies's records indicate that the dimensions of the footprints were 12 in. by 8 in., giving a breadth/length index of 67 which is more bear-like than human-like or ape-like. The outline of the foot is bear-like and not ape-like, and the behaviour of the animal, which clearly crossed several glacial streams, definitely favours bear rather than an ape, for whom water provides an impenetrable barrier. The length of the step, according to Squadron-Leader Davies, is 'twice that of a man', which admittedly argues against the bear theory. Bears do not walk bipedally for long distances and their step is very short. When walking quadrupedally, the distance between the back of one hindfoot impression and the preceding one may be 3 ft. or more. When the bear breaks into a fast gallop the interval rises to 7 ft.–10 ft.

Davies further comments that on very steep slopes his creature apparently slid down on its rump. Otters slide on snow slopes, so do penguins, and so — according to Marcel Couturier, who has made an exhaustive study of the brown bear throughout the world[6] — do bears, but not on their rumps. Couturier observes that when descending slopes of deep snow, bears make a snow-plough of their chests. He also states that when the snow is not so deep, the bear glissades down the slope on its fore- and hindfeet, much as a skier would perform a *schuss*. Couturier has never seen or heard of a bear coming down a slope on its rump. If Squadron-Leader Davies can show clear evidence that his creature came tobogganing down on its bottom, then his quarry was probably a hominoid creature and not a bear. Ralph Izzard and Gerald

Russell also saw evidence of tobogganing by something believed by them to be a Yeti in the Dudh Kosi Valley.

The Hillary Expedition of 1960–61 was planned as a physiological rather than a mountaineering venture; it also came up with a few so-called Yeti tracks. On October 15th, 1960, on the Ripumu Glacier a set of footprints were found which – for all the world – appeared to have been made by a naked human foot. This in itself is not unreasonable (see p. 154), but the tracks were rather too big to be wholly acceptable. Furthermore, as Edmund Hillary and Desmond Doig[7] rather disarmingly put it, they had one glaring anomaly – *they had toes on their heels*. This valiant attempt by the authors to keep the Yeti-ape image alive while damning it right, left and centre with other evidence (see chapter 2) is not very convincing. The authors remark that when an ape walks, it walks on the bent knuckles of its hands; its fingers therefore point backwards – hence the 'toes-on-the-heels' bit (point taken but definitely not accepted).

The other two sets of tracks discovered by the 1960 Hillary Expedition were even more destructive to the myth. Let Hillary and Doig tell the story as they saw it:

> To us, alas, they were plainly and obviously the tracks of a small quadruped, the pugmarks placed close enough together to form one large imprint ... As we followed the track we were confronted with 'footprints' that on the shady side of the snow ridge were unmistakably a rosette of small pug marks, but on the top of the same ridge were expanded by the sun into vast fifteen-inch 'feet', the slightly misplaced pugs forming toes and heels. On the downhill slope the 'footprints' either reverted to bouquets of pugmarks or took on the appearance of small elephant-like tracks ... Fascinated we watched small paws become giant feet, claw marks turn to toes, enormous 'Yeti' feet become the pugmarks of an animal no bigger than a fox.

But perhaps the most telling feature of Hillary and Doig's account was the fact that the Sherpas were convinced that the tracks were those of a Yeti. As one Sherpa observed ' ... and no better could you hope to find anywhere'. Sherpas were positive that the expanded pugmarks were your actual Snowman. So much for native know-how. So much for the naive assumption by Europeans that to be a child of nature is to be automatically an informed student of natural history.

The most recent tracks to be reported were seen by Don Whillans late in March 1970 while reconnoitring the approach to the south face of Annapurna. Whillans's track, which was discussed in chapter 2, is shown in plate 3. The footprints were 12 in. deep and about 9 in. or 10 in. long, and appear to have been made by a quadruped taking bounding leaps in soft snow. The nearest impression seen in the photograph presumably represents the two hindfeet, close together and separated by a ridge of snow; the right hindfoot is slightly in advance of the left. Then follows the right foot and, further on, the left forefoot. The track then slightly changes direction but the same foot sequence continues. The track is quite unlike a bear's; bears gallop, but they do not bound. In this depth of snow, a bear's tracks, as it snow-ploughed its way along, would look more like a pair of continuous channels.

Don Whillans observed that his creature was bounding across the snow. The bound is a springing action initiated by the hindlegs held close together, projecting the body into the air at each step. The function of the forelimbs in bounding animals is to absorb the shock of landing, and for this purpose they may be held slightly apart or close together. Whillans also commented that the creature he saw was ape-like, but great apes—the gorilla, the chimpanzee or the orang-utan—do not bound. On the other hand, some monkeys, particularly langurs, do. Bounding on the ground requires the same locomotor mechanisms as leaping in trees, and this type of gait is one at which langurs are particularly adept. The length and narrowness of the footprints are rather suggestive of the langur and are quite dissimilar to those of the bear or even the snow leopard (plate 3). The only alternative explanation for the footprints is that they were made by some species of ungulate, of which there are many in the Himalayas, including the ibex, the goat and the goat-antelope. The tracks seem to be rather elongated for a hoofed animal, and rather narrow for a snow leopard—another possibility. Could Don Whillans have mistaken a goat, an antelope or a leopard for anything else? He states quite unequivocally that the creature he saw in the bright moonlight was ape-like. Did he really mean 'ape-like', or simply 'primate-like'? The word 'ape' is used by most non-scientists in an imprecise way to mean any primate. The Barbary Ape and the Celebes Ape (both monkeys) are names in common use even amongst primatologists. It is significant that Don Whillans was struck by the ape-like nature of the animal he saw. He might have said bear-like, leopard-like, or goat-like, but he said ape-like, so ape-like is probably what it was. As there is no suggestion of two-footedness either in the tracks photographed by Whillans or in his report, the provisional assumption must be that what he saw was a quadrupedal monkey, possibly a langur. This is by no means as outrageous a conclusion as it might sound. People tend to think of monkeys as animals of tropical forests, but langurs, according to many authorities including the Rev. Robert Everest,[8] are frequently to be seen above the snowline in the Himalayas. At least two observers (see chapter 2) have seen langurs at 13,000 feet and 19,000 feet respectively, although admittedly the latter report is somewhat suspect. An altitude of 13,000 ft.–15,000 ft., though high for a langur (see table 4, p. 214), is not entirely impossible. There for the moment the matter rests. The langur with its long, narrow foot, bounding gait and 'ape-like' appearance, seems to be by far the most promising suspect for this particular incident. In no sense, however, can Don Whillans's sighting be said to underwrite the existence of the Yeti.

Charles Stonor in his book *The Sherpa and the Snowman* recounts how he saw his first footprint a few hours' climb from Namche Bazar, Nepal, at 13,000 feet in the no-man's-land between the treeline and the snows. On a patch of relict snow in an area of heath-like upland he found a medley of 'very man-like' prints, one of which he photographed. His photograph shows a typically well-melted print, 10 in. by 5 in., with rolled edges and no toe-marks or other details; it would be impossible to guess its provenance. From the appearance in the photo it could be any-thing one liked to think it was—even 'man-like'. Pranavanandra, already mentioned in connection with the philology of Tibetan names of the Yeti, saw a set of giant footprints 21 in. long when crossing the Khandosanglam Pass in 1941. A pass, he notes, that is crossed by pilgrims intent on circumnavigating the holy Kailas Mountain. Pranavanandra ascertained that a lama had crossed the pass some twenty-five days earlier, and he believes that what he saw were the lama's prints enlarged out of all proportion by the warm summer sun. In the light of the snow experiments reported above this seems rather excessive, indicating at least 100 per cent increase in length; but it may not be an exaggeration for enlargement by sublimation or evaporation.

Another footprint, once officially attributed by the British Museum (Natural History) to a langur, as I mentioned earlier, was the famous print discovered by Shipton and Ward in 1951. What-ever made this remarkable track on the edge of the Menlung Glacier, it was certainly no langur. As I have indicated elsewhere, this footprint is a critical one simply because a number of writers, on seeing it, have made up their minds that it provides sufficient evidence to erect a whole phylogenetic history for the Yeti. The footprint was 'ape-like', therefore it was made by an ape. What ape? By a reasoning typical of the Goblin Universe, *Gigantopithecus* (see chapter 7) was cast in the role of the favourite son. The fallacy, of course, occurs at the very beginning of the inductive process. What justification is there for considering the footprint to be ape-like?

Lawrence Swan was struck by the similarity of Shipton's foot-print to a photograph published some years ago by Carl Akeley, the well-known American naturalist, of the foot of a dead gorilla. Footprints, it will be remembered, are records not simply of the shape of a foot but of the style of walking. The footprint of a living gorilla is distinctive, and does not in the least resemble

Shipton's track. In Akeley's picture the big toe is bent downwards and inwards in a grasping position (opposed position) and the other toes are curled up in the spasm of death. In spite of a superficial resemblance to Shipton's footprint, the comparison is meaningless, as a gorilla does not walk with its foot in the position of rigor mortis. Furthermore, the dimensions are wrong. The gorilla's foot has a breadth/length index of 45 per cent compared with 37 per cent for the human foot (table 3, p. 213) and 61 per cent for the Shipton print. A similarity to the gorilla's foot has been proposed by many other authors, who have then proceeded to explain the obvious differences by implying that the footprint was not made by a living gorilla but by an 'extinct' form like *Gigantopithecus*, which, they imply, quite without justification, possessed a gorilla-like foot. The role of *Gigantopithecus* in the Yeti myth is discussed in chapter 7, but it would not be out of place to recall that there are no fossil remains of this creature below the level of the teeth and jaws. Theories about the foot of *Gigantopithecus* must be regarded as wholly speculative.

A very striking characteristic of the Shipton footprint is what seems to be a much enlarged second toe. This feature – it has seriously been suggested – is a rock-climbing adaptation, a sort of fleshy piton to be wedged into the crevices of vertical rock faces. Even in the Goblin Universe it is going a bit far to invent a purely hypothetical pattern of behaviour to explain a shadowy impression seen in a footprint photograph.

Shipton's photograph has been published many times in various books, magazines and newspapers but never before, as far as I am aware, has the whole area of the original negative been shown. This omission is rectified in plate 1. What the whole negative reveals throws a deal of new light on the much-discussed print. First of all, it shows the thickness of the snow on the underlying glacier ice; second, it demonstrates (at the bottom of the picture on the right) the presence of what may be *another footprint*. My suspicion that there was more to the negative than met the eye in the published versions stems from past experience of art editors for whom tight framing is an article of faith. Thanks to the efficiency and enthusiastic cooperation of the Mount Everest Foundation and its secretary, T. S. Blakeney, Shipton's original negatives were found among their files, and to my delight they not only confirmed my suspicion of picture editors but also added a new dimension to Shipton and Ward's remarkable discovery.

The particular features shown by Shipton's photograph are as follows:

1. The foot is not excessively long, even by human standards (13 in. approx.), but is extremely wide (8 in. across the forefoot and 6½ in. across the heel).

2. The presumptive big toe is short, slightly separated from the big toe and has an almost circular outline; behind it is a sharp v-shaped indentation.

3. The 'second' toe is the longest and appears to be hook-shaped and bent at the tip, which is possibly an illusion created by the shadow pattern; two further toes can be seen and there may also be a fifth toe which has left little in the way of an indentation.

4. Judging by the shadows and highlights, the imprint of the foot is convex in the region of the ball precisely where one would expect it to be concave.

5. The deepest parts of the imprint are on the outer side of the heel and the inner side of the sole.

Further analysis of the anatomical characteristics would be not only tedious but misleading, because *there is no certainty that the footprint as photographed is identical with the footprint as made*. There is ample evidence that footprints exposed to hot sunlight at high altitudes, where atmospheric pressure is low, are liable to undergo extreme changes in size and outline as a result of melting or sublimation. This phenomenon was discussed earlier in this chapter, and its effect on footprints has been described by Hillary and Doig.[9] As a reminder of what can happen, the following personal communication from Lawrence Swan is very appropriate:

The tracks were indeed those of a small wolf or fox, more

likely the latter. Sublimation of the snow left the large prints relatively clean-cut and fresh appearing. It was apparent that paw marks lengthen in the sun and orient their length with the midday sun. Snow at high altitudes tends to become 'fluted'. The peaks have these fluted ridges all over them, and it seems that on the sunny side of a depression in the snow, small flutings appear. These are the 'toes'. All this was fairly obvious when the tracks were followed round a half circle. Instead of the feet pointing in the direction of a bipedal walking individual, they oriented into a single direction opposite the sun. Hence, half way round half a circle, that is after 90°, the feet were sideways to the line of progression and at 180° they were facing backward to the original direction of movement. Hence of course, they lend support to the legend which maintains that Yeti's feet face backwards.

For my own part I was not prepared to accept that Eric Shipton's print might have been distorted by melting or sublimation until I was able to study the entire field of Shipton's negative. With the new evidence it provided it became clear that in the interval between the imprint being made and the photograph being taken, the snow in the lower half of the picture had melted and re-frozen. In the upper half, the substrate is still crystalline, lying one inch deep on the glacier ice. This immediately suggests that the dark area at the outer side of the heel is not simply the heavy impression of a heel at the 'heel-strike' phase of human walking, as has been assumed, but an area (comparable to that seen at the left-hand side of the lower footprint) where sublimation has taken place. With this observation, the footprint loses one of its principal claims to be man-like.

The lower footprint is a bit of a puzzle in itself. The general fluffiness of the outline is in contrast to the punched-out appearance of the main print, a difference that may be related to the texture of the substrate — ice in the case of the former and snow in the latter. The suggestion of claw-marks in the lower print is rather intriguing, but these are probably, as Lawrence Swan believes, examples of the 'fluting' that he refers to in the quotation above.

The recognition that melting and sublimation have probably played some part in the dimensions of the footprint does not excuse one from the obligation of explaining its origin, but it lightens the burden by providing one with a little more room for manoeuvre.

As it stands, the footprint is not human; nor was it made by an ape or an ape-like creature known to science. What are the alternatives? There are very few. No known creature anywhere in the world could leave a spoor like this. However, if we make the assumption that the footprint as photographed is not in its original form, then the perpetrator could have been a bear, a langur, a fox, a snow leopard or even one of the many bovid creatures living at this altitude (table 4, p. 214). Without knowing all the rules that govern melting and sublimation it would be impossible, bearing in mind Lawrence Swan's observations on the footprints of the Ripumu Glacier, to designate the villain of the piece. Eric Shipton agrees that melting or sublimation might be responsible for the appearance, but he points out quite correctly that it would be reasonable to expect the narrow ridges behind and between the little toes to be the first features to disappear in these circumstances.

There is one further possibility, and one that I strongly favour: that the footprint is double—two tracks superimposed. But a double—what? I don't know. I have experimented with all possible combinations: the superimposed fore- and hindfeet of bears, a human print impressed upon a bear print, an adult female bear and a cub, and even a palimpsest made by a naked human foot treading in the tracks of a shod one. None of these combinations, except the last, is even remotely convincing. Lawrence Swan, who was kind enough to re-study the Shipton photograph at my invitation, has suggested that the footprint is made up of the superimposed pugmarks of the fore- and hindfoot of the snow leopard, the forefoot in front and the hindfoot behind. This is a very reasonable suggestion as long as one accepts that a great deal of melting has also taken place because, as Lawrence Swan points out, the leopard that made the tracks would have to be somewhat of a monster in its own right. Snow leopard's prints have a width of $3\frac{1}{2}$ in.–4 in. at the most; and with the best will in the world it is difficult to explain how such pugmarks can expand to $7\frac{1}{2}$ in. and still leave an impression so sharply defined as Shipton's print.

Something must have made the Shipton footprint. Like Mount Everest, it is there, and needs explaining. I only wish I could solve the puzzle; it would help me sleep better at night. Of course, it would settle a lot of problems if one could simply assume that the Yeti is alive and walking about the Himalayas on gigantic feet with two big toes on each foot, and leave it at that. The trouble is that such an assumption conflicts totally with the principles of biology as we know them. Rightly or wrongly, in the absence of any other form of natural evidence, I would rather put my money on biological principles than on imaginative speculation.

To some enthusiasts, quite understandably, Shipton's footprint is proof of the existence of the Yeti; but to me it is proof of absolutely nothing. I am not prepared to accept it on its face value. I do not believe that, as it stands, it is the print of an unknown ape-like creature. I accept that melting and sublimation can convert a fox's pugmark into a vaguely human-like or ape-like footprint, but I am not at all convinced that this is the whole story. If I had to make a guess—and this is all it is—I would say the print was composite, made by a naked human foot treading in the track of a foot wearing a leather moccasin. Surprisingly enough, pilgrims *do* walk barefoot through the Himalayas (see chapter 6). The curious V-shaped kink behind the big toe, which has no apparent biological function, could then be explained in terms of a deep fold in the leather of the moccasin, the product of many years' alternating wetness and dryness. That there should be humans at the edge of the Menlung Glacier following the same route as Shipton and Ward is not an unreasonable assumption considering, as Shipton admits in his most recent book,[10] that he and Ward were on the very frontier between Nepal and Tibet.

I find it sad to have to end this chapter on a note of anticlimax.

At first sight the Shipton print seems to offer unequivocal evidence for the reality of the Yeti; but perhaps it is too much to expect that the Himalayas would surrender one of its outstanding mysteries as easily as that.

6. The Evidence of Natural History

It must by now be clear that at least some of the sightings and footprints, particularly in the Himalayas, are attributable to many creatures, including man. In this chapter we shall be looking at some of the mammals (and birds) which can legitimately be regarded as suspects. We will start with bears.

In the popular view, bears are lovable, clever and amusing, with just the touch of gruffness that reminds one of a favourite uncle. With the cosy image of their own childhood in mind, parents expose their young to the Pooh complex at the earliest possible age, just as if it were chicken-pox or measles to be got out of the way before adulthood sets in. A teddy-bear is not simply a toy that is taken up and quickly discarded; it is a way of life, a doppelganger, and the confidant of children's most intimate thoughts that could not possibly be revealed to anyone else. Teddy-bears have a cultural function in the life of man, and parents, on the whole, are probably acting sensibly. Normally, young children grow out of the Pooh complex, just as adolescent girls ultimately make a complete recovery from the Horse obsession.

The prevalence of the Pooh complex is particularly odd inasmuch as bears are really extremely savage animals and not at all cosy. Zoo-keepers will readily admit that bears, particularly polar bears, offer the biggest security problem of all caged animals. The problem is not so much that of keeping the bears in as of keeping the children out. The cuddly image is a tender trap.

Bears have always played a very important part in mythology and ancient religions. They have a particularly important role in North American Indian myths, where they are regarded as healers and the guiding spirits of legendary heroes. Bear dances and other ceremonial rituals involving bears are traditional among the Plains Indians. Bear myths are particularly well entrenched in the mythology of peoples living close to the Arctic Circle, such as the Finns, the Lapps and the nomadic tribes of northern Siberia. Bear worship was practised amongst the Ainu tribes of northern Japan. Spring festivals in many parts of Europe feature the bear to symbolize rebirth at the end of hibernation.[1] Bear cults, along with ibex cults, are among the most ancient known, dating back some 100,000 years. Bear cults are particularly associated with the Neanderthal race in Eastern Europe. Several examples of burials decorated by the skulls of the cave-bear (an extinct species of the living brown bear) arranged in a ritualistic fashion are known from France and Eastern Europe. Man's earliest ancestors must have been extremely wary of the cave-bear before the discovery of fire by Pekin Man (*Homo erectus*) some 500,000 years ago; in fact, one theory suggests that the start of cave-dwelling by man dates back to this momentous event. Contrary to popular belief, very early man was not a cave-man. No one would have dared enter — let alone sleep in — a cave before investigating it thoroughly by torchlight and, if necessary, smoking out its sitting tenants, bears, hyaenas or leopards.

Man and bears must have been in competition with each other in the northern hemisphere for many thousands of years simply because their food requirements are similar. Both are omnivorous, which means that they will eat practically anything. Their dietary tastes are catholic, ranging from roots and tubers through fruit and honey to other animals, including fish; neither are they averse to carrion, nor even to a little bit of cannibalism on the side. Man however soon grew out of his *ad hoc* feeding behaviour with the development of agriculture and livestock farming; and as the diets of man and bears grew apart, so did their ways, and competition between them gradually ceased. The status of the bear in the eyes of man has changed, too. From a highly respected but much feared enemy, the bear came to be tolerated by most civilized peoples in most parts of the world as a non-competitor. Consequently the bear has become a plaything — an animal to be killed for sport or to be captured and trained for the entertainment of the masses in bear-pits, in circuses and on village greens around the world.

Unlike monkeys, which as animal entertainers have always been regarded as objects of fun and derision, the bear has retained a large measure of human esteem and respect, perhaps because of its great size and anthropomorphic qualities. It is somewhat ironical that monkeys, which actually *are* man-like, should be denied the respect that bears, which are zoologically far removed from man, are universally accorded. Perhaps the trouble is that monkeys are too much like man, too uncomfortably reminiscent of man's baser elements, to be tolerated. Bears inspire no fear in civilized communities, and in fact enjoy an ambience of awe and even reverence which makes it easy to understand the epidemiology of the Pooh complex.

In view of the major role that bears have played in the life of man, it is not surprising that every now and then a theory of human evolution involving the ancestral role of bears crops up at the fringes of science. The most recent example of the genre was reported in *The Times* early in 1970. An Italian biologist, psychologist and palaeontologist, Dr Luigi Ammendola, is said to have resurrected the theory once again. As is so often the case, the 'evidence' put forward (at least as reported in the press) is so palpably ridiculous that in an inverted sort of way all efforts at rebuttal tend to bestow the seal of approval on the very statements one is attempting to disparage.

Dr Ammendola, according to *The Times* correspondent, holds that monkeys lack powers of reflection and are garrulous and superficial, whereas man is not; he is introspective and reserved — like bears. Leaving aside the problem of assessing 'superficiality' in monkeys and taking the statement on its face value, it is a vile canard. Garrulous a chimpanzee may be, and superficial, perhaps, but its reflective powers are considerable, as anyone who knows anything about chimpanzees will agree. Orang-utans and gorillas are the least garrulous animals alive; their solemnity and introverted personalities are a by-word. There are of course noisy, bouncing primates, but the vast majority are silent and circumspect.

Bears, Dr Ammendola avers, have an advanced cooperative

hunting technique unknown to primates. On the contrary, bears are solitary animals, and they do not hunt in the accepted sense of the word. Non-human primates do not hunt either, but they do have a tendency to form complex, highly integrated social units in the form of troops or bands in which cooperative behaviour is paramount.

Monkeys copulate in front of the children, says Dr Ammendola, but bears have a much greater sense of propriety and 'purposely send their young away'. Begging the question of the evidence for the remarkable observation that bears purposely send their young away, and the significance of 'propriety' in the life-style of a bear, it is worth commenting that copulating in front of the children is a very human sort of thing to do. It is known in fact as sex education and people make films about it.

There is no doubt that the principal rationale for man-bear evolutionary theories is the fact that bears are *ad hoc* bipedalists. As a result their hindlimbs show a certain number of convergent characters with man. The late Professor F. Wood Jones, the great comparative anatomist, was wont to say that the femur of the bear could easily be confused with the femur of man. He was stretching the point a bit in the cause of dramatic illustration of the evolutionary phenomenon of *convergence*, and in fact, the bear's bipedal action has been over-stressed as a characteristic of the species. A bear will freely stand on its hindlegs and will totter a few paces, but bipedal walking is not a normal feature of its repertoire.

There is considerable confusion between the functions of standing and walking in animals. Animals, including many primates, of course, will stand up for reasons that are quite unconnected with locomotion. The act of standing in normally quadrupedal animals serves two purposes: first, it increases the animal's range of vision by extending the horizon, and second, it frees the arms from their weight-bearing function. In the case of the monkey, which possesses *hands*, this emancipation allows it to extend its manipulative range and capabilities. In the case of the bear, which has *paws*, bipedal standing serves only to bring these powerful weapons into offensive action. Unlike monkeys, bears do not carry objects in their paws, so there is no particular advantage to be gained by two-footed walking. Bears are quadrupeds, and four-footed walking for them is both faster and safer. Any explanation of footprints that depends on bipedal walking by a bear for more than a few steps is quite unacceptable. It is significant that by far the commonest Sherpa description of the Yeti is that it is partly a bipedal and partly a quadrupedal creature.

The bear on the face of it is one of the most likely candidates for the role of a Yeti-substitute. It stands upright; it is brown or reddish-brown in colour; it is about the right height; it leaves footprints that in certain circumstances can look remarkably similar to a human's; and it eats most of the things that a man-like monster might be expected to eat. Above all, its zoological distribution overlaps the theoretical range of Bigfoot; this is not only true of the Himalayas but of Asia, Canada and the north-western United States as well. The bears merit serious consideration.

There are four genera of bears in Asia, only two of which are relevant in the context of the Yeti — the brown bear (*Ursus arctos*) and the Himalayan black bear (*Selenarctos thibetanus*). The sloth bear and the Malayan sun bear don't really come into it. Of the brown bear genus, one race, *Ursus arctos isabellinus*, the so-called red bear or snow bear, has considerable relevance. Another race, *Ursus arctos pruinosus*, the Tibetan blue bear, has probably contributed something to the myth but is unlikely to be more than an 'extra'. The red bear, which has been recorded at altitudes of 16,000 feet, above the snowline, ranges from Kashmir in the west, south-eastwards to the Bheling Valley and the upper reaches of the Ganges near the mountains of Kamet and Nanda Devi. Further east, in Nepal, there are no positive records (in the shape of specimens or photographs) of *Ursus a. isabellinus*, but there is indirect evidence that red bears do extend somewhat further eastwards than is generally supposed. The type-locality of Horsfield's *Ursus isabellinus* is given as the 'mountains of Nepal'. B. H. Hodgson recorded in 1832 that both snow bear and Asiatic black bear are 'common' in the central and northern regions of Nepal where they are said to be 'very dangerous and troublesome'. In more recent times (1923) the Mammal Survey of Nepal, under the auspices of the renowned Bombay Natural History Society, noted the occurrence of red bear in the Kachar, the northern region of Nepal, though no specimens of red bear from this region have been collected.

Considering how many bears have over the years been shot by British big-game hunters in the western Himalayas and in Tibet, there are remarkably few specimens available in the collections of the British Museum (Natural History). When Dr R. I. Pocock came to write his classic monograph on the brown bear in 1932 he found it necessary to make a public appeal for bear-skins and skulls. Even today there are only thirty specimens of *U. a. isabellinus* in the British Museum in London, and only seven specimens of the blue bear, *U. a. pruinosus*. Thus, according to British Museum records, no red bear is known east of the Bheling Valley, Uttar Pradesh, India, and no blue bear south of Lhasa in Tibet. Museum specimens, however, are not the only evidence that should be taken into account. Horsfield, Hodgson and the Bombay Natural History Society, presumably as a result of direct sightings, have stated that red bear *does* occur in Nepal. This somewhat unsatisfactory position regarding the eastward extension of the red bear should be viewed in the context of Nepal's long history of political and social isolation which ended a bare thirty years ago. During the heyday of the big-game hunter, Nepal was forbidden territory. Now that it is open there are no more big-game hunters; there are only mountaineers. The Everest Expedition of 1953 was the first to approach the mountain from the south; the expeditions of 1924 and 1933 were obliged to attack it from the Tibetan side. Now, of course, the conditions are reversed: Tibet is closed and Nepal is open.

The evidence for red bear in Nepal is, for whatever reason, unsatisfactory. We can certainly assume that at present it is not as common in this region as it is in the western Himalayas. There is, possibly, a very simple ecological explanation for this state of affairs. The south-west monsoon brings its heaviest rainfall to Darjeeling (88° E) where 90 per cent of the annual rains of 121 inches fall between May and September. At the other end of the Himalayas, in Peshawar (72° E), the effect of the monsoon is minimal. Between these two extremes, the rainfall figures increase from west to east. Nepal lies to the west of Darjeeling, and while in its eastern parts its rainfall is just about as high as in Darjeeling, the maxima fall off as one progresses further westward. May to September is the period when the red bear, accompanied by the young cubs born during the hibernation period of November to March, moves up to feed on the new grass of the high-altitude yak pastures. Heavy snowfalls at this time of year would have tended to limit the feeding range of bears and force them to seek areas further west where the snowfall is not so high. Due to a rain-shadow effect, the snowline on the Tibetan or northern side of the Nepalese Himalayas occurs at a higher altitude than it does on the southern slopes. So, once again, conditions on the northern side would be better for red bear than on the southern side.

The red bear, locally known as the *Lal-bhalu* (meaning red or brown bear), is a race of the European brown bear, *Ursus arctos*, and is a large animal which averages 5 ft. 8 in. head and body length; the largest specimens may reach 7 ft.–8 ft. Body weight is approximately 500 lb. Their habitat lies between the treeline and the perpetual snow, an altitudinal range of 6,000 ft.–16,600 ft. During the winter the red bear hibernates for three or four months in caves or snow-covered rocky shelters at about 8,000 feet.

The diet of the red bear is truly omnivorous, consisting of a variety of such items as grass, roots, tubers, pikas, voles, insects and carrion. Red bears have been known to kill and eat sheep, goats and ponies. They are also fond of fruit, and will raid fruit-trees in season; this, incidentally, is about the only time they are seen to climb trees.

Their coat colour shows considerable variation owing to seasonal moult. The summer coat is dark-brown, grading through café-au-lait to cream; the winter coat is coarse and matted and the brown hairs develop pale-coloured tips. It will be noted that, as is so often the case, the common name is misleading. No red bear is actually 'red', although it may have a reddish glint to the fur.

The chief point of interest in the present context is the tracks that bears leave. The following remarks apply to all brown bears, including the 'red' and 'blue' varieties. The brown bear takes a greater proportion of its body weight on its forefeet, and consequently the front prints are usually better defined than the back ones. Fore- and hindfoot prints are quite distinct (figure 3). The bear walks in a *digitigrade* fashion on its forefeet but in a *plantigrade* fashion on its hindfeet. The difference between these two walking styles is exemplified by the dog and the cat which walk on the pads of their fingers and toes (digitigrade), and monkeys which walk on the flats of their hands and feet (plantigrade). A characteristic of the bear is that the forefoot is in-turned when walking. That is to say that as far as its front feet are concerned the bear is pigeon-toed. The hindfoot of the bear is remarkably human-like; it has five toes, a shank, a heel, and the foot is 10 in. in length, roughly that of the average man. The differences, however, are equally obvious. Bears have non-retractible claws, which almost invariably leave narrow impressions – particularly in snow – ahead of the toe-pads. The toe-pads themselves are rounded and quite separate from the ball of the foot; the largest pad often occurs on the *outer* border of the foot in contrast to man's big-toe print which is on the *inner* border. The sole of the foot is extremely broad in front and narrows acutely to a slender heel behind. Nevertheless, it is easy to understand how a bear's footprint could be mistaken for a human footprint, particularly in snow where melting or evaporation has obscured the finer details.[2]

Claw marks are not a particularly consistent feature of bear tracks. A bear recently out of hibernation has long claws, which can hardly fail to leave an impression, but towards the end of summer the claws have become worn and blunted and may not show up at all. So the absence of claw marks in a given footprint does not wholly rule out the bear as the perpetrator. It would seem that the easiest way to distinguish the tracks of a man and a bear would be to look out for prints of the forefoot, which should clinch the matter; but it is not quite so easy as that. When a bear is ambling along in no particular hurry, the forefoot comes down in front of the hindfoot; but the faster the bear walks the more the hindfoot creeps up on the forefoot. At moderate speeds, the hindfoot overlaps the forefoot track; and at fast speeds, the hindfoot strikes the ground well in front of the forefoot (figure 3). At moderate speeds the track is often a composite one, with the fore- and hindfoot superimposed; in these circumstances it can give the appearance of a single track made by a bipedal creature. The outline of the composite track, particularly in snow that has been subjected to melting, is, at first sight, extraordinarily human-like. The footprints photographed by Professor Williams on the Sim Gang Glacier in the Karakorams were almost certainly made by a red bear pacing at moderate speed (figure 4).

The dimensions and appearance of Squadron-Leader L. W. Davies's prints from the Kulti Valley, Lahoul, are also suggestive of red bear. Both the Kulti Valley and the Biafo Glacier lie within the known geographical range of the red bear subspecies. In 1956, Pranavanandra discovered some recently made footprints measuring 5¾ in. by 2¾ in. in the region of Rupkumu in the Garwhal Himalaya. He states that they were 'just like those of a human boy', but expresses the belief that they were of a young bear. Again, both red and black bear are known to occur in this area.

As we have seen, Sherpa folklore recognizes two creatures that may loosely be described as Abominable Snowmen – the Dzu-teh and the Meh-teh (or Yeti). The Dzu-teh is said by Sherpas to be rare in Nepal but common in the west and to the north. The description of the Dzu-teh given to many travellers, Charles Stonor for example, would fit a red bear or possibly a blue bear. The Yeti however is clearly a different kettle of fish; the frequency with which it uses bipedalism is not particularly bear-like, but nevertheless the reports *could* refer to the Asiatic black bear (*Selenarctos thibetanus*) which, unlike the red bear, is common in Nepal, albeit at lower altitudes. Possibly the black bear may account for some of the footprints seen in the eastern Himalayas at moderate altitudes, for instance those seen at 12,000 feet by Abbé Bordet in the Dudh Kosi Valley.

The black bear occurs from the Hindu Kush in the west throughout the Himalayan foothills to Assam in the east. It is also found in Balukhistan, Thailand, Indo-China, Manchuria, China, on the offshore islands of Hainan and Formosa and in Japan. In contrast to brown bears, whose habitat is high montane moorland, black bears are essentially forest-dwellers. Their recorded upper altitudinal limit in the Himalayan part of their range is 11,000 feet. They are a little smaller than brown bears, never exceeding 6 ft. 6 in. in head and body length. Black bears do not need to hibernate, as an all-the-year-round food supply is guaranteed by the simple expedient of descent to lower altitudes for the winter months. Being forest-dwellers, black bears climb trees more freely than the brown variety, but as far as diet is concerned they differ from them not at all, except perhaps that they eat less grass, roots and tubers, and more fruit and insects. The tracks of the two bears are very similar, the only difference being that the forefoot of the black bear has two separate pads of flesh, one behind the other, whereas in the brown bear there is only a single pad. Black bears are primarily nocturnal, often living near towns and villages, and they are extremely aggressive towards man. Bears can inflict the most terrible wounds by the raking action of the fore-paws. A Colonel Markham recounts the appalling injuries to the face and scalp inflicted on one of his porters by a black bear.[3]

It is quite conceivable that these two genera of bears, the red and the black, have helped to perpetuate the Yeti legend in Nepal, Sikkim, Bhutan and Tibet; but whether they were responsible for initiating it is quite another matter. The red bear may account for some of the sightings and footprints seen in remote regions at high altitudes and particularly west of the Bheling Valley, while the black bear, which lives at lower altitudes and haunts the vicinity of villages, could well be a factor in the numerous sightings reported in the neighbourhood of villages and monasteries. The central character in the story told to Lord Hunt by the Abbot of Thyangboche could well have been an Asiatic black bear. I am not suggesting that the Yeti is simply a bear, and that all who have seen it are either, at best, so hallucinated or so ignorant that they do not know a bear when they see one or, at worst, so mendacious that their stories can be discounted. I am simply stressing that Yetis and bears apparently share a common range, as well as a similarity in a number of structural and behavioural characters – footprints included.

The Himalayas are extremely well endowed with mammalian fauna, and many species live at altitudes above 17,000 feet (see table 4, p. 214). Although none are likely to be confused in good visibility with the Yeti, all leave footprints of one sort or another in the snow. Any of these prints, if subjected to melting, sublimation or to the effects of high winds or blizzards, could easily become so distorted that precise identification becomes impossible. Hence, another 'mysterious footprint' goes on record.

Birds are not the most obvious Yeti-substitute, but in view of a letter recently published in a weekly magazine it appears that we may have been neglecting an important source of footprints. While in the Austrian Tyrol, the writer (clearly a keen ornithologist, who lives in a house called Chiffchaffs), looking down from a high peak, observed a line of human steps traversing a cornice of snow at a precarious angle. As he watched, two Alpine choughs landed and hopped along the cornice breast-deep, leaving behind them a row of 'human' footprints![4] Choughs are common birds in the Himalayas, and the yellow-billed variety have been observed at 26,000 feet. Footprints apart, the choughs deserve some attention for their high-pitched mewing call. This could conceivably be interpreted as the yelping call of a Yeti, which is heard so much more frequently than the animal itself, or its tracks, is actually seen.

Man himself is also part of the fauna of the Himalayas, even if only in a migratory capacity. Mountaineers, the now-extinct big-game hunters, escapees from Siberian prison-camps, mineral prospectors, geographers and tax-collectors apart, the snows of the Himalayas are traversed annually by a cadre of devotees, dedicatedly plodding their—often barefooted—way along the caravan routes towards the high passes like Nangpa-la, the corridors of Nirvana, that lead to the holy city of Lhasa or further west, to the sacred mountains of the Kailas range. In 1896[5] S. J. Stone met a holy man who had been wandering through the mountains for twelve years. Stone recalls how the fakir, barefoot and dressed only in a tattered coat and a pair of torn pyjamas, sat in the snow and talked to him 'in seeming comfort'. Stone remarks that he smoked marijuana. As mentioned on p. 136 Pranavananda encountered the tracks of one such pilgrim crossing the Khandosanglam Pass east of the Kailas Mountain. In 1930, Colonel Henniker, an officer in the British Army, met with a *sadhu*, a Hindu pilgrim, crossing the Ladakh range in northeast Kashmir at 17,000 feet, barefoot, clad simply in a loincloth and carrying a wooden staff. Barry Bishop recounts how a Nepalese holy man walked into their camp at 18,000 feet high up the Mingbo Valley. He was barefoot and dressed in light garments (plate 8). For two nights he slept in the snow with no coverings, suffering little apparent harm except for swollen hands and feet, which soon returned to normal with treatment. His feet were bare and wherever he walked he must of course have left footprints—man-like footprints.

Apart from pilgrims *en route* for elsewhere, the Himalayas and adjacent ranges have their share of hermits and mystics.[6] Pater Franz Eichinger, the German doctor and missionary, described in an interview in the *News Chronicle* (1959) how in many areas of Tibet there are ascetics who live solitary lives, roaming naked through the mountains at high altitudes, and capable of enduring intense cold and severe privation. Eichinger stressed that these people were not members of primitive races, but were religious mystics of Tibetan or Mongolian origin who are much respected and even feared by nomadic tribes. Eichinger met one of these mystics who wandered into a nomad tent-village in the Tsinghai Province of western China. These people, too, must leave footprints.

The langur has already been mentioned several times, and

without doubt has a role in the Himalayan Bigfoot legend, albeit a minor one. Apart from being one of the principal suspects in the Don Whillans case, it has figured in at least two other Yeti incidents (see chapter 2). Langurs are essentially quadrupeds, and they have long tails. They may briefly stand upright on two legs, but they certainly never walk on them. I have seen langurs 'dancing' or hopping on their hindlegs, but that's all. They can probably be excluded from any incident in which protracted bipedal walking is involved.

Other than men and langurs, the only primate which has been mentioned in the context of Himalayan Bigfoot is the orang-utan. As a very large Asiatic ape, red or reddish-brown in colour, capable of walking short distances on two legs, the orang would seem a natural suspect for a Yeti-substitute. The only trouble is that orangs do not exist outside South-East Asia, and even in their present-day habitat of Borneo and northern Sumatra they are all but extinct. Moreover, they are tropical animals and are essentially tree dwellers. There is no doubt whatsoever that orangs should be excluded from any *present* participation in the Bigfoot affair, but there are some cogent reasons why they might be apportioned at least part of the blame for the birth of the legend.

When Charles Stonor[7] was journeying through northern Nepal in search of information on the Sherpas' attitude towards the Yeti, he made a habit of showing photographs of various animals to the villagers he met on his travels, and noting their reaction. The animals included bears, langurs and orangs. He made a point of keeping the picture of the orang to the last. When finally he unveiled it, with the showmanship of a conjurer producing a rabbit out of a hat, the instantaneous reaction on several separate occasions was a chorus of 'Yeti, Yeti!' Further questioning revealed that the picture did not recall the local Yeti but a creature that was believed to live in the mountains far away towards the north in Tibet. Perhaps the photographs of the orang recalled the image of the Dzu-teh which, as all Sherpas agree, is somebody else's headache and not in their bailiwick at all. Some orang-utans, particularly those from Sumatra, can look extraordinary human-like, which may possibly account for their being cast in the role of ape-men (plate 9).

From the Lepchas in Darjeeling, Stonor heard of a legendary monster of Tibet called the Thloh-Mung. Apart from its reputation for cunning and ferocity, the following account could apply to orang-utan as well as to anything else:

> Long ago there was a beast in our mountains, known to our forefathers as the *Thloh-Mung*, meaning in our language Mountain Savage. Its cunning and ferocity were so great as to be a match for anyone who encountered it. It could always outwit our Lepcha hunters, with their bows and arrows. The *Thloh-Mung* was said to live alone, or with a very few of its kind; and it went sometimes on the ground, and sometimes in the trees. It was only found in the higher mountains of our country. Although it was made very like a man, it was covered with long, dark hair, and was more intelligent than a monkey, as well as being larger. The people became more in number, the forest and wild country less; and the *Thloh-Mung* disappeared. But many people say they are still to be found in the mountains of Nepal, away to the west, where the Sherpa people call them *Yeti*.

One of the Lepchas told Stonor that he had seen such a creature in captivity in the zoo in Calcutta. Stonor satisfied himself that the animal in question was, indeed, an orang-utan.

It is interesting to speculate how the orang of faraway Borneo and Sumatra got itself involved in Yeti mythology at all. The obvious explanation is that orang-utans were once widespread over much of the southern regions of continental Asia. One is constantly falling into the trap of imagining that because certain species are *now* to be found in particular areas, their distribution has always been the same. It is necessary to remind oneself that today we are looking at a very narrow slice of geological time — a second, as it were, in the twenty-four-hour span of mammalian history. In terms of the orang, it would not be possible from scientific records alone to state categorically that *it did not exist* on the Asian mainland five hundred years ago, or even two hundred years ago for that matter. When the scientific records of living animals fail us we still have two resources left: folklore, for what it is worth, and the fossil record.

Van Gulik[8] believed that the Fei-fei of China mentioned in the *Erh-ya*, the Chinese dictionary of the Chou period of 200 B.C., could refer to the orang. The Fei-fei is described (*inter alia*) as having a human face with long lips and long red hair. To homologize this description with the orang is fair enough on the face of it, but it is not proof; only the fossil record can provide this.

The early evolutionary history of the orang-utan is shrouded in mystery. The fossils most likely to be ancestral to living orangs are those of *Dryopithecus sivalensis*, found in the Siwalik Hills, foothills of the Himalayas, in north-west India and West Pakistan. Their attribution to the orang is possible but by no means certain. The date of the Siwalik deposits is uncertain too but probably they were laid down in the region of 10 million to 14 million years ago. During this period of time, which corresponds with the late Miocene and early Pliocene geological epochs, the ape and human stocks are thought to have separated into two independent families—the Pongidae (the ape family) and the Hominidae (the human family). It is reasonably safe to make the assumption that ancestral orang-utans were represented in the Siwalik fauna at about this period. No further information is forthcoming about the early history of orangs until the Pleistocene, the geological epoch that started between 2–3 million years ago. During this period we know from fossil evidence that there was a continental species of orang living in southern China. The orang was also much more widespread in south-east Asia than it is now, being known from central Sumatra and Java, regions where it is not found today. After the end of the middle Pleistocene (250,000 years ago) apparently there are no further records of orangs in fossil deposits on the mainland but this does not necessarily mean that they had become extinct. Absence of fossils proves little. There is good reason for assuming the existence of a continental orang in the Pleistocene and it is reasonably safe to assume that if such a creature was roaming the forests of the Yunnan province of China in the middle Pleistocene it was likely to have lived in the intermediate regions of Laos, Vietnam, Thailand and Malaya.

There is some evidence that orang-utans were still found on the island of Java (and possibly the mainland of Asia) up until the eighteenth and nineteenth centuries. Jacob Bontius, a doctor living in Batavia (now Jakarta), published in 1718 an account of an animal in Java called an 'Ourang-Outang'. Neither the description nor the illustration, which was of a rather hairy woman, has much relationship to the orang as we know it. Bontius had heard rumours of the orang-utan but, clearly, had never seen one. His illustration of a hairy woman is quite fortuitous and, incidentally, had already been used twenty years previously by Edward Tyson in his famous monograph on the chimpanzee. Bontius was very much in the position of present-day authors who have heard of – but never seen – the Yeti or the Sasquatch, but are prepared to describe and even supply an illustration of one, and – if necessary – give it a scientific name to boot. Bontius referred to this creature as *Homo sylvestris*. Linnaeus, in the 1758 edition of his *Systema Naturae*, absorbed *Homo sylvestris* (based on Bontius's illustration and description) into his species *Homo troglodytes* (*Homo nocturnus* was an alternative name used by Linnaeus). Also in 1758, Edwards in his *Gleanings of Natural History* provided a figure illustrating an 'Orang-autang', otherwise known as 'The Man of the Woods', '*L'Homme Sauvage*' or *Homo sylvestris*. This time the illustration really *looked* like an orang and nobody doubts its authenticity. In 1760, Hoppius reproduced Edwards's orang and called the creature *Simia pygmaeus*. Bontius's human-like creature still continued to influence later authors and until 1834 in many books of natural history the geographical range of the orang included the island of Java. It is difficult to decide whether Bontius's hirsute female was based on an orang-utan that actually lived in Java or on rumours of such a creature from the neighbouring islands of Borneo and Sumatra.

The mainland orang was mentioned specifically in *The Natural History of Monkeys* by Sir William Jardine, published in 1833. Reference is made to the distribution of the orang as Sumatra, Borneo and 'the peninsula of Malacca'. Geoffroy in his *Catalogue des mammifères* (1851) mentions that the habitat of the orang is possibly on the mainland of Asia, as have several other authors. It is quite likely, of course, that there was confusion between the orang and the gibbon, or more probably the slightly larger siamang, common in this area. In spite of the uncertain nature of the evidence, a wider distribution of the orang-utan a mere 150 years ago is a distinct possibility. It is not really necessary for orang-utans to have lived in Nepal or Tibet, or even particularly close to these countries, for the orang image to have become identified with a local monster myth. However, it is not out of the question that orangs were once to be found in the high-altitude montane forests of Himalayan valleys such as the Arun river valley in eastern Nepal. Conceivably they could still be living there today.

The ethnic and cultural history of the Tibetans and their off-shoots, the Sherpas of the Khumbu in northern Nepal, is linked with China – unlike their Buddhist religion which derives from India. It would be from China that the legend would have spread. Bearing in mind the view expressed by many authorities (von Fürer-Haimendorf, see, for example, p. 55) that Yeti legends have little if any religious significance, it seems likely that the myth of the Yeti owes more to Sino-Tibetan culture than to Mahayana Buddhism of India. The orang-utan overtones of the Yeti are therefore more likely to have been derived from a Far Eastern culture where orang-utans were at one time a familiar element of the fauna, than from an Indian source where there is no fossil evidence of more recent date than ten million years ago to support such an idea.

Circumstantially, orang-utans appear to be deeply involved in the tales of the Himalayan Bigfoot, and indeed may account for the giant-ape element that is so pervasive. The teeth of middle Pleistocene orangs from southern China are considerably larger than those from the later Trinil deposits in Java or from Sumatra. Orang teeth from fossil deposits in Sumatra have been estimated by the Dutch palaeontologist D. A. Hooijer to have been 16 per cent larger than in modern forms. Thus the continental orang may well have been a large and fearsome creature though not, I am convinced, a cunning or ferocious enemy of man or of his domestic beasts.

A totally unsolicited fragment of 'evidence' came into my hands recently. A letter arrived on my desk from Mr L. Hindmarch, the proprietor of a restaurant in Devonshire. He states that in conversation with a lama in eastern Tibet two or three years ago, he was told of a creature called a Baja which '*has a face similar to an orang-utan* and has toes and fingers like a man, with similar nails, and leaves footprints similar to a human's ... it is *frequently seen walking on its hind legs and brushing the hair from its eyes with its hands*'. The pen sketch of the Baja drawn by the lama resembles a yak more than anything else, but Mr Hindmarch assures me that in the lama's view it looked like a cross between a bear and an ape. The alleged facultative bipedal gait and the floppy frontal hair are classics of the Yeti legend. The lama told Mr Hindmarch that he himself had seen one of these creatures and that he had also seen an orang-utan in a zoo so could not possibly have confused the two.

The circumstantial evidence in favour of the Orang Theory is derived from a number of pointers, insignificant by themselves but quite impressive taken collectively:

1. The fossil record of the orang-utan.
2. The 'consensus' description of the Yeti from Sherpa folklore.
3. Van Gulik's 'evidence' regarding the Fei-fei.
4. Charles Stonor's experiences with Sherpa villagers on showing them a photograph of an orang-utan.
5. Charles Stonor's account derived from the folklore of the Lepchas of Darjeeling concerning the Thloh-Mung.

12. John Green studying
15 in. Sasquatch prints on
Blue Creek Mountain,
Northern California, in
1967

13. One variety of the
'hourglass' Sasquatch print
from the Bluff Creek area,
Northern California

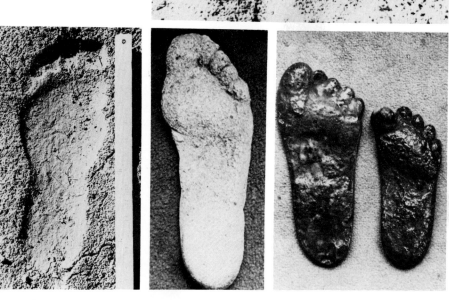

14. Cast of a human walking-print (*left*), and casts of footprints
of Neanderthal Man impressed in clay and found in a sealed
cave near Toirano, Italy

15. (*above*) Sasquatch prints of two different sizes from the Bluff Creek area. (*below left*) Another variety of the 'hourglass' type, where the toes are like 'peas in a pod'. (*right*) Human footprints in damp sand, and (*below right*) the position of the toes at the toe-off stage of striding; note that the little toes are bent up and the big toe is flattened

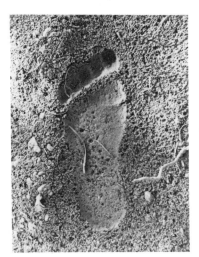

6. The identification by a Lepcha of an orang-utan in Calcutta zoo as a Yeti.

7. B. H. Hodgson's comment in 1832 on the possible nature of the creature sighted by his porters.

8. Mr L. Hindmarch's testimony of a Lama's description of a 'Baja' as having a face similar to an orang-utan.

9. The zoogeographical history of the orang in eighteenth- and nineteenth-century zoological texts.

Although the orang is now extinct on the mainland of Asia, it is not difficult to see how the tradition of the orang-utan might have persisted, becoming transformed into the Yeti in the process. When the present-day mongoloids of Tibet and their off-shoots, the Sherpas of Nepal, arrived in the area, they brought with them the tales of the orang-utans of the tropical forests of south China (and possibly, too, of the tropical montane forests of western China, north Vietnam and northern Burma). Even supposing orangs have never existed in Tibet or northern Nepal, there would have been plenty of sources of local reinforcement to keep the legend alive such as bears, langurs and snow leopards. Contributions in the form of tales told by new immigrants arriving from the east would also have helped to keep the pot boiling. As a result of its new environment, the legend would have undergone certain modifications in which orang-like characters became submerged, through lack of specific reinforcement, and were replaced by the zoological hotch-potch that so puzzles us today.

I have left to the last any consideration of the role of bears, pilgrims or orang-utans in the growth of the Sasquatch legend. Neither pilgrims nor orangs would seem to come into the American Bigfoot story but—to a limited extent—bears do. By 'limited' I mean that none of the published footprints (the only objective source of evidence for the existence of the Sasquatch) could conceivably have been made by a bear. This leaves only the possibility that some of the sightings were of bears. This must be accepted as a possibility, but to try and shrug off the

Sasquatch as just a bear would be a ludicrous attempt at simplification: whatever the Sasquatch is, it is not a bear. However, having made a categorical statement I am, like any sensible person, anxious to qualify it. Assuming for the moment that what hundreds of people are reported to have seen was an illusion, a *déja vu* or something of the sort, it could well be that the image of the bear has played a dominant role in the general tenor of their descriptions. Bears (principally the American black bear, *Ursus americanus*) are indigenous to the regions where Sasquatch sightings are most common. Can one totally exclude the fact that the image of the bear, hairy, omnivorous and partially bipedal, must be uppermost in the minds of people entering the boreal forest wildernesses of the north-west? After all, the black bear is the only animal, other than the rare mountain lion, the bobcat, and the even rarer wolverine, that they need to fear in these regions. What is more likely than that a close brush with a black bear should become a horrific encounter with a Sasquatch; after all, it is a sight easier to admit fear when face-to-face with an unknown monster than with a bear—just a little ol' bear! Who has ever cast doubt on the courage of a man frightened by a ghost?

Bears, I am sure, play a part in the legend of the Bigfoot in North America, just as they do in Asia. However, to explain away the sightings and the footprints simply in terms of bears alone is like describing gravity as a phenomenon by which apples are found on the ground.

*   *   *

Edo ergo sum is one of those handy aphorisms that sound best in the original. For all that the message is clear, one must eat to live. If one is going to insist on the reality of a mythological animal, then one must be prepared to obey the ground rules, the most important of which is to provide a milieu that meets the minimum requirements for the creature's survival in terms of food supply. Yetis and Sasquatches fall into the category of giants, and giants have prodigious, gargantuan, appetites. An adequate food supply for a population of Bigfoot would presuppose a pretty lush environment all the year round. Significantly, the alleged environments of Bigfoot are singularly barren.

The mountain gorilla, the bulkiest of all primates, provides a useful analogy. In the wild, they may weigh up to 450 lb, and in captivity they have been known to tip the scales at 600 lb. In order to survive, a gorilla has to spend a large part of each day eating bulk foodstuffs. George Schaller[9] in his intimate study of mountain gorillas estimates that at least eight out of the twelve waking hours are spent in feeding. The gorilla is lucky inasmuch as it lives in the sort of environment that can supply its needs all the year round. Actually, of course, the question of 'luck' doesn't come into it, the truth is that it is only in areas where the food supply is adequate that gorillas can survive.

Present-day gorilla habitats are rather restricted, and probably represent only a small proportion of the areas they once occupied before the African forests started to shrink during the period of relative dryness that followed the last of the great Pleistocene Ice Ages. It has been suggested that gorillas are primarily mountain-forest dwellers, and that as the climate changed and the extent of high altitude forests was reduced many ancestral populations of gorillas were forced to migrate into the lowland forests of East and West Africa—their principal home today. Colin P. Groves[10] suggests that the thickset, barrel-chested build of the gorilla is an adaptation for relatively cold climates at high altitudes. At first sight, a theory that holds that ancestral gorillas were inhabitants of mountainous regions would seem to be rather relevant to the giant-ape theory of the nature of the Yeti. However, what is important is that they live in forests.

The mountain gorilla habitat in Africa on the lower slopes of the Virunga Volcanoes and Mount Kahuzi lies between 5,000 and 10,000 feet; rainfall is high, and vegetable food is available all the year round. Comparable forests are not found much above 5,000 ft.–6,000 ft. either in the Himalayan foothills or in the deep river gorges that transect the Himalayas from north to south. The Arun is one of the most spectacular of these river valleys. The river arises in the Tibetan plateau; it enters Nepal east of Mount Everest and finally leaves it as the Sapt Kosi to empty into the Ganges. The floor of the valley is heavily forested with tropical montane vegetation. The sides of the gorge are steep. At about 6,000 feet, montane forest degrades into bamboo forest and higher still to rhododendron forest which in turn gives way to moorland; and at 14,000 feet the snowfields begin. There is no doubt that the Arun Valley and others like it could theoretically support an ape-like creature very easily. Much of the forests are unexplored so there is no *a priori* reason why unknown creatures could not be living there. The Arun Valley could still house a relict population of orang-utans, or Yetis for that matter. The foregoing argument is based on the assumption that the Yeti has a gorilla-like diet and, thus, needs to live under subtropical conditions.

However, the Yeti or its footprints are most often seen at altitudes of 14,000 feet or over, so the question remains as to what a subtropical forest creature is doing swanning about the snowfields and glaciers at heights up to 20,000 feet. It might be supposed that Yetis do not live at this height, but are simply visiting there. For what purpose? It has been suggested that Yetis, like many human populations living far inland, would suffer from an iodine deficiency, and a particularly nutritious type of moss, rich in iodine, to be found at high altitudes provides the attraction. The alternative suggestion is that when seen they are *en route* for new feeding grounds. What new feeding grounds? There are other, less richly vegetated valleys to the west, like the Honghu Kosi and the Dudh Kosi, but they are a long trek from the Arun. It is difficult to accept that Yetis are sufficiently plastic in physiological make-up to cope with such extreme climatic contrasts, or sufficiently motivated to make such epic journeys. However, it is known that the mountain gorillas in passing from one forested region to another reach as high as 13,500 feet.

Let us suppose that the Yeti actually *lives* at high altitudes, making its home among rocks or in caves. The possibility that the Yeti is a descendant of the fossil ape *Gigantopithecus* is reviewed in chapter 7. From the evidence of the teeth, their wear pattern and relative proportions, it has been proposed that *Gigantopithecus* was a 'graminivorous' feeder living on small food objects (see chapter 7), like the present-day gelada 'baboon' of the Ethiopian highlands.[11] But in the Himalayas even such a rugged feeder as the gelada would have little to live on above 15,000 feet. In their snow-free, natural habitat in Ethiopia, food is available to geladas all year round, and they have the added advantage of being able to utilize the side-products of human agriculture; the threshing-floors of the villages, for instance, provide food for geladas for days on end. The Yetis would have none of these advantages. Yetis could conceivably be 'graminivorous' feeders, but their habitat has few of the all the year round resources that characterize the home of the gelada.

The only alternative is that the Yeti is an omnivorous feeder like a man or a bear. Both man and bears will eat anything in the animal line that doesn't eat them first, and they are partial to fruit, vegetables, honey, roots and tubers. In spite of his lack of specialized teeth, man is able to include animal flesh in his diet because his technology, in the widest sense of the word, facilitates both the killing and cooking of animals. Bears have no technology but they *do* have carnivorous teeth. Yetis, apparently, have neither the technology nor the appropriate teeth; nevertheless the only possible diet on which they could survive at high altitudes would be an omnivorous one. Omnivorous diets must of course include flesh, and one might argue that this would provide no great problem for a Yeti. Pikas or Himalayan mouse-hares are common enough and live at very high altitudes (up to 20,000 feet), and a few pikas a day would provide quite an adequate diet for a creature of the size of a Yeti, which in terms of consensus opinions of observers (see chapter 4) is far from gigantic.

Let us summarize this see-saw argument. A Yeti could theoretically survive in the tropical montane forests of the major river valleys as a gorilla-like vegetarian; it could conceivably survive as a 'graminivorous' feeder at high altitudes below the snowline; and a rather inadequate case could be made out for its surviving during the winter above the snowline as an omnivore, primarily by flesh-eating — during the spring and summer, as the snows melted on the lower slopes, it could revert, as a bear does, to the more vegetarian elements of its dietary range.

The diet of the American Bigfoot is another matter altogether. Not only is the Sasquatch larger than its Himalayan cousin, but its habitat, in terms of vegetational type, is totally different. Sasquatch country broadly speaking is coniferous forest. Summers are cool (except in some extreme coastal areas) and winters are long and humid. Heavy snow occurs above 2,000 feet. Coniferous forest in this area provides, according to Frank L. Beebe, the poorest quality of high-energy plant food. This is accounted for by the low solar energy input resulting from the dense forest cover and the almost continuous overcast.

In summer the dietary opportunities (for the bear, for instance) include insects of various sorts, berries, roots of bracken, spruce tips, skunk-cabbage and so on, but in the winter these resources do not exist and, to survive, the bear must either hibernate or migrate.

A few primates have become adapted for life in extremely adverse climatic conditions. In Shimokita, the northernmost peninsula of Honshu, Japan, at a latitude of 41° 20′ N, troops of macaque monkeys ride out the snowy winters subsisting on little more than the cambium layer of trees. As Japanese macaques weigh approximately one-sixteenth of a large male gorilla and one-thirtieth to one-fortieth of a ten-foot Sasquatch, their survival problems are proportionately less intense. Recent studies have shown that Japanese macaque monkeys also kill and eat rabbits, which observation may give us a lead to the winter diet of the Yeti and the Sasquatch.

What exactly does the Sasquatch eat? Observers have seen and reported the Sasquatch eating berries, fruit, leaves, spruce tips, water-plants, tubers, fish (salted and fresh), rodents, deer, as well as sheep, cows, horses and Indians [*sic*]. John Green mentions that in his extensive file of eyewitness reports, vegetable-eating and flesh-eating occur in the proportions of 6:5. Except possibly for the Indians, the Sasquatch diet has the catholic qualities of a bear, but bears, even the giant Kodiak bears of north-west Canada and Alaska, are not true predators in the style of the feline carnivores. It is for this reason that bears find it necessary to adopt a form of hibernation during winter.

Hibernation is the only alternative, other than migration, to winter starvation for many mammals. True hibernation as practised by dormice or marmots, for instance, is a physiological process by which the metabolism of the body is reduced to the minimal level consistent with life; the animal rolls up into a tight ball with its paws firmly clenched and its tail wrapped over its body. The heart-rate slows and the body-temperature drops. The torpor of hibernation is triggered off by low environmental temperatures and thus, even within a single zoological group distributed over a wide range of latitude and altitude, there is considerable variability in the time of the onset of seasonal torpor.

Bears are not true hibernators. When 'denned-up' for the winter, the body temperature remains almost normal although the heart-rate falls. The Asiatic black bear seldom dens-up, preferring to migrate for the winter to lower altitudes where food is plentiful. The sloth bears and the sun bears of the tropics, of course, have absolutely no need to sign-off; neither, in the warmer parts of its range, does the American black bear although in the more northern latitudes it dens-up in the winter months just as do the grizzly bear (*Ursus horribilis*) and the Kodiak bear (*Ursus middendorffi*). For all bears who 'hibernate', the lean season is also the birth season, which is one reason why one so seldom sees the cubs born to zoo bears until they are several weeks old; old habits die hard.

Primates, being tropical animals, neither hibernate nor den-up; even in the rare cases when they live in temperate to cold regions, they tend to soldier on, subsisting on very little. If the

Sasquatch hibernates, the chances are that it is no primate. But, as it happens, the evidence for hibernation of the North American Bigfoot is not very strong. Sightings have been recorded during all months of the year, and if Sasquatches appear to be rather thin on the ground during November-December-January, the reason may be that the depth of winter is the time when man does a bit of denning-up on his own account.

One thing seems fairly certain. Whatever the Sasquatch is – man, ape or bear – it is not a professional predator. In spite of scattered reports of predation of domestic animals – and even humans – this behaviour is not characteristic. If it were, you may be sure that in North America, Bigfoot would rapidly become Public Enemy No. 1 which assuredly it is not.

Let us attempt to sum up the ecological argument to date. If the Sasquatch is as big as his footprints make him out to be, if he is not a predator (in the sense of a carnivore), and if he does not hibernate or den-up in the winter, then just what does he do for a living in the cold quarter of the year? Short of retiring to a cave, building a fire and living on canned food, how does an 800 lb creature keep itself going in boreal forests under winter snows? One possible solution is that, like some bears, it migrates towards the coast, where it lives on sea-food. The present evidence for this wintering behaviour is not very persuasive. All in all, the ecological situation facing the Sasquatch in winter does not argue in its favour but, bearing in mind the extraordinary resilience of some primates (including man) in adverse conditions, the ecological case against the Sasquatch is far from proven.

One further aspect of animal ecology, which is relevant to feeding behaviour, is the pattern of activity during a twenty-four-hour period. According to general zoological principles, animals may be *diurnal* (active from sunrise to sunset), or *nocturnal* (active from sunset to sunrise). In practice there are a number of variants on this simple box-and-cox arrangement; some tropical animals are *crepuscular*, being active in the cool periods of dawn and dusk. Most of the Malagasy lemurs, for example, follow this regime. Other mammals—like the bears—appear to be indiscriminately nocturnal or diurnal.

The activity rhythm of animals is closely related to diet. Strictly nocturnal animals are either insect eaters or flesh-eating predators. Grass-eaters, such as cattle, graze by day as well as by night and cannot easily be classified. The hippopotamus is mainly a nocturnal grazer and a diurnal wallower. Monkeys and apes, whose diet is omnivorous but principally vegetarian, are strictly diurnal. The only species of monkey that fails to toe the line is *Aotus*, the night-monkey of South America. In the tropics, animal life works on a twenty-four-hour principle; there is but one period of the day in which no sensible animal is active—only mad dogs and Englishmen go out in the midday sun.

From the evidence presented in chapter 3, the Sasquatch is observed at night as well as during the day, an activity rhythm which is similar to a bear's but quite unlike that of a higher primate. We obviously know nothing of the periodicity of early man, but it is fairly safe to assume that, like the really primitive tribes that still exist today, he lived by the sun as a good primate should.

While on the subject of nocturnal-diurnal behaviour, there is the little matter of retinal reflection—a trivial thing, no doubt. A number of observers of the Sasquatch have commented on its 'eye-shine' and described it as red, green, yellow or white. In diurnal animals there is a minimum of shine because the retina has an in-built mechanism (comparable to the black backing of a photographic plate) which absorbs the light falling on it. The retina of nocturnal animals, on the other hand, is adapted for *reflecting* light; this is a practical device for bouncing back the light, such as it is, thus giving the retina a 'second chance'. The reflecting layer of the 'nocturnal' retina is called the tapetum, and at night, when light falls on the eye, some of it instead of being bounced back escapes through the pupil and is seen as 'eye-shine'. The colour of light reflected from the tapetum of nocturnal animals is green; diurnal animals, which lack a tapetum, give a red, pale-pink or white reflection. John Green's records provide one instance of green reflection and five of red or white. On the basis of these paltry observations, the most one could deduce is that the Sasquatch is not obviously adapted for a nocturnal existence. I do not recall a single instance where the 'eye-shine' of the Yeti has been commented upon.

In the popular imagination, monsters tend to be both solitary and male. We talk of *the* Abominable Snowman just as we refer to *the* Loch Ness Monster. If monsters are to be taken seriously they must learn to conform to the basic biological rule that— amongst vertebrates at any rate—it takes two to make a species and, by the nature of things, they must be of opposite sex.

Female monsters do occur in mythology, but they are in the minority. Perhaps it is significant in this connection that in the records of Yeti sightings (as opposed to Yeti-lore) a female Yeti has only once been specifically mentioned. This occurred in Rawicz's suspect account quoted in chapter 2. Although he does not specifically mention a female, the implication is clear on the basis of size difference. Sherpa tales told round the fire, with *chang* and buttered tea flowing freely, invariably include an account of the Yeti females who are forced to throw their large and pendulous breasts over their shoulders when running. If Rawicz's female really was a female one wonders why he missed such an obvious embellishment to his tale. Perhaps the lack of female sightings simply reflects a measure of reticence amongst the Sherpas. North Americans seem to be less inhibited. My own records (table 2, p. 210) include eight instances where Sasquatch females were specifically mentioned; John Green cites fifteen instances. Family groups are unknown for the Yeti, but have been observed several times in North America. Juveniles are also unrecorded in the Himalayas, but are fairly commonly seen in Sasquatch sightings; John Green's records show that approximately 4 per cent of all individuals sighted are juveniles. There is no doubt that as a biological entity the Sasquatch is a much more satisfactory fellow than his Himalayan counterpart.

If we accept Bigfoot as a living creature we must be prepared to acknowledge that there must be *populations* of these animals in the eastern Himalayas and in the mountains of north-west United States and Canada. Bearing in mind the vast area covered by the purported range of the species (approximately 125,000 square miles for the Sasquatch, and 150,000 square miles for the Yeti), one might expect populations of at least several hundred to a thousand or more in each region. Even these extremely low population density estimates (or guesses, rather) put a further strain on credulity. Is it really possible that a population of up to 1,000 Bigfoot could exist in remote, but by no means untravelled, regions without being formally recognized by zoology? The American puma or mountain lion is widespread from British Columbia to Patagonia in quite large numbers. Yet it is so elusive that few people have seen it in the wild, and fewer still have been able to photograph it. Nevertheless, in spite of its retiring habits, the mountain lion is well-known to science.

England admittedly is a small country, but the following has some relevance to the argument. Unknown to all but a few experts and a handful of local people and visitors, there are populations of Australian wallabies living freely in two fairly remote regions in England at present. The areas they occupy are very small, and their population numbers are very low. In one area the numbers had built up to an estimated 40–50, but the severe winter of 1962–3 all but wiped them out; they are now slowly building up again.[12] Wallabies are relatively small animals and extremely difficult to spot when lying low, it is true, but this example demonstrates that it is perfectly possible for a strange animal population to exist in our midst unknown to the general public. But of course *they are not unknown to science.* I can see this example being thoroughly worked over by the fans of mysterious animals and strange phenomena as a classic example of the scientific plot called the Conspiracy of Silence. Scientists *know*, but they are keeping the information from the public for disreputable reasons of their own. My reasons are far from disreputable. I am not specifying the areas where free-living wallabies are to be found simply because I wish to protect them from intentional or unintentional harassment by thoughtless people. When their numbers build up they will become more widely known; but by then they will be in a stronger position to cope with human interference.

Perhaps scientists know more about the Sasquatch than they are telling, for similar reasons. Perhaps they are, but I doubt it profoundly. Scientists are very incompetent plotters.

Frank L. Beebe (to whom I am indebted for much of the foregoing ecological information relating to north-west America) and Don Abbott of the Provincial Museum, Victoria, B.C., have come up with a most ingenious 'model' for the Sasquatch's feeding habits. They base it on the life-style of the wolverine, a weasel-like mustelid of large proportions (3 ft. or more including tail). This extraordinarily interesting animal has a wide home-range of 200 miles or more, is largely carnivorous and rapacious with it (not for nothing is it known as the 'glutton'). Wolverines, broadly speaking, occupy the same habitat as the Sasquatch. A particularly relevant aspect of their behaviour is that wolverines cache their food in natural 'deep-freeze' lockers above the snow-line, winter and summer. They range upwards into the snowfields when food is scarce at lower altitudes, open their lockers and (presumably) carry the food down to altitudes where it gradually thaws. This model might explain how the Sasquatch survives through the winter, and why so-called Sasquatch footprints have been observed at high altitudes by skiers and snow-mobilers; equally, of course, the habits of the wolverine might account for the very existence of these amorphous tracks. Let me give full rein to imaginative speculation: could deep-freeze behaviour patterns also explain the apparently inexplicable occurrence of Yeti footprints high above the snowline in the Himalayas?

7. The Evidence of Fossils

Correlating monsters present with monsters past is a favourite exercise of their devotees. As a means of rationalizing an otherwise unlikely story, it has much to commend it. By postulating that a monster is a relict form—a hangover from the past—monster fans feel absolved from the necessity of explaining how such an outrageously unsuitable creature has evolved in the light of present-day ecology. Actually, of course, there is still the obligation, often ignored, of explaining how an archaic form has achieved the remarkable feat of surviving beyond its time.

In this chapter, the possibility that monsters today are relict forms surviving in isolated pockets in various parts of the modern world will be considered as a serious proposition. To begin with, we will examine the fossil record in pursuit of likely candidates who, were they living today, might be looked upon as monsters; and, second, we will try and assess the odds for and against such creatures surviving through the intervening millennia.

All eyewitness accounts indicate quite clearly that Bigfoot is more man-like than ape-like. The principal reason for this conclusion is the consensus view, deduced from footprints as well as actual sightings, that emphasizes two-footedness. In the light of our present understanding of primate evolution bipedalism—*habitual* bipedalism that is—is the prerogative of the family of man, the Hominidae.

While it is true to say that, universally, Bigfoot is more like an ape than a man, it will already have become apparent that certain monsters, the American Bigfoot for instance, are more human, less bestial, than their Himalayan counterparts. The American footprints are reminiscent of a gigantic human foot, whereas the Himalayan variety, occurring as they do in a bewildering variety of shapes and forms, are, on balance, decidedly less than human.

173

Eyewitness accounts point to the same conclusion. The general tenor of the descriptions from the Himalayas indicate that the Yeti is a man-like beast, while those from America suggest that the Sasquatch is a beast-like man. Thus of the four candidates for Bigfoot ancestry discussed below, the first two, *Gigantopithecus* and *Paranthropus*, appear to be natural antecedents for the Himalayan Bigfoot while the last two, *Homo erectus* and *Homo sapiens neanderthalensis*, are custom-built suspects for the American variety.[1]

The Hominidae include all species, both living and extinct, that have evolved since the moment in time when the human stock and the ape stock separated and went their different ways. The timing of this event is a matter of contention among anthropologists. The issue is not *if* (we are almost all agreed on that), but *when*. There are two schools of thought, which may be labelled the 'early' school and the 'late' school. The early school is in favour of the hypothesis that separation occurred 15–20 million years ago. The late school adheres to the idea that this critical event took place much more recently than that. There is even an 'early-early' school who place the dichotomy further back in time than do the 'early' school; they contend that man became separated from the apes during the Oligocene epoch 25–30 million years ago. The late school derives its inspiration from the fashionable scientific beliefs of the 'twenties and early 'thirties, which in turn owed their popularity to the well-reasoned arguments of Sir Arthur Keith in Britain and Dr William K. Gregory in the United States. In the early 'twenties Keith proposed that the close similarity of the physical adaptations of the gibbon—a brachiating, arm-swinging ape of exclusively arboreal habits—and of man, indicated that the latter had evolved from a highly specialized ape-like brachiating ancestor. Keith's 'brachiating theory' has fallen into disrepute in most quarters; indeed, Keith himself, towards the end of his long life, withdrew in principle his earlier beliefs. There are still pockets of resistance here and there, however.

The late school, whose opinions heretofore have been based entirely on anatomical and fossil evidence, have recently received

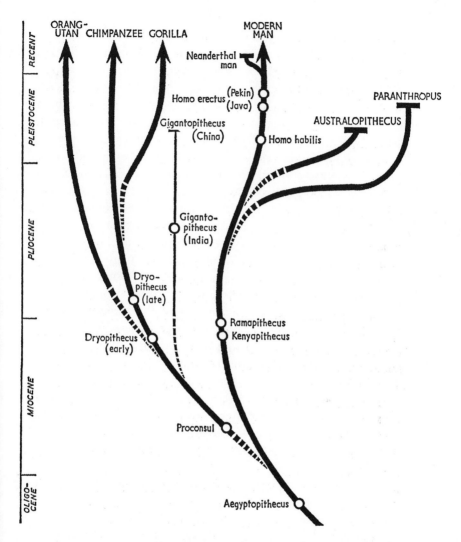

FIG. 5. Author's interpretation of the evolutionary relationship of man and the great apes. The time-scale spans about 30 million years, but the lengths of the epochs are not in proportion.

significant support from a most unexpected quarter—molecular chemistry. Studies of protein substances in the blood, albumin for example, show that the constituents of primate albumins differ from each other in the sequence of their amino-acids. Such differences in sequence are believed to have been brought about by mutations occurring at a constant rate in the basic chemical components of the genes. If this is so—and it has yet to be proved to everybody's satisfaction—the biochemical study of serum proteins provides a sort of evolutionary clock by which the length of time that two groups of primates have been separated can be estimated by a simple mathematical equation. The close similarity of human and chimpanzee albumins indicates that these two stocks have been separate for a relatively short period of time, less than five million years, in fact. What makes it particularly difficult for the scholars of the early and early-early schools to accept findings of the late school is that their results wholly contradict the evidence of the fossil record. At present the earliest generally recognized member of the human family, *Ramapithecus*, whose remains have been found in both India and Africa, dates back to a period between 12 million and 14 million years ago, nearly three times the age predicated by the molecular chemists.

The exact date of separation of ape and human families does not affect the present issue unduly except that the ensuing discussion will be based on the views of the early school, with which I align myself, and may conflict with views which the reader holds for himself.

The four possible candidates for immortality as progenitors of Bigfoot are as follows: *Gigantopithecus*, *Paranthropus*, Java Man (now called *Homo erectus*) and Neanderthal Man (*Homo sapiens neanderthalensis*). There may be others that for the lack of fossil evidence we know nothing about. Figure 5 indicates the relative positions of the candidates on the family tree of apes and man.

The discovery of *Gigantopithecus* is a romantic, often-told story that will bear repetition. In 1935, Professor von Koenigswald was sifting through the stock of 'dragon's-teeth' offered for sale

16. A statue of a Sasquatch. Carved in redwood by Jim McClarin, it is on permanent exhibit at the township of Willow Creek, California

17. Casts of a pair of human-type footprints of the Bossburg Sasquatch. Note that the footprint on the left suggests a severe club-foot deformity; the print on the right is apparently normal

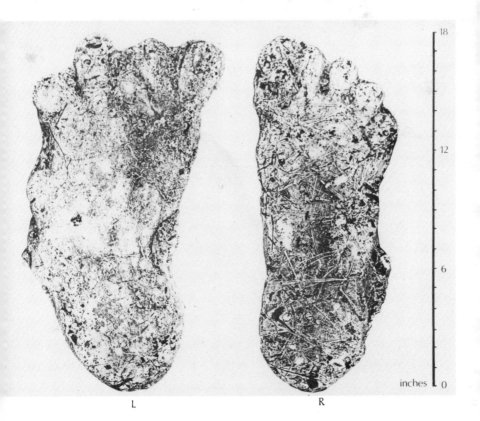

18

12

6

inches 0

L   R

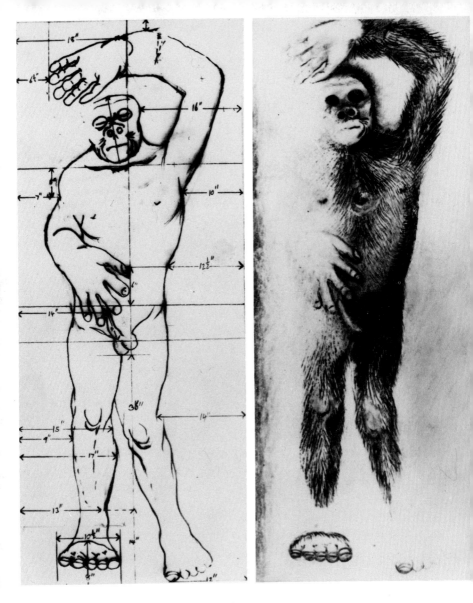

18. Scale drawings of the Iceman prepared by Ivan T. Sanderson

in a Chinese pharmacy in Hong Kong when he came across two teeth which he believed to be of giant ape.[2] As a result of this and subsequent searches in the late 1930s, von Koenigswald discovered three more giant-sized molar teeth. These proved to be so extraordinarily large, and seemed so typically ape-like to von Koenigswald that he described them in the scientific press and assigned them to a new genus—*Gigantopithecus*, the giant ape. This procedure may seem to have been somewhat risky, recalling perhaps the formal naming of the Iceman, but the circumstances are rather different. Von Koenigswald could hold the type specimen of *his* genus in his hand, he could examine it by several different techniques in order to verify its authenticity; furthermore, he could (and did) place the teeth in the Geological Institute, Utrecht, where for ever afterwards students will be able to confirm or deny his assertions. Nevertheless, the naming of *Gigantopithecus* was a bold stroke but one that in the light of subsequent events paid off handsomely. Further individual molar teeth, about fifty in all, and four mandibles (lower jaws) of this creature have now come to light in places as far apart as the Kwangsi province of southern China and the Siwalik Hills of northern India.

The jaws and teeth are peculiar; they are neither typically ape-like, nor typically man-like. The molars are huge and the cusps are worn down to a flat surface; the canines are only moderately large and thick and are also ground down to stubs. In the jaw discovered recently in the Siwalik Hills, the canines are so worn down that they barely project beyond the level of the other teeth.[3] The provenance of *Gigantopithecus* is not yet really understood. Clearly it is neither a typical ape nor a typical human but, rather, is something of an evolutionary by-blow. Its direct antecedents were probably an ancient, forest-living, anthropoid ape, perhaps similar to *Dryopithecus indicus*, a species known from the Siwalik Hills in northern India in the late Miocene times. As *Gigantopithecus bilaspurensis* and its possible predecessor *Dryopithecus indicus* have both been found in the region of the Siwalik Hills, part of the foothills of the Himalayas, it would be reasonable to expect that Bigfoot devotees would offer their fervent thanks to scientists for demonstrating that, slap-bang on the doorstep, there once lived a giant creature that was half-man and half-ape. What, they say, is more reasonable than that *Gigantopithecus* should have been an ancestor of the Abominable Snowman, the Bigfoot of the Himalayas? Some authorities such as Dr Bernard Heuvelmans are already convinced that the Yeti is a descendant of *Gigantopithecus*, a proposal which has achieved recognition even in the correspondence columns of *Nature*.[4] Quite apart from the fact there is no evidence whatsoever to link *Gigantopithecus* with the Yeti (even supposing the latter exists), there are a number of points that make such a relationship rather unlikely.

First of all there is the time element. The two jaws found in 1968 and 1970 in the Siwalik Hills area of northern India are dated, according to the faunal horizon in which they were found, at 4–8 million years (*Gigantopithecus*) and 12 million years old (*Dryopithecus indicus*). The Kwangsi jaws, as well as von Koenigs-wald's pharmacy teeth, are much younger than that, perhaps between half a million and a million years old. Clearly, then, *Gigantopithecus* was no flash-in-the-pan species, but part of an established and successful lineage that survived for 10 million years or so. Recent geological deposits bear no signs of this giant near-ape-man, so as far as palaeontologists are concerned, *Gigantopithecus* became extinct in the middle Pleistocene.

Second, the principal physical characteristic that makes *Gigantopithecus* an alluring ancestor for the Bigfoot is its inferred gigantism. Admittedly, the size of the molar teeth and jaws of *Gigantopithecus* suggest that the rest of the body would have been equally vast, and so it would have been if growth occurred proportionally throughout the body, which it does not. There is a well-established principle in biology called 'allometry', which states that when an animal's body-length is doubled, its volume is tripled. This can be expressed in another way: volume is proportional to the cube of the length. Thus large animals have disproportionately *larger* bones (and teeth) than one might expect from their stature. The gorilla has a much heavier jaw, much larger teeth than the tallest man; but in terms of stature, an average man stands higher than an average male gorilla. *Gigantopithecus* was probably a large, ground-living ape, but was certainly not a 9 foot giant.[5]

Third, *Gigantopithecus*, from the evidence of his teeth and jaws, was a vegetarian, not at all the sort of creature that one would expect to find wandering about the Himalayas at 15,000 feet in winter, far from an appropriate source of food supply.

However, there is another side to this question of diet. *Gigantopithecus* shows a number of characters that bear distinct functional similarities to the teeth of the gelada 'baboon'. The gelada is a baboon-like creature living in the High Semyen Mountains in central Ethiopia. Clifford Jolly, a British anthropologist now working at New York University, has named the dental functional complex shown by the gelada the 'T-complex' after the generic name of the creature, *Theropithecus*. Jolly surmises that the dental characters are secondary to a specialized form of diet which he calls 'graminivorous', the principal components being seeds, stems, roots and rhizomes. All these are hard, high-energy items which necessitate a lot of grinding and chewing, and hence require heavily built, deep-crowned, closely packed molar teeth. Geladas live at high altitudes up to 15,000 feet. Their habitat is moorland, where the grass is sparse and tussocky and the living conditions are rugged. Viewed in this light, the hypothesis that makes the Himalayan Bigfoot a relict *Gigantopithecus* becomes a little more plausible. The high yak-pastures of the Himalayas offer no less in the way of food-reward than the moorlands of the High Semyen. For instance, even at 18,000 feet, where Shipton and Ward photographed their famous footprint, there are regions of alpine moorland totally devoid of snow in the spring. Indeed Shipton's team camped in such an area after the footprint sighting. These regions are inhabited by pikas and other small mammalian species and are visited in season by bears, snow leopards and a variety of bovid species. Ecologically, the persistence of a 'graminivorous' ape-like form in such an area is not wholly ridiculous. It may be unlikely, but it is not impossible.

Fourth, and finally, there is no evidence that *Gigantopithecus* was bipedal. Its ape-like affiliations strongly suggest that it was not; rather we would suppose that it was a pseudo-quadruped, a knuckle-walker, like present-day chimpanzees. We have no fossil evidence to argue one way or another; once again, it is possible, but scientific understanding of the anatomical and ecological significance of bipedalism makes it rather improbable.

The footprints of the Yeti do not tell a consistent story because no two prints are exactly alike. Shipton's print, the clearest and the best ever recorded, as it stands is not the footprint of an ape (nor for that matter of a human). As we know nothing of the foot of *Gigantopithecus*, nor of the anatomy of the maker of Shipton's print, there is little profit in further speculation.

In the terms of the monster enthusiasts, *Gigantopithecus* is not really such a bad candidate as all that. It is possible that these creatures, thought by anthropologists to be long extinct, survived in refuge areas such as some of the deep forested river gorges of the Himalayan range until relatively recent times. The absence of a fossil record is not necessarily evidence of extinction. The memory of such creatures could well be enshrined in the folktales of ancient races. The myth of the Yeti could, in fact, be a legend, the hazy, unwritten record of an ancient relict race of man-like apes, which lingered on in isolated enclaves until a few thousand years ago. The question 'did such creatures exist', however, is a very different one from 'do such creatures exist'.

Paranthropus robustus (*Australopithecus robustus* according to some), to give the devil his full taxonomic due, is a very problematical creature and has certainly worried palaeontologists since 1949. This does not mean that its very existence is in doubt; in fact it is exceptionally well represented in the fossil record from both South African and East African fossil sites. The crucial issue is just how closely it was related to *Australopithecus africanus*, the near-men of South Africa, and *Homo habilis*, the threshold humans of Bed I, Olduvai Gorge, Tanzania.

Many authorities would identify *Paranthropus* zoologically as *Australopithecus robustus*, indicating his close relationship to the true pre-human stock. There are a few of us, headed by no less an authority than Professor J. T. Robinson, the successor to Robert Broom and the discoverer of many fossils of both *Australopithecus* and *Paranthropus*, who hold that *Paranthropus* belongs to a distinct and separate genus and is therefore only remotely related to man (figure 5). *Paranthropus* never had much chance of becoming a man; there was always too much competition from more advanced species of humans living contemporaneously. *Paranthropus* had no more chance than the gorilla or chimpanzee has today of climbing to the top of the hominid ladder. I suppose one might say therefore that *Paranthropus* was a failed human, but this would pre-suppose that it was in the running in the first place. One might sigh deeply and refer to its species as an unsuccessful one, but *Homo sapiens* has still got three million or so years to go before he can afford to assume a patronizing attitude over the non-success of *Paranthropus*, whose career spanned at least three and a half million years.

Until a few years ago, *Paranthropus* was known only from two middle Pleistocene sites in South Africa, but now remains of this creature have been discovered at Olduvai Gorge in Tanzania from a much earlier geological period, at Lake Natron also in Tanzania, at Omo in Ethiopia, at Koobi Fora to the east of Lake Rudolf, and at several sites in north-west Kenya. His remains indicate that he was living over a wide area of South and East Africa for a period of at least 3–5 million years.

Paranthropus, like *Australopithecus* the 'southern apes' of the Transvaal with whom it was contemporaneous, was a bipedalist, but not apparently a very good one. His gait was believed to be inefficient and clumsy, and under conditions of stress it may even have deteriorated into a form of four-footed walking. In other words, *Paranthropus*, in respect of his bipedalism, may have been only a little more advanced than a bear.

The teeth and the size of the jaws of this by-product of human evolution argue strongly for a vegetarian way of life, somewhat similar to that of the living gorilla. *Australopithecus*, his contemporary at Omo in Ethiopia, Olduvai Gorge in Tanzania and in South Africa, was – at least in part – a carnivore. The way of life attributed to *Australopithecus* and to his early descendants is very broadly equivalent to that of a modern hunter-gatherer society. This socio-economic system is to be seen today in some of the few remaining primitive tribes of human being such as the Hadzas, the Kalahari Bushmen, the natives of central New Guinea and the few remaining free-living Australian aborigines. Under this system, the men are the hunters of the steak and the women are the gatherers of the french fries. In hunter-gatherer societies it has been estimated that meat constitutes only about 25 per cent of the total intake, so probably women contribute more to the daily menu than do the men in terms of staple foods. Theoretically the differences in diet between *Paranthropus* and *Australopithecus* (a genus which, as we see it, later evolved into true man) would have permitted them to have lived cheek by jowl, just as carnivores and herbivores do today in the grasslands of Africa. This does not mean that there was no friction between the two groups: carnivores prey on herbivores, but they are not in competition with each other in the strict meaning of the word. *Australopithecus* (or early *Homo*) was not a meat-eater like a lion or a leopard; nevertheless I feel sure Australopithecines would not have been averse to a *Paranthropus* chump-chop if it happened to be available. In spite of a predator-prey relationship, I see no reason why they should not have survived side-by-side to their mutual advantage as lions and wildebeeste do in East Africa today.

Paranthropus may also have been living in the Far East, although there is no certain evidence for this in the fossil record. However, it could be argued that *Paranthropus* is found in association with developing man elsewhere in the world, so why not in Asia?

Even if we accept the remote possibility that *Paranthropus* existed in Asia 500,000 years ago, there does not seem to be any particular reason for proposing a link between this long extinct form and the Himalayan Bigfoot. But we are committed to investigating all *possible* candidates for an ancestral role in the Bigfoot family tree, and *Paranthropus* must be considered a likely lad. *Paranthropus*, like *Gigantopithecus*, was a vegetarian and had a quasi-upright gait and he was unquestionably more man-like than *Gigantopithecus*.

The third of our candidates is so-called Java Man and his lineal successor, Pekin Man. Unequivocally both of these creatures are *men* and are classified as *Homo erectus* within the genus *Homo*. Pekin Man, the more advanced species, was a hunter and a tool-maker; he had discovered the functions of fire—a means of keeping warm, a means of providing light, a means of cooking food and a means of defending himself against predators. With fire at his command, Pekin Man was able to make good use of cave shelters, as the famous site at Choukoutien near Pekin clearly attests. The discovery of fire also permitted man to spread his growing sphere of influence outside the tropics. Choukoutien lies on the 40° N parallel; the present climate offers cold, dry winters and hot, wet summers, but in mid-Pleistocene times, when Pekin Man was a resident of the limestone caves of Choukoutien, the climate was considerably cooler. The vegetation, as determined from studies of fossil seeds, seems to have been almost boreal in nature, consisting of conifers and hardy deciduous trees and shrubs, not unlike the present vegetation of the forests of British Columbia where the Sasquatch now reigns.

The evidence of Pekin Man's cultural life indicates that he knew about fire, was a hunter of large animals and was a toolmaker. His brain, which was quite respectably large by modern standards, supports the contention that Pekin Man—or *Homo erectus* as he should more properly be called—was probably quite an advanced human being, with some power of speech. His limb-bones, as we know them from the fossil record, do not indicate any great differences from modern man in posture or style of walking.

For Pekin Man to stand in an ancestral relationship to either the Himalayan or American Bigfoot, he would have had to have deteriorated rather considerably. I find it impossible to believe that a human being who had discovered fire, who could work stone into serviceable tools and who could hunt large game could conceivably end up naked and culture-less, prowling the high yak-pastures of the Himalayas or the boreal backwoods of north-west America.

Our last candidate is the much maligned offshoot of human evolution, Neanderthal Man. Never have any members of the human species suffered such a barrage of undeserved insults as poor *Homo sapiens neanderthalensis*. When this new fossil man was discovered in the Neander Valley in Germany in 1856, Darwin's *The Origin of Species* was yet to be published. As John Pfeiffer expressed it, 'Neanderthal Man came into the world of the Victorians like a naked savage into a ladies' sewing circle.'⁶ In the public eye Neanderthal Man was a monstrous intrusion, half-man half-ape, and a shameful blotch on the fair name of mankind.

After 1859, the scientists were deeply divided on the issue of Darwinism. For the fundamentalists among them, Neanderthal Man was a horrible embarrassment. Many curious suggestions were proposed to 'explain' the discovery without loss of orthodoxy. One of the most imaginative was that the Neanderthal skull was that of a soldier of Napoleon's army, suffering from water on the brain, who met his death by the wayside on the retreat from Moscow. A popular device of the time to keep embarrassing by-blows from sullying the human lineage was to label them as imbeciles. One such account, quoted by John Pfeiffer, of the Man of the Neander Valley was as follows: 'It may well have been one of those wild-men, half-crazed, half-idiotic, cruel and strong, who are always more or less to be found living on the outskirts of barbarous tribes, and who now and then appear in civilized communities to be consigned perhaps to the penitentiary or the gallows' (p. 60).

The denigration of Neanderthal Man following the discoveries of other skeletons at La-Chapelle-aux-Saints in 1908 and La Ferrassie in 1909, both in the Dordogne, extended well into the twentieth century. To sum up the consensus view of the time, Neanderthalers were nasty, brutish and short, and, what's more, they were bent over in a ludicrous posture half-way between a four-footed and a two-footed stance. It took about a hundred years from the date of the initial discovery for the process of upgrading Neanderthalers to start. Two anatomists, one British and one American, pointed out that the 'old man' of La-Chapelle-aux-Saints was victim of severe arthritis, and if he was bent double he deserved our sympathy rather than our scorn.[7] Since then we seem to have reverted to obloquy. Recent reports suggest that Neanderthalers were (1) rachitic dwarfs and (2) congenital syphilitics. Perhaps the grossest insult of all has been to imply that *Homo sapiens neanderthalensis* is the natural forebear of the Minnesota Iceman (see chapter 4).

If the truth were known, Neanderthal Man — as many authorities have stated — would pass for human if dressed in contemporary clothes and placed in a contemporary situation. The human race is infinitely variable and one may see good Neanderthalers all over the place — in tubes and subways, in supermarkets, on the terraces and in the bleachers of stadiums around the world, but not, I think, stomping the snowfields of the high Himalayas or the dirt roads of California.

As a candidate for Bigfoot ancestry, Neanderthal Man is a very long shot. By the standards of *Gigantopithecus, Paranthropus* and even *Homo erectus*, Neanderthalers are sophisticated humans who had an advanced stone-tool technology, were capable hunters and fire-users. Moreover, they appear to have advanced sufficiently in the ability to conceptualize their thoughts to have conceived of an after-life. They buried their dead with enough personal belongings to give the departed a good start in the next world. Neanderthalers might conceivably be the progenitors of the Almas of Central Asia, but they are certainly not acceptable to me as ancestors for the ape-like Yeti of the Himalayas or the wild men of North America. However, Neanderthal Man has so often been mentioned in the context of Bigfoot that its claims merit a little further examination.

Most anthropologists recognize that there are two grades of Neanderthal Man, the 'classic' and the 'early'. Few would quibble about the status of classic Neanderthalers, the populations living a snow-beleaguered existence in Europe during the last glacial period. The classic Neanderthalers were a very specialized race of European 'eskimos', with short, sturdy bodies adapted to conserve heat, large knobbly joints, massive jaws that could chew tough or partly cooked meat, and a tool-kit in which 'survival' tools such as cutters, scrapers and skinners predominated; in those days there was no time for delicacy or for the pursuit of liberal arts. Little in the way of costume jewellery, no ritual figurines, or the decorative cave murals typical of the later Cro-Magnon people and their descendants, have been discovered in the caves and rock shelters of the Neanderthalers. It would seem Neanderthal Man had not time to spare for frivolities; he was up to the eyes with the day-to-day problems of survival. Perhaps Neanderthalers were barbarians, but who could afford to be anything else within a few hundred miles of the polar ice-sheets? The classic Neanderthalers, it is generally agreed, were too specialized a race to have evolved into the post-glacial populations of modern man *Homo sapiens sapiens*. There is no evidence for a gradual transition from Neanderthal to Cro-Magnon; in fact, as we shall see below, archaeologists have been able to demonstrate from a study of living-floors that the break between the two cultures was abrupt.

The early human populations of the last interglacial period were a pretty variable bunch, but probably no more so than we are today. A spectrum of geographic types existed, ranging from the Neanderthal-like Rhodesian Man through intermediate populations like those of Ehringsdorf and Krapina to less Neanderthal-like populations like those of Fontéchevade and Kanjera. In the area of Mount Carmel in Israel, two caves, adjacent geographically though disparate in chronological terms, give expression to this diversity; a neanderthaloid-type is present at Tabūn and a more advanced sapiens-type at Skūhl. It is not yet agreed from where-abouts in the spectrum modern human populations evolved.

Another major issue concerns the fate of the Neanderthal race. What happened to the 'classic' Neanderthalers when the ice-sheets finally withdrew? It is certainly true that they disappeared completely from the fossil record, but did they disappear from the face of the earth? One view holds that they did, being exterminated by the Cro-Magnon people, the ultimate inheritors. The 'catastrophic' view receives strong support from the evidence of certain cave sites in France where the Mousterian tool-culture of the Neanderthalers was abruptly replaced by tools of a more advanced technology, typical of the Cro-Magnon people. Both Neanderthalers and their tools disappeared with remarkable suddenness. A more moderate view suggests that they were absorbed into the Cro-Magnon race by a process of cross-breeding or hybridization, in which case the genes of the Neanderthal race would not have been lost, but would still be part of the genetic bank account upon which mankind draws to this day. If this moderate view is the correct one, as I believe it is, all of us are carrying a few Neanderthal genes in our current account and it is no wonder a few cave-man types turn up from time to time in our society. Many Neanderthal characters are found in living human populations. The Eskimos of East Greenland, for instance, show a high frequency of 'taurodontism' — an enlargement of the pulp cavity of the molar teeth — characteristic of the Neanderthalers. It is not impossible that pockets of Neanderthalers living in geographically remote regions of Eastern Europe, Siberia and Mongolia could have avoided the consequences of either physical extermination or racial absorption and still be surviving as relict populations in these regions today.

The mountains of central Eurasia from the Carpathians and the Caucasus to the Altai and the Tien-Shans in the north and the Himalayas in the south, by virtue of their remoteness and rugged inhospitality, have always been off the beaten track and closed to immigrants. Even today these areas are inhabited by culturally backward peoples, by-passed by the tide of human affairs. Neanderthalers are known from several sites, one in the Zagros Mountains of Iran (Shanidar); two in the Crimea, Kiik-Koba and Staroselj'e, and one in Uzbekistan at Teshik-Tash in the Pamirs, seventy-eight miles south of Samarkand. The Teshik-Tash child was questionably 'classic', and may have been a representative of the 'early' group. Nevertheless, its remains may flag the geographical location of a population living today in these remote mountain areas, where they are being regarded by their sophisticated human cousins as simply 'wild men'. Yet, somehow, it is difficult to conceive that a relatively advanced people like the Neanderthalers should have reverted to the very lowly status that all the reports of Almas seem to imply. If the possession of human characteristics, particularly a large brain, means anything at all, then for all their primitiveness these people should pass as human. Of course, it can be said that in many ways they appear to do so. Witness, for instance, as recounted in chapter 2, the Almas female discovered breast-feeding a human infant, the group of Almas found warming themselves at an abandoned camp fire, and the reputed hybridization between a human male and an Almas female. On the other hand, the physical descriptions (see below) of an Almas male and female are not particularly reminiscent of what we can glean of the Neanderthalers from the fossil evidence.

Bernard Heuvelmans quotes the Russian zoologist and explorer V. A. Khaklov, whose journeys in search of 'wild men' in the desert and mountainous regions of Dzungaria led him to summarize the principal traits of the Almas from the evidence of witnesses in the following terms: 'They are of medium height, with hair all over the body, absence of a forehead but prominent brow-ridges and heavy lower jaw and no chin, long arms and short legs, feet broad with big toe shorter than other toes but massive and broad and projecting inwards, other toes fanned out.' When this description is compared with that of Neanderthal Man we find a certain amount of correspondence but also a number of major differences. Khaklov states that Almas were of 'medium' height, which accords well with the 5 ft. 5 in.–5 ft. 6 in. estimated for Neanderthal males. The Almas forehead is rather receding, its brow-ridges were prominent and the jaw heavy. Again, these are features that are in accord with the skull of 'classic' Neanderthal Man. The bodily proportions of Almas, however, are not like Neanderthalers who did not have the long arms and short legs of Khaklov's description but virtually the same relative proportions as in modern man. Almas, according to one of

Khaklov's Kazakh witnesses, have narrow chests (a surprising feature to find associated with long arms), while Neanderthalers were exceptionally 'barrel-chested'. Almas are not reported to be muscular; in fact the eyewitness evidence credits them with a rather slender build. Neanderthalers, as Professor Carleton Coon observes,[8] were built like the squat and powerful men of the Italian and Austrian Alps.

Khaklov's description of the feet of the Almas has certain points of correspondence with those of Neanderthal Man's. The foot of both is rather broad, the big toe is stout and the other toes are splayed. All these characteristics can be seen in living populations that are neither Almas nor Neanderthalers; the Alakaluf Indians of the Southern Archipelago of Chile have exceptionally broad feet, as Coon points out. Khaklov also observes that the big toe was shorter than a man's, set apart and projecting inwards. A short big toe occurs in some Neanderthal skeletons (from Kiik-Koba, for instance) and is not at all rare in modern populations. This particular conformation of the foot is referred to as the Greek Ideal and can be seen in the majority of Greco-Roman statues. 'The inwards projection' of the big toe of Khaklov's description is not precise enough to comment upon; it might imply an anthropoid-like condition, but on the other hand it might simply describe an exceptionally mobile and divergent big toe.

Curiously enough, the footprints of Neanderthal Man are known. The imprints of human feet were found impressed in clay in a sealed section of a cave near Toirano in Italy in 1950. The prints are not at all exceptional by modern standards (plate 12). The feet are broad, but not exceptionally so; the big toe is massive, but not unduly; and in both footprints the big toe is longer than the little toes. The Toirano prints do not show that the toes were fanned, but this may well have been the effect of the wet-clay texture of the substrate at the time that the prints were made; in wet mud the toes tend to curl downwards and become squeezed together in an attempt to counteract slipping and sliding. Another footprint (the oldest human print known) was found in 1967 at Vertesszöllös near Budapest on a living-floor, or hearth, in association with primitive tools and weapons and the bones of animals killed and eaten by hunters. This print dates back to a very much earlier period than the Toirano Cave prints. Vertesszöllös Man, living some three to four hundred thousand years ago, seems to have been a descendant of Pekin Man (*Homo erectus pekinensis*) and a possible forerunner for the later, more sapient, populations of Europe.

The general conclusion seems to be that with a bit of give and take and a measure of allowance for the errors of eyewitness descriptions, the Almas cannot be excluded as relict members of the Neanderthal populations of the last glacial period. But it must be emphasized that, to date, there is really not one shred of hard evidence pointing to the present existence of such creatures.

Neanderthal Man has clearly no place in the lineage of the ape-like Himalayan Bigfoot; but could he be ancestral to the North American variety of Bigfoot, the Sasquatch? It is not theoretically impossible that some of the eastern Neanderthalers migrated even further to the east during or after the last Ice Age. Except in the immediate neighbourhood of the high mountain blocks, the southern two-thirds of eastern Eurasia was relatively free of the encroachment of glaciers. There is no ecological reason why Neanderthalers, well adapted to cold conditions, should not have blazed the trail into the New World.

The time and manner of man's first invasion of the Americas is unknown. Generally the date is thought not to be earlier than 15,000–20,000 years ago. The port of entry would almost certainly have been Alaska via the Asian-Alaskan land bridge, which at this time was a low-lying plain many hundreds of miles wide, and rich with game. Man at this time was an accomplished hunter and would have entered the New World on the heels of the migrating herds. Recently it has been suggested by the world-famous Kenyan anthropologist Louis Leakey that humans were occupying North America between 60,000 and 80,000 years ago at the time when the Neanderthalers were living in Western Europe and points east. According to Leakey, the evidence for this assertion has been discovered at the foot of the Calico Hills, near Yermo in south California, where a large collection of very crude stone 'tools' have been excavated from an old alluvial fan. The issue is whether these 'tools' are man-made or are natural phenomena. Most geologists and anthropologists in America do not find the evidence for human technology very convincing. Even if this material could be shown, unequivocally, to be man-made, there is no evidence as to the identity of the toolmaker. In the spirit of the Goblin Universe might one suppose that these very early North Americans were Neanderthalers?

While zoogeographically there may be no particular problem in erecting Neanderthal Man as the lineal ancestor of the Sasquatch, the theory is insupportable from every other point of view. The Sasquatch, according to all observers, is not a human being. It may leave hominoid footprints, but it neither looks nor behaves like a man, except in a most superficial way. Unless something very extraordinary took place in the evolution of Neanderthalers, any connection between the relatively sophisticated people of the Mousterian cultural period and the lumbering hair-clad giants of the Cascade Mountains is highly improbable.

The problem of Neanderthal Man in North America was discussed by Dale Stewart of the Smithsonian Institution, Washington, D.C.[9] A number of skulls found in different parts of the country, including Iowa, have at various times been attributed to this lineage. Stewart categorically rejects neanderthaloid affiliations and points out that the lowness of the brows, the principal criterion for such an affiliation, is characteristic of many modern Indian tribes such as the Sioux and the Arikara, who are of course good *Homo sapiens* types.

Perhaps the Calico Hills people, should they be shown to exist, were derived from an earlier stock than that of the relatively sophisticated Neanderthalers. But could they, on the other hand, be descended from some relict groups of middle Pleistocene near-human species like *Gigantopithecus blacki*, which were primitives in their own time? Could they have found their way into the New World from Asia? As we have no evidence to suppose that the Asian species of *Gigantopithecus* had any culture, we would have to assume the Calico Hills artefacts were the products of a progressive North American branch that had acquired a crude stone culture independently of the mainstream of human evolution. Attractive, and even to some reasonable, as this hypothesis may sound, it is based on the most florid of speculative reasoning.

Finally, what about the Iceman? I do not intend – even in terms of the Goblin Universe – to take its antecedents very seriously. My conviction is that the Iceman is a model made of synthetic materials, in which case its ancestors are more likely to have consisted of carbon rings than purine bases. If there is any physical similarity between Neanderthal Man and Minnesota Man, then all credit must go to the Frankensteins of Hollywood who, in my view, created the monster; the diligence of their anthropological research is beyond reproach.

Of all the candidates for Bigfoot ancestry, the claims of *Gigantopithecus* and *Paranthropus* are by far the strongest. *Homo erectus* and Neanderthal Man are altogether too advanced towards the *sapiens* grade to merit serious consideration as antecedents, although the latter may well be the source of the legends of the Asian Almas. If we are to designate possible ancestors for problematical creatures, then the procedure must be internally consistent. From what we know of these two forms, either would do. *Gigantopithecus* is generally regarded as an aberrant ape, while *Paranthropus* is conceded to be, by some authorities at least, an aberrant human. It would be a neat solution to allocate the ape-like *Gigantopithecus* to the Himalayas and the more human-like *Paranthropus* to North America, but it would be a shockingly unscientific thing to do.

8. *Conclusions*

Man has an insatiable appetite for ghouls and bogles, and large sections of the entertainment business make it their concern to see that his tastes are well catered for. Horror-films, horror-comics, horror-exhibits are big business; ghost stories and stories of the supernatural are perennial best sellers, and magazines that specialize in inexplicable phenomena are sell-outs on the news-stands. Even the most staid of national newspapers such as *The Times* is right up there with the worst of them when a monster story breaks. This determination of mankind to frighten itself to death can perhaps be regarded as an endearing trait, an expression of a touching, child-like naiveté in the face of the Monstrous Forces of the Unknown. On the other hand, perhaps it is just a cult that owes nothing to nature, religion, philosophy or the mainstream of folklore, but is simply another form of self-indulgence.

Anthropologists, who see folktales as dynamic themes ebbing and flowing with time, would probably not agree that present-day monster worship is simply a cult. In their eyes, customs and superstitions are amoeba-like entities, constantly changing shape as they adapt to the contemporary scene. Flying saucers may be a modern phenomenon, but they come from the same stable as Pegasus, the flying horse of Mount Helicon. I see the contemporary monster cult in much the same light. For me it provides a perfect example of the primeval urge to regard with awe forces that are outside the normal range of human experience. Man possesses a potential for idolatry. The sun, the moon and the stars are favourite targets; so are the trees and the mountains; and so are superhuman figures that are as tall as trees and as massive as mountains. Man admires bigness for its own sake, and if physical bigness is linked with psychological bigness, whether of natural or supernatural origin, then the combination cannot fail. The

Himalayas and the western coastal ranges of North America are worthy of respect in their own right, but give them a Bigfoot roaming their slopes and they become modern Valhallas, the awe-inspiring homes of the latter-day gods.

As I suggested in chapter 1, a belief in myth and legend must have a survival advantage for mankind, as otherwise it would not have gained such a strong hold on the human mind. Of course, like many cultural characteristics, a belief in monsters could simply be acquired, a matter of learned behaviour unconnected with genetic inheritance—something, as it used to be said, that a child learned at its mother's knee. However, studies in animal behaviour in recent years suggest that few aspects of human culture are wholly learned or wholly inherited. For instance, in song-birds the capacity to sing is inherited, but the species-song has often to be learned. I would suggest that monster worship has both a learned and an inherited component: the potential is inborn, but the object of the worship has to be discovered by learning. If any of this is true, then it is necessary to demonstrate the advantage that monster worship bestows on the human race. Let us try a few ideas and see how they stand up. First, the Bugbear Hypothesis.

The traditional bugbear was a sort of evil spirit that took the form of a bear. It was supposed to devour naughty children, thus providing parents and nannies with a potent weapon with which to control their charges. Bugbears were the ultimate deterrent of the nursery. Sherpa Tensing Norgay told an interviewer in 1955 that as a child he was hushed to silence at the mention of the Yeti. Michel Peissel recounts how the head lama of the Monastery at Thyangboche told him that the Yeti was a sort of bogeyman invoked to frighten naughty children. The Bugbear Hypothesis provides one possible rationale for the ubiquity of the Bigfoot tale.

In this book we are taking a very narrow view of a phenomenon which is universal in time and space. In terms of all their manifestations, hominoid monsters appear to possess some of man's worst characteristics, and in this sense they could be looked upon as scapegoats, the traditional means by which man exorcizes the burden of his own frailties. The scapegoat of the Bible (Lev. xvi, 7–10) was one of a pair of goats that was driven into the wilderness bearing into oblivion the sins of the people. Hominoid monsters are convenient repositories for all that is savage, ignoble and libidinous in man. But the Scapegoat Hypothesis appears to have only minor relevance to Bigfoot. It seems to me that despite its size, it is altogether too decent a type to be a dustbin for human frailties; but perhaps I am biased.

Finally, there is the Grooming Hypothesis. On the face of it, Western societies do not need bugbears, scapegoats or idols any more than they need their little toes, their appendixes or the lobes of their ears; but they do need comforting — today more than ever. Grooming or mutual fur-cleaning is a pattern of behaviour that plays a very important role in the lives of higher primates. More important than its hygienic function is the personal contact that it facilitates. Western man does not *need* to have his fur attended to regularly (except for his head fur), but the cultural importance of grooming as a social adhesive has not been lost. Grooming is expressed in the dozens of intimate actions between human individuals such as touching, stroking, brushing, which involve close contact and promote a sense of physical togetherness — of belonging. The conventions of social intercourse, the formalized exchanges with a new acquaintance, for instance, are the social skirmishes that determine whether or not a grooming relationship should be entered into. Once established, grooming in humans takes many physical forms, depending largely on regional cultural influences. Arab men hold hands, Frenchmen bestow the ceremonial kiss, Britons and Americans go in for the grip on the upper arm or the punch to the shoulder to communicate their sense of one-ness. But above all, grooming expresses itself verbally. There is comfort to be gained in the local coffee shop or pub from experiences shared, common enemies to hate, universal fears to be exorcized and mysteries to be solved. In Britain the effectiveness of verbal grooming was never better exemplified than in the early years of the Second World War, when what was called the Dunkirk spirit prevailed throughout the land. Might one suppose that it played a major part in Britain's ultimate survival?

Fundamentally, I do not think that there is much difference between the functions of Bigfoot tales in Asia and North America, in spite of the obvious differences in the standard of living, education and culture of these regions. To the Sherpas of Nepal, the Lepchas, the Tibetans, the Bhutanese and the Sikkimese, the Yeti is today important to their way of life. A belief in the Yeti helps, perhaps, to unify the community in the spirit of the Grooming Hypothesis, but I have no doubt that the Bugbear, and even the Scapegoat, also contribute in a measure to the perpetuation of the tale.

One curious aspect of the Bigfoot tales that has not yet been mentioned but may be significant, is the almost total absence of sexuality. Sexuality plays a major role in myths and legends but it is an inconspicuous element in folktales. The strange story of Helen Westring, who claimed to have been raped by an Abominable Snowman [sic] in the woods of Minnesota (see chapter 4) can almost certainly be disregarded, if only for its sexual content. To my knowledge only once amongst the hundreds of eyewitness accounts of the Himalayan or American Bigfoot on record have the sexual organs of the male been remarked upon. This was in the course of a taped interview between Rene Dahinden and Albert Ostman. Ostman recalls that the penis of the old male was very small and discrete and hardly discernible. The breasts of the female Sasquatch have been noted on several occasions, but the primary female sex organs remain properly shrouded in mystery. Bigfoot seems to be neither a rapist nor an abductor of women. Its 'raw lust' ratio is low; its image, on the other hand, is really rather benevolent, recalling the cuddly bear rather than the sexually agressive ape. (Ironically, of course, it is the lovable bear that is aggressive – though not sexually so, to humans at any rate – while the rapacious ape is the gentle giant.) The one thing that bears and apes do have in common is the discreteness of their genitalia. Only in truly upright man have the sex organs swivelled round to the front of the body.

This has led to a lot of interesting cultural consequences. The invisible genitalia of Bigfoot and its lack of overt sexuality does not prove anything, but at least it suggests that the function of the myth is social rather than sexual.

The time has come to try and draw together the threads of a rambling discussion that has been going on for long enough. Is Bigfoot an *idea* or an *animal*? This is the only real question. If it is an idea, then the ball is firmly in the court of the folklorist; if it is an animal, then the zoologists have something to explain.

This is not a classic detective story. There can be no neat resolution, no country-house dénouement when the detective-inspector takes up his position in front of the fireplace, face to face with the principal characters, and resolves the mystery with a few well-chosen phrases: ' … so, when one realized that his wife was a nymphomaniac, it became perfectly clear why Sir Henry said that he had taken the Rolls that night, the night when the dog was found dead with its throat cut from ear to ear … '

With Bigfoot there can be no unmasking, no Q.E.D. There can only be value judgments based on such evidence, direct or indirect, as is available.

The question of whether Bigfoot is a living animal or a cultural cliché can only be assessed on the basis of evidence. If we confine ourselves rigidly to what most scientists would regard as hard evidence, then the answer is heard loud and clear: *Bigfoot does not exist.* There is no scrap of hard evidence that such creatures are roaming the snows of the Himalayas or the woods of the coastal ranges of the American north-west today (whether such creatures were to be found yesterday is quite another question). There are no skulls, no postcranial bones, no captive animals, no photographs or ciné films of unquestionable probity. What possible justification is there for intelligent people to countenance such a wraith?

But nevertheless there is a certain amount of soft evidence: there are eyewitness accounts, there are footprints galore and there are a few supplementary items such as scalps, hairs, mummified hands and droppings, although none of them, as far as I know, have been underwritten by any scientist or scientific institution that has investigated them; all have turned out to be either unidentifiable, or clearly attributable to some well-known animal. Even if footprints and travellers' tales cannot prove the existence of Bigfoot they indicate the presence of something that needs explaining. First, let us consider eyewitness accounts.

Eyewitness accounts offer considerable problems of interpretation. Individually, they can probably be ignored; who knows under what conditions of exhaustion, mental stress, alcoholism or drug addiction, etc., the sighting was made? Was the eyewitness motivated by a spirit of scientific advancement, an urge for a spiritual experience or was he simply concerned with publicity and self-aggrandizement? Was he hallucinated, fooled or simply lying in his teeth? There is no certain way of telling what factors were influencing his judgment.

Man is a complex creature whose inventiveness is unlimited and the depths of whose motivations are unplumable. While paying lip-service to moral principles like telling the truth, for instance, man is also a master of expediency who can rationalize the most blatant of falsehoods by beatifying them as 'white lies'. Many of the eyewitness accounts of the Yeti and the Sasquatch have an air of impressive sincerity, but without careful checking for possible motivations they cannot be accepted as primary data. Serious investigators of U.F.O.s have reached the same conclusion; the reports of solid citizens can be as false as the ramblings of the town drunk.

Consensus opinions, on the other hand, stand on slightly firmer ground. I would stress that by 'consensus opinions' I do not mean 'group opinions'. To be of any value, consensus opinions must be the result of random sampling. Group opinions such as those eagerly voiced by a convivial gathering of Sherpas or by a group of lumberjacks drinking beer in a bar owe little to chance.

The consensus opinions of North Americans are rather impressive, because the same or very similar characteristics crop up time and time again in, apparently, wholly independent observers. It is important to bear in mind that the sightings of Sasquatches have had a great deal of publicity in newspapers, magazines and on television, so it is impossible to be certain that an eyewitness account is truly first hand. Nevertheless there are a number of eyewitnesses who aver that they have never read a published account nor talked to anyone who claims to have seen a Sasquatch. Often, of course, there is such wide disparity in detail that no consensus is possible. In the case of the Surrey puma, which enthralled all England in 1964, the mysterious creature was described variously as 'a small cheetah, a monkey, or an alsatian dog'.[1] I have tried to discount eyewitness reports as primary data, although as reinforcing data they have considerable value, but the case has first to be proved on the basis of harder evidence. I say 'tried' because I know it is impossible to be totally objective. Footprints are another matter.

In the last column of table 1 I have indicated my own interpretation of the provenance of the so-called Yeti footprints. Six of these implicate the bear, and several others, particularly Izzard's, Russell's, Smyth's and Lees's, could well be bear on the basis of altitude and foot proportions. The bear is a popular suspect, and at least three mountaineering observers have concluded that a bear was responsible for the footprints they saw. Dyrenfurth[2] in an authoritative review of Yeti sightings and footprints places the bears as his second choice, his first being the langur. The renowned American comparative anatomist W. L. Straus Jr of Johns Hopkins University comes out strongly on the side of the Bear Theory.[3] The late Professor F. Wood Jones also leaned towards this view. Of course there are plenty of anti-bear people, including, for some reason, most of the professional writer-naturalists. Perhaps they think such a simple explanation is altogether too dull and facile.

The Himalayan langur must also figure as an important suspect. The somewhat dubious report by Thorberg and Frostis (see chapter 2) places their maximum altitudinal range at 19,000 feet, and Don Whillans's recent sighting, which *might* have been a langur, was between 13,000 and 15,000 feet. The langur, a monkey of the forested foothills, possesses a moderately long, though narrow, foot. Clearly, these creatures, which normally descend to lower, warmer altitudes during the winter, cannot be held responsible for all of the footprints. If the langur is involved in reinforcing the Yeti myth, then its role is entirely subsidiary.[4]

The pilgrim, sadhu, ascetic, lama or holy man have earned the right to be included in this list of suspects if only on account of their dedicated plodding through Yeti country. In terms of the breakdown of Himalayan footprint characteristics given above, humans don't come out too badly except in respect of overall proportions. A step of $1\frac{1}{2}$ ft.–2 ft. would be perfectly acceptable for a man walking in snow, and a foot length of 10 in.–12 in. is within the normal human range; but a foot width of 6 in. is excessive for man (see table 3, p. 213). Once again the question of melting or sublimation, discussed in chapter 5, must be taken into account. Pranavanandra claims that he has evidence that a holy man had crossed the Khandosanglam Pass into Tibet some three weeks before he discovered his footprints. Time enough it would seem for, let us say, 10 in. prints to have swelled into 21 in. depressions. Tombazi thought that the 6 in.–7 in. prints he saw on the Zemu Glacier might possibly be a pilgrim's, but pilgrims don't come all that small; footprints may swell in the sun but they don't shrink in the cold. Pater Franz Eichinger was definitely a pilgrim-man, and so up to a point was Dyrenfurth. Against the pilgrim theory is the rather important point that no unequivocally human footprint has ever been demonstrated in the snows of the Himalayas.

The other possible suspects are snow leopards, foxes, wolves, ungulates of various breeds and even Alpine choughs. It may well be that *some* of these animals have been responsible for *some* of the footprints, but they cannot be regarded as major contributors to the Yeti story.

One possible explanation is that the Yeti is not a real animal existing today but rather a legendary creature—a chimera, part-ape, part-langur, part-bear and part-human. But even legendary creatures must have roots, and what is more likely than that the prototype was some ape-like or man-like creature that in time past formed part of the fauna of mainland Asia but which has now disappeared from these areas. The fossil record attests that a form of ape called *Gigantopithecus* once lived several million years ago in northern India. Nearer our own time, about 750,000 years ago, members of the same genus were to be found in the Kwangsi province of China. Even more recently, 250,000 years ago, a species of orang-utan roamed the forests of southern China and, as discussed in chapter 7, such creatures may well have survived until relatively modern times. Today the only ape found on the continent of Asia is the gibbon which is so familiar to most Asians, and relatively so small, that it is unlikely to have provided the root or branch of the Yeti folktale. Undoubtedly the most likely model is the orang-utan. Finally there are those who believe that the Yeti is real, and is a relict form of *Gigantopithecus*. H. W. Tilman holds this view,[5] as do W. Tschernezky and Bernard Heuvelmans.

Footprints of the Sasquatch, the American Bigfoot, are a much bigger problem. Certainly no bear, mountain lion or other innocent denizen of the forests can be held responsible for this gigantic spoor. There are no wild orang-utans in North America and there never have been, but this does not exclude the orang from providing the roots of the Sasquatch legend, if indeed this is what it is. The earliest inhabitants of North America were mongoloids; of this there is no shadow of doubt. Their port of entry was Alaska and their route from Siberia was a land bridge spanning what is now the Bering Strait.

Throughout the Quaternary period the sea level underwent vertical oscillations as water pre-empted during the glacial periods was released as the glaciers melted. Thus, in these shallow seas, dry land would make its appearance in glacial times only to be cut again as the sea transgressed the land during the interglacials. The last time a continuous connection between Asian and the American continents existed was at the end of the Würm-Wisconsin glaciation, about 10,000 years ago; since that time the sea has been steadily rising, until about three thousand years ago when it reached its present level.

On this evidence, it seems that the first wave of immigrants entered North America between 15,000 and 20,000 years ago, and it appears that their migration didn't stop until they had reached the sun; the oldest archaeological evidence of human occupation (stone tools) is found in Venezuela. Might one suppose that the continent of America filled up from the bottom, the earliest immigrants continuing their unimpeded southward spread until they had reached the warmth of the subtropics, and the late-comers, finding the lower latitudes already occupied, taking up residence at points progressively further north? This is highly speculative, but it might explain why the earliest remains of the American Indians are no older than 10,000 years, if that. There is every likelihood, but no certain evidence, that immigration continued in a west–east direction until the Bering land bridge became totally impassable some time between 5,000 and 10,000 years ago. Thereafter the route to America was by sea. Just how late mongoloid invasions of North America continued is not known.

It is not particularly outrageous to suggest that the legend of the orang-utan reached America with some of the later immigrants to persist as part of the verbal tradition of their North American descendants. The consensus description of the Sasquatch as a large, hairy, bipedal creature with a very short neck, wide shoulders, deep chest and long arms is consistent with the general image of an ape, but it is also consistent with the hypothetical image of a primitive sort of man. Specific orang-like characters are missing from descriptions of the Sasquatch: the long, shaggy fur of reddish hue (characteristic of orangs) has become brown, black or grey. The partly bipedal, partly quadrupedal gait characteristic of contemporary Yeti descriptions has become wholly bipedal; and the cone-shaped head of the male orang, and sometimes of the Yeti, is seldom strongly emphasized in the context of the Sasquatch.

As might be expected in a zoogeographical realm, which has no wild apes to reinforce the image, the original — imported — mythological model has lost some of its ape-like specifications and has become man-like with bear-ish overtones.

Few would deny that today the tales of the Sasquatch are

subject to intense cultural reinforcement. The direction in which the modern legend is going appears once again to be ape-orientated. As we see in Roger Patterson's film, the Sasquatch is acquiring a somewhat gorilla-like image superimposed on a basically human framework. This turn of events has done nothing for the credibility of the legend. The body of a man and the legs of a horse may be all right for an out-and-out mythological creature like a centaur, but the body of an ape and the legs of a man are just not on for a creature that is supposed to be alive today and living in Bluff Creek, California. Chimeras are fun, but they do not make convincing next-door neighbours.

Further research into the folklore of the ethnic groups of mongoloid origin may turn up an acceptable 'common ancestor' for the Yeti and the Sasquatch. It may turn out to be something like the *Fei-fei* (see p. 31), or something quite different. The mythology of the American Indians, the Tibetans and the Chinese will have to be combed in order to find clues to the 'adaptive radiation' of the legend of Bigfoot.

Inevitably a theory which proposes that the Sasquatch is an insubstantial being, a wraith, an Amerindian legend, must be tested in the hard light of footprints and in the softer glow of eyewitness reports. If the Orang Theory is valid, then Bigfoot in America exists only in the minds of men, and the footprints and sightings are quite irrelevant, *but I am not convinced that this is so*. Elsewhere I have stressed the seeming impossibility that every single track among the tens of thousands scattered over 125,000 square miles of Sasquatch territory in the Pacific north-west is a hoax; and that every eyewitness account of the many hundreds on record is either a deliberate falsification or a matter of imperfect identification. No one doubts that some of the footprints are hoaxes and that some eyewitnesses are lying, but if *one* track and *one* report is true-bill, then myth must be chucked out of the window and reality admitted through the front door.

The dilemma is simple enough. Either some of the footprints are real, or all are fakes. If they are all fakes, then an explanation invoking legend and folk memory is adequate to explain the mystery. But if any one of them is real then as scientists we have a lot to explain. Among other things we shall have to re-write the story of human evolution. We shall have to accept that *Homo sapiens* is not the one and only living product of the hominid line, and we shall have to admit that there are still major mysteries to be solved in a world we thought we knew so well.

Don Abbott, an anthropologist from the Provincial Museum, Victoria, B.C., has said of the footprints, 'If the evidence of which I am aware has been the work of hoaxers, it would be one of the most elaborate hoaxes ever perpetrated. I find this possibility almost as incredible as that of the existence of such a creature.'[6] Don Abbott speaks for all of us who have become involved in this strange story. The evidence that I have examined persuades me that some of the tracks are real, and that they are man-like in form. One might expect that having accepted these propositions one could pursue them painlessly to their logical conclusion — that they have been made by a man-like creature. But when the *size* of the tracks is taken into account, and the conclusion is reached that the man-like creature in question has a stature of at least 8 ft. and weighs upwards of 800 lb, the mind starts to boggle at such a preposterous idea. The vision of such creatures stomping barefoot through the forests of north-west America, unknown to science, is beyond common sense. Yet reason argues that this is the case.

Dr Johnson's view that 'all power of fancy over reason is a degree of insanity' provides a crumb of comfort. But Thomas Henry Huxley's aphorism that 'logical consequences are the scarecrows of fools and the beacons of wise men' puts steel into my soul.

The Yeti of the Himalayas has little going for it. Eyewitness accounts are quite valueless as primary data. Sherpa reports are suspect because Sherpas do not distinguish between the 'reality' of the real world and the 'reality' of their myth-ridden religious beliefs. Sightings by Western man are of two kinds: those in which the fictional element appears to take precedence over actuality (Rawicz, Thorberg and Frostis); and those which by the nature of the distance involved (Tombazi and Whillans) are too imprecise to be of any real value as evidence.

So-called Yeti footprints, though useless in proving the existence of a Himalayan Bigfoot, do at least offer some hints of the origins of the folktale. Unlike the Sasquatch, there is little uniformity of pattern, and what uniformity there is incriminates the bear. Undoubtedly interpretation of footprints is complicated by the virtually unknown effects of melting and sublimation. There is only one footprint which disturbs me, and that is Shipton's (see chapters 2 and 5); this is my chief hang-up over the Yeti problem. It could be the one single piece of evidence that underwrites the existence of the Yeti, but I don't think it is. Sherlock Holmes, perhaps, would not have agreed with me. How often he must have bored kind, patient Dr Watson with the aphorism ' ... when you have eliminated the impossible, whatever remains, *however improbable*, must be the truth'. The Shipton print, at the moment of writing, is the one item in the whole improbable saga that sticks in my throat; without it I would have no hesitation in dismissing the Yeti as a red herring, or, at least, as a red bear. As it is, the issue must lie on the table unresolved.

From the point of view of evidence, the Sasquatch business is altogether a different proposition. Eyewitness reports which provide strictly circumstantial evidence are very persuasive, and the more direct evidence of footprints is quite impossible to dismiss in all instances.

I am convinced that the Sasquatch exists, but whether it is all that it is cracked up to be is another matter altogether. There must be *something* in north-west America that needs explaining, and that something leaves man-like footprints. The evidence I have adduced in favour of the reality of the Sasquatch is not hard evidence; few physicists, biologists or chemists would accept it, but nevertheless it *is* evidence and cannot be ignored.

I have suggested that myth and legend have survival value for mankind, and are therefore subject to natural selection like all physical and many behavioural characteristics of man. We are far from understanding exactly what the role of a hypothetical myth-gene could be, but perhaps it is connected with man's highly socialized state. Bonds and allegiances are the bedrock of our society, as they are of many nonhuman primate societies. There is the pair-bond of husband and wife, the family-bond, the village-bond and the national-bond; to say nothing of the sex-bond, school-bonds, club-bonds and innumerable, unclassifiable religious and ideological-bonds. But mankind needs more than bonds, and the comforts of grooming they involve; we need to experience feelings of awe. Husbands, fathers, elders, statesmen, dictators, presidents, chairmen and grand masters are all very well as god-figures, but they are inadequate because they lack the essential ingredient of remoteness. Man needs his gods — and his monsters — and the more remote and unapproachable they are, the better.

Postscript

A year or so ago I was taking leave of Lord Hunt, the leader of the triumphant Everest Expedition of 1953. After a long and pleasant discussion on mountains and Yetis he saw me to the lift, talking all the way. As the gates closed he added ' ... and don't be too hard on the Yeti.' Because Lord Hunt is a gentle and persuasive person I was deeply impressed and I sincerely hope that he will settle for the Sasquatch even if I cannot oblige him by validating the Yeti on the present state of the evidence.

Perhaps by the time this book is published somebody will have discovered a Bigfoot. I hope so; but if not, I will happily settle for the myth.

TABLES

TABLE I. *Sightings and footprints of Yeti in the Himalayas since 1915* (in chronological sequence)

Observer	Region	Month and year	Nature of observation	Altitude	No of toe
J. R. P. Gent	Phalut, Sikkim	Dec. 1915	F	—	—
C. K. Howard–Bury	Lhakpa–La	Sep. 1921	F	20–22,000	—
N. A. Tombazi	Zemu Glacier	Spring 1925	S & F	15,000	5
R. Kaulback	Upper Salween	Dec. 1935	F	16,000	—
F. S. Smythe	Bhundar Valley, Garwhal	June 1937	F	20,000	5
H. W. Tilman	Zemu Gap	July 1937	F	19,276	—
John Hunt	Zemu Gap	Nov. 1937	F	19,230	—
S. Pranavanandra	Khandosanglam Pass	July 1941	F	18,000	—
Eric Shipton	Menlung Glacier	Nov. 1951	F	18,000	4 ?5
Wyss–Dunant	Khumbu Glacier	Apr. 1952	F	19,000	5
Charles Stonor	Near Namche Bazar	Jan. 1954	F	14,000	—
Ralph Izzard	Dudh Kosi Valley	Feb. 1954	F	15,000	—
John Jackson	Khumbu Glacier	Feb. 1954	F	19,000	—
Abbé Bordet	Dudh Kosi Valley	May 1955	F	12,350	4
A. J. M. Smyth	Kulti Valley	June 1955	F	12,375	5
L. W. Davies	Kulti Valley	June 1955	F	12,000	5
E. S. Williams	Sim Gang Glacier, Karakorams	Sept. 1956	F	17,000	—
Desmond Doig	Ripumu Glacier	Dec. 1960	F	18,000	—
Don Whillans	Machapuchare, Nepal	Dec. 1970	S & F	13–15,000	—

NOTE. The width/length index for all prints is well outside the range for Sasquatch, fossil man and modern human prints (see table 3). Only observations with adequate data are listed. S = sighting, F = footprint.

Step length	Print length	Print width	Width/length index	Observer's interpretation	Author's interpretation
—	18–24 in.	6 in.	—	Feet point backwards	—
—	—	—	—	Grey wolf	—
1½–2 ft.	6–7 in.	4 in.	63	Man–like	Black bear
—	—	—	—	Bare–foot man	—
1½–2 ft.	12–13 in.	6 in.	48	Probably bear	Red bear
—	—	—	—	Booted tracks	—
—	—	—	—	Two sets of tracks	—
—	21 in.	'Broad'	—	Bare human foot	Pilgrim
—	13 in.	8 in.	62	—	Double Origin?
1 ft. 2 in.	10–12 in.	5–6 in.	50	Quadruped ? Bear	Bear
—	10 in.	5 in.	50	Yeti	Black bear
2 ft. 3 in.	8–9 in.	4–5 in.	53	Unknown biped	—
—	10–11 in.	5–6 in.	52	—	—
1½–2 ft.	8 in.	—	—	'Like Shipton's'	Black bear
—	12 in.	6 in.	50	—	—
4–5 ft.	12 in.	8 in.	67	Yeti	Red bear
1½–2 ft.	10½ in.	6 in.	57	—	Red bear
1½–2½ ft.	11–14 in.	'Broad'	—	Bare human foot	? Pilgrim
—	9–10 in.	'Narrow'	—	Ape–like creature	Langur

TABLE 2. *Sightings of footprints of the Sasquatch of north-west America since 1920*

Locality	Observer	Year	Month	Time	Sex	Stature	Footprint dimensions	Category
BRITISH COLUMBIA AND ALBERTA								
Toba Inlet	Ostman	1924	Summer	N	M & F	7–8 ft.	—	S
Ruby Creek, Fraser river	Chapman	1940	Oct.	D	M	7–8 ft.	—	S
New Hazelton	Luxton	1949	?	N	—	8 ft.	—	S
Nr Chilliwack	Gregg	1952	Nov.	N	M	7 ft.	—	S
Mica Mt., Tete Jaune Cache	Roe	1955	Oct.	D	F	6 ft.	—	S
Yale, Fraser river	Hunt	1956	May	N	—	—	—	S
Nr Enderby	Bellevue	1959	Sept.	D	—	7–9 ft.	—	S
Nr Nelson	Bringsli	1960	Oct.	D	—	7–9 ft.	16–17 in.	S & F
Pitt Lake	—	1961	?	N	—	9 ft.	—	S
Pitt Meadows	Welch	1965	June	D	—	10–12 ft.	24 × 12 in.	S & F
Richmond	—	1966	July	N	—	7–8 ft.	—	S
Nr Thompson Valley	—	1966	Oct–Nov.	—	—	—	14–16 in.	F
S.W. of Nordegg (Alberta)	Roan	1968	Summer	—	—	—	15 × 6–7 in.	F
Windy Point, Alberta	Harris	1968	Fall	—	—	—	17 & 13½ in.	F
Squamish	—	1969	Mar.	D	—	—	—	S & F
Powder Mt.	Osborne	1969	Apr.	—	—	—	12–14 in. (snow)	F
Merrit, Nicola Valley	Group	1969	May	N	—	?10 ft.	—	S
Lytton, E. of Squamish– Pemberton road	Wally	1969	Nov.	N	—	7 ft.	—	S
	Anon.	1970	Jan.	D	—	9 ft.	—	S
Q. Charlotte Islands	—	1970	June	N	—	7 ft.	—	S

NOTE. This table lists the sightings of Sasquatch and discoveries of footprints since 1920 on my files. There are hundreds more, although those given here are probably among the best documented. The surname of the observer is given where known. The designation 'Anon.' respects privacy where requested. 'Group' indicates sightings by a number of people together. Indication of 'day' or 'night' is relevant only in the case of sightings. Sex is listed only where positive evidence is available. Stature is based on the observer's estimate. S = sighting, F = footprint.

TABLE 2 (contd)

Locality	Observer	Year	Month	Time	Sex	Stature	Footprint dimensions	Category
WASHINGTON STATE								
Ape Canyon	Hennrich	1963	July	D	—	—	16 in.	S & F
Cascade Crest Trail	Fox	1965	Summer	—	—	—	17 in.	F
Yakima, W. of	Pellishon	1966	July	N	—	7 ft.	—	S
Bear Creek, Skamania Co.	Closner & Wright	1969	Mar.	—	—	—	22 × 7½ in. (snow)	F
Skamania County	Cox	1969	Mar.	N	—	8–10 ft.	—	S
Skamania County	Group	1969	Apr.	—	—	—	20 in.	F
Bossburg	—	1969	Apr.	D	—	7 ft.	—	S
Hoquiam	Herrington	1969	July	N	F	7–7½ ft.	18½ in.	S & F
Deception Pass	—	1969	Sept.	N	—	? 5½ ft.	—	S
Marietta	—	1969	Sept.	N	—	—	13½ in.	S & F
Tacoma	—	1969	Sept.	N	—	—	—	S
Bossburg	Marx	1969	Oct.	—	—	—	17½ × 7 in.	F
Woodland, Seattle–Portland road	Kent	1969	Nov.	N	—	—	12 × 4 in.	S & F
Bossburg	Dahinden & Marx	1969	Dec.	—	—	—	Snow	F
Whistle Lake	Grover	1969	Dec.	—	—	—	17 in.	F
Colville	—	1969	Dec.	—	—	—	17 in.	F
St Helens Mt.	Morgan	1970	June	—	—	—	16 × 7 in.	F
Carson	—	1970	June	—	—	—	13 in. and 16 in.	F
Stevens County	—	1970	Nov.	—	—	9 ft.	—	S
OREGON								
Three Sisters Wilderness	Hunter	1942	Sept.	D	—	—	—	S
Wanoga Butte	—	1957	Oct.	D	—	9 ft.	—	S
Tenmile, Nr Roseburg	Johnson & Stork	1959	Oct.	D	—	?14 ft.	11 in.	S & F
Mt. McLoughlin	—	1962	Aug.	—	—	—	—	F
Nr Portland	—	1963	July	N	—	9 ft.	—	S
The Dalles	Group	1967	June	N	—	7 ft.	19–24 × 8–10 in.	S & F
Nr Portland	—	1967	Nov.	D	—	—	—	S
Area unnamed	Anon.	1967	Nov.	D	M & F	6 ft.+	12–15 in.	S & F
Estacada	Kiggins	1968	Jan.	—	—	—	14 in.	F
Clackamus River	Anon.	1968	Dec.	D	F	—	Snow	S & F
Myrtle Point	Woodruff	1969	Feb.	—	—	—	20 in. (snow)	F
Copper	—	1969	Aug.	—	—	—	18 in.	F
The Dalles	Brown	1971	June	D & N	—	8 ft.	20 × 9½ × 3½ in.	S & F

TABLE 2 (contd)

Locality	Observer	Year	Month	Time	Sex	Stature	Footprint dimensions	Category
N. CALIFORNIA								
Mt. Bally	—	1936	Jan.	—	—	—	—	F
Bluff Creek	Crew	1958	Oct.	—	—	—	16 × 7 in.	F
Bluff Creek	Titmus	1958	Nov.	—	—	—	15 in.	F
Bluff Creek	Tripp	1958	Nov.	—	—	—	17 in.	F
Bluff Creek	Byrne	1960	July	—	—	—	16 in.	F
Hoopa, Humboldt Co.	—	1962	Sept.	—	—	—	14 × 7 in.	F
Hyampom	—	1963	May	—	—	—	17 in. & 13 in.	F
Blue Creek Mt.	—	1967	Aug.	—	—	—	·15 in., 12½ in., 13¼ in.	F
Bluff Creek	Patterson	1967	Oct.	D	F	7½ ft.	14½ in.	S & F
Blue Creek Mt.	Graves	1969	Jan.	—	—	—	—	F
Stirling City	—	1969	Apr.	N	—	6 ft.	—	S
Bluff Creek	Frey	1969	May	—	—	—	—	F
Bluff Creek	Northrup	1969	May	—	—	—	—	F
Trinity Nat. Forest	Foster	1969	June	D	—	6 ft.	14 in.	S & F
Siskiyou Co.	Hardasty & Carroll	1969	June	—	—	—	15 in.	F
Trinity Center	—	1969	July	D	—	8 ft.	—	S
Train, Nr Oroville	—	1969	July	N	—	—	—	S
Oroville	Jackson	1969	July	D	F	7–8 ft.	—	S
Oroville	Stickley	1969	July	N	F	—	—	S
Oroville	Anon.	1969	July	N	—	8 ft.	—	S
Yolla Bolla District	Haas & Dana	1969	July	—	—	—	16 in.	F

TABLE 3. *Dimensions and indices of Sasquatch and human footprints*

Status	Dimensions (in.)	Foot width/length index	Big toe width index	Estimated stature	Known stature
SASQUATCH					
Bluff Creek	15·0 × 6·3 × 4·8	42·0	28·7	8 ft. 3 in.	—
Blue Creek	12·25 × 4·7 × 3·7	38·4	20·9	6 ft. 9 in.	—
Blue Creek	15·0 × 7·0 × 4·8	46·6	25·6	8 ft. 3 in.	—
Blue Creek	15·0 × 6·3 × 4·3	42·0	23·1	8 ft. 3 in.	—
Bluff Creek	13·0 × 3·8 × 2·5	29·2	18·2	7 ft. 2 in.	—
Onion Mt.	11·5 × 4·5 × 2·8	39·1	—	6 ft. 4 in.	—
Bluff Creek	11·5 × 4·8 × 3·3	41·7	—	6 ft. 4 in.	—
Bluff Creek	15·0 × 5·6 × 4·4	37·3	25·0	8 ft. 3 in.	—
Bossburg	17·5 × 6·8 × 5·5	38·6	35·7	9 ft. 7 in.	—
NEANDERTHAL					
Toirano, Italy	10·8 × 4·7 × 3·3	43·5	36·8	5 ft. 11 in.	—
Toirano, Italy	9·0 × 3·4 × 2·9	37·7	32·0	4 ft. 11½ in.	—
HOMO SAPIENS					
Male	11·3 × 4·0 × 3·1	35·4	32·3	6 ft. 2½ in.	6 ft. 1 in.
Male	11·5 × 4·0 × 3·0	34·8	33·3	6 ft. 4 in.	6 ft. 1 in.
Male	12·0 × 5·0 × 3·1	41·7	31·1	6 ft. 7 in.	6 ft. 7 in.
Female	10·5 × 4·0 × 2·6	38·1	31·3	5 ft. 9 in.	5 ft. 9 in.
Female	9·3 × 3·8 × 2·5	40·9	36·5	5 ft. 1½ in.	5 ft. 1 in.
Female	9·6 × 3·6 × 2·7	37·5	32·3	5 ft. 3½ in.	5 ft. 2 in.

NOTE. All dimensions are derived from photographs of footprints except for the Neanderthal dimensions which were obtained from casts.

Dimensions = greatest length, greatest width forefoot, greatest width heel

$$Width/length\ index = \frac{length \times 100}{width\ forefoot}$$

$$Big\ toe\ index = \frac{width\ of\ big\ toe \times 100}{total\ width\ of\ all\ toes}$$

Note the uniformity throughout of width/length index, but the marked difference in big toe index, which is much higher in *Homo sapiens* and Neanderthal Man than in Sasquatch. Note, especially, that the Bossburg prints belong with man in this respect. All measurements by the author.

TABLE 4. *Mammals of the Himalayas*

Maximum altitude	Common name	Scientific name
20,000 ft.	Yak	*Bos grunniens*
	Bharal (blue sheep)	*Pseudois nayaur*
	*Pika (mouse hare)	*Ochotona roylei*
19,800 ft.	Woolly hare	*Lepus oiostolus*
19,500 ft.	Ibex	*Capra sibirica sacin*
19,000 ft.	*Woolly wolf	*Canis lupus chanco*
	Argali (Tibetan wild sheep)	*Ovis ammon hodgsoni*
18,500 ft.	*Hill fox	*Vulpes vulpes montana*
18,000 ft.	Lynx	*Lynx lynx isabellinus*
	Kiang (wild ass)	*Equus hemionus kiang*
	Chiru (Tibetan antelope)	*Panthalops hodgsoni*
	Goa (Tibetan gazelle)	*Procapra picticaudata*
	Marmot	*Marmota bobak*
	Marco Polo's sheep	*Ovis ammon poli*
17,000 ft.	Weasel	*Mustela altaica*
	Field vole	*Pitymys leucurus everesti*
16,600 ft.	*Brown bear (red bear)	*Ursus arctos isabellinus*
	*Tibetan sand fox	*Vulpes ferrillata*
16,000 ft.	Himalayan weasel	*Mustela sibirica*
15,000 ft.	Pallas' cat	*Felis manul*
14,000 ft.	Shapu (Astor wild sheep)	*Ovis orientalis*
	Stoat	*Mustela erminea*
	Ghoral	*Nemorhaedus goral*
	Hangul (Kashmir red deer)	*Cervus elephas hanglu*
	Long–tailed marmot	*Marmota caudata*
13,500 ft.	Otter	*Lutra lutra monticola*
13,000 ft.	Red panda	*Ailurus fulgens*
	Linsang	*Prionodon pardicolor*
	*Langur	*Presbytis entellus ajax*
	*Snow leopard	*Panthera uncia*
12,500 ft.	Musk deer	*Moschus moschiferus*
12,000 ft.	Markhor	*Capra falconeri*
11,500 ft.	Beech marten	*Martes foina*
11,000 ft.	Tahr (Himalayan tahr)	*Hemitragus jemlaicus*
	Shou (Sikkim stag)	*Cervus elephas wallachi*
	Sikkim vole	*Pitymys sikimensis*
	Yellow–bellied weasel	*Mustela kathiar*
	Asiatic jackal	*Canis aureus*
	*Serow (Tibetan)	*Capricornis sumatrensis milneedwardsi*
	*Asiatic black bear	*Selenarctos thibetanus*
	Wild dog	*Cuon alpinus*
	Yellow–throated marten	*Charronia flavigula*
10,400 ft.	Tiger	*Panthera tigris*
10,000 ft.	Elephant	*Elephas maximus*

NOTE. This table lists actual sightings of mammals on north and south slopes of the Himalayas. Altitudes represent the highest recorded. An asterisk indicates mammals involved — in one way or another — with the Yeti legend.

Appendix

DR D. W. GRIEVE'S REPORT ON THE FILM
OF A SUPPOSED SASQUATCH

The following report is based on a copy of a 16 mm. film taken by Roger Patterson on October 20th, 1967, at Bluff Creek, Northern California, which was made available to me by Rene Dahinden in December 1971. In addition to Patterson's footage, the film includes a sequence showing a human being (height 6 ft. 5½ in.) walking over the same terrain.

The main purpose in analysing the Patterson film was to establish the extent to which the creature's gait resembled or differed from human gait. The bases for comparison were measurements of stride length, time of leg swing, speed of walking and the angular movements of the lower limb, parameters that are known for man at particular speeds of walking.[1] Published data refer to humans, with light footwear or none, walking on hard level ground. In part of the film the creature is seen walking at a steady speed through a clearing of level ground, and it is data from this sequence that has been used for purposes of comparison with the human pattern. Later parts of the film show an almost full posterior view, which permits some comparisons to be made between its body breadth and that of humans.

The film has several drawbacks for purposes of quantitative analysis. The unstable hand-held camera gave rise to intermittent frame blurring. Lighting conditions and the foliage in the background make it difficult to establish accurate outlines of the trunk and limbs even in un-blurred frames. The subject is walking obliquely across the field of view in that part of the film in which it is most clearly visible. The feet are not sufficiently visible to make useful statements about the ankle movements. Most importantly of all, no information is available as to framing speed used.

Body shape and size

Careful matching and superposition of images of the so-called Sasquatch and human film sequences yield an estimated standing height for the subject of not more than 6 ft. 5 in. (196 cm.). This specimen lies therefore within the human range, although at its upper limits. Accurate measurements are impossible regarding features that fall within the body outline. Examination of several frames leads to the conclusion that the height of the hip joint, the gluteal fold and the finger tips are in similar proportions to the standing height as those found in humans. The shoulder height at the acromion appears slightly greater relative to the standing height (0·87:1) than in humans (0·82:1). Both the shoulder width and the hip width appear proportionately greater in the subject creature than in man (0·34:1 instead of 0·26:1; and 0·23:1 instead of 0·19:1, respectively).

If we argue that the subject has similar vertical proportions to man (ignoring the higher shoulders) and has breadths and circumferences about 25 per cent greater proportionally, then the weight is likely to be 50–60 per cent greater in the subject than in a man of the same height. The additional shoulder height and the unknown correction that should be allowed for the presence of hair will have opposite effects upon an estimate of weight. Earlier comments[2] that this specimen was 'just under 7 ft. in height and extremely heavy' seem rather extravagant. The present analysis suggests that Sasquatch was 6 ft. 5 in. in height, with a weight of about 280 lb (127 kg.) and a foot length (mean of 4 observations) of about 13·3 in. (34 cm.).

Timing of the gait

Because the framing speed is unknown, the timing of the various phases of the gait was done in terms of the numbers of frames. Five independent estimates of the complete cycle time were made, from 'R. toe-off', 'L. toe-off', 'R. foot passing L.', 'L. foot passing R.' and 'L. heel strike' respectively giving:

Complete cycle time = 22·5 frames (range 21·5–23·5). Four independent estimates of the swing phase, or single support phase for the contra-lateral limb, from toe-off to heel strike, gave:

Swing phase, or single support = 8·5 frames (same in each case). The above therefore indicates a total period of support of 14 frames and periods of double support (both feet on the ground) of 2·75 frames. A minimum uncertainty of ± 0·5 frames may be assumed.

Stride length

The film provides an oblique view and no clues exist that can lead to an accurate measurement of the obliquity of the direction of walk which was judged to be not less than 20° and not more than 35° to the image plane of the camera. The obliquity gives rise to an apparent grouping of left and right foot placements which could in reality have been symmetrical with respect to distance in the line of progression. The distance on the film between successive placements of the left foot was 1·20 × the standing height. If an obliquity of 27° is assumed, a stride length of 1·34 × the standing height is obtained. The corresponding values in modern man for 20° and 35° obliquity are 1·27 and 1·46 respectively.

A complete set of tracings of the subject were made, and in every case when the limb outlines were sufficiently clear a construction of the axes of the thigh and shank were made. The angles of the segments to the vertical were measured as they appeared on the film. Because of the obliquity of the walk to the image plane of the camera (assumed to be 27°), the actual angles of the limb segments to the vertical in the sagittal plane were computed by dividing the tangent of the apparent angles by the cosine of 27°. This gave the tangent of the desired angle in each case, from which the actual thigh and shank angles were obtained. The knee-angle was obtained as the difference between the thigh and shank angles. A summary of the observations is given in the following table.

FRAME NO.	EVENT OR COMMENT	ANGLES MEASURED ON LEFT LIMB					
		Apparent on film			Corrected for 27° obliquity		
		Thigh	Knee	Shank	Thigh	Knee	Shank
3	R. toe-off	+ 7	14	− 7	+ 8	16	− 3
4		+ 1	19	− 18	+ 1	21	− 20
5		− 7	10	− 17	− 8	11	− 19
6	blurred	− 18	3	− 21	− 20	3	− 23
7	R. foot pass L.	UNCERTAIN					
8		OF					
9		LIMB					
10		OUTLINES					
11	} R. heel strike	HEPE					
12		− 27	13	− 4υ	− 30	13	− 43
13	L. toe-off	− 25	22	− 47	− 28	22	− 50
14		0	61	− 61	0	64	− 64
15		+ 10	63	− 53	+ 11	67	− 56
16	L. foot pass R.	+ 10	64	− 54	+ 11	68	− 57
17		+ 13	62	− 49	+ 14	66	− 52
18		+ 17	45	− 28	+ 19	50	− 31
19		+ 23	38	− 15	+ 25	41	− 16
20		+ 28	29	− 1	+ 31	32	− 1
21	} L. heel strike	+ 17	6	+ 11	+ 19	7	+ 12
22		+ 20	10	+ 10	+ 22	11	+ 11
23		+ 19	16	+ 3	+ 21	18	+ 3
24	} R. toe-off	+ 17	18	− 1	+ 19	20	− 1
25		+ 19	33	− 14	+ 21	36	− 15
26		+ 8	15	− 7	+ 9	16	− 7
27		+ 2	19	− 17	+ 2	21	− 19
28	} R. foot pass L.	+ 4	28	− 24	+ 4	30	− 26
29		NO MEASUREMENT					

The pattern of movement, notably the 30° of knee flexion following heel strike, the hip extension during support that produces a thigh angle of 30° behind the vertical, the large total thigh excursion of 61°, and the considerable (46°) knee flexion following toe-off, are features very similar to those for humans walking at high speed. Under these conditions, humans would have a stride length of 1·2 × stature or more, a time of swing of about 0·35 sec. and a speed of swing of about 1·5 × stature per second.

Conclusions

The unknown framing speed is crucial to the interpretation of the data. It is likely that the filming was done at either 16, 18 or 24 frames per second and each possibility is considered below.

	16 fps	18 fps	24 fps
Stride length approx.	262 cm.	262 cm.	262 cm.
Stride/Stature	1·27–1·46	1·27–1·46	1·27–1·46
Speed approx.	6·7 km./hr	7·5 km./hr	10·0 km./hr
Speed/Stature	0·9–1·04 sec.[1]	1·02–1·17	1·35–1.56
Time for complete cycle	1·41 sec.	1·25 sec.	0·94 sec.
Time of swing	0·53 sec.	0·47 sec.	0·35 sec.
Total time of support	0·88 sec.	0·78 sec.	0·58 sec.
One period double support	0·17 sec.	0·15 sec.	0·11 sec.

If 16 fps is assumed, the cycle time and the time of swing are in a typical human combination but much longer in duration than one would expect for the stride and the pattern of limb movement. It is as if a human were executing a high speed pattern in slow motion. It is very unlikely that more massive limbs would account for such a combination of variables. If the framing speed was indeed 16 fps it would be reasonable to conclude that the metabolic cost of locomotion was unnecessarily high per unit distance or that the neuromuscular system was very different to that in humans. With these considerations in mind it seems unlikely that the film was taken at 16 frames per second.

Similar conclusions apply to the combination of variables if we assume 18 fps. In both cases, a human would exhibit very little knee flexion following heel strike and little further knee flexion following toe-off at these times of cycle and swing. It is pertinent that subject has similar linear proportions to man and therefore would be unlikely to exhibit a totally different pattern of gait unless the intrinsic properties of the limb muscles or the nervous system were greatly different to that in man.

If the film was taken at 24 fps, Sasquatch walked with a gait pattern very similar in most respects to a man walking at high speed. The cycle time is slightly greater than expected and the hip joint appears to be more flexible in extension than one would expect in man. If the framing speed were higher than 24 fps the similarity to man's gait is even more striking.

My subjective impressions have oscillated between total acceptance of the Sasquatch on the grounds that the film would be difficult to fake, to one of irrational rejection based on an emotional response to the possibility that the Sasquatch actually exists. This seems worth stating because others have reacted similarly to the film. The possibility of a very clever fake cannot be ruled out on the evidence of the film. A man could have sufficient height and suitable proportions to mimic the longitudinal dimensions of the Sasquatch. The shoulder breadth however would be difficult to achieve without giving an unnatural appearance to the arm swing and shoulder contours. The possibility of fakery is ruled out if the speed of the film was 16 or 18 fps. In these conditions a normal human being could not duplicate the observed pattern, which would suggest that the Sasquatch must possess a very different locomotor system to that of man.

D. W. GRIEVE, M.SC., PH.D.,
Reader in Biomechanics
Royal Free Hospital School of Medicine
London

References

1. Grieve D. W. and Gear R. J. (1966) The relationships between Length of Stride, Step Frequency, Time of Swing and Speed of Walking for Children and Adults. *Ergonomics*, **5**. 379–399; Grieve D. W. (1969) The assessment of gait. *Physiotherapy*, **55**. 452–460.
2. Green J. (1969) *On the track of the Sasquatch*. British Columbia Provincial Museum. Cheam Publishing Ltd.

Notes

1. Man and his Monsters

1. P. B. Medawar. *The Art of the Soluble*. London: Methuen, 1967; Pelican Books, 1969.
2. R. von Nebesky-Wojkowitz in a letter to the Directors of the British Museum (Natural History). Nebesky-Wojkowitz is the author of *Where the Gods are Mountains*. London: Weidenfeld and Nicolson, 1956.
3. Ivan T. Sanderson, Eton and Cambridge, a member of many learned societies and contributor to zoological journals, is now resident in U.S.A. His book *Abominable Snowmen: Legend come to life* is published by the Chilton Co. of Philadelphia and New York, 1961.
4. Colin P. Groves. *Gorillas*. New York: Arco, 1970.
5. Vernon Reynolds. *The Apes*. New York: E. P. Dutton, 1967. See also: Desmond and Ramona Morris. *Men and Apes*. New York: McGraw-Hill, 1968.
6. George Schaller. *The Mountain Gorilla*. Chicago: University Press, 1963.
7. Bacil F. Kirtley. Unknown Hominids and New World Legends. *Western Folklore*, **23.** 77–90.
8. Harold Stephens. Abominable Snowmen of Malaysia. *Argosy Magazine*. August 1971.
9. W. D. Skeat and C. O. Blagden. *The Pagan Races of the Malay Peninsula*. London: Macmillan and Co., 1906.
10. This intriguing scrap of ancient folklore has cropped up again recently in connection with the Russian Almas (Almasti). A Russian scientist, Igor Bourtsev, and his wife Alya Bourtseva working in Azerbaydjan in the Southern Caucasus in 1971 discovered in various areas a number of mares whose manes had apparently been 'plaited' overnight; the mares were tired and sweating as if they had been ridden hard and fast. The significance of 'plaiting' or 'braiding' is unknown, but in some areas tradition has it that in this

way the hairs of the mane of mares with foals are converted into a sort of stirrup into which the Almas insert their feet so that—lying under the body of the mare—they can suck her milk as she gallops along. I am grateful to Rene Dahinden for this curious tale, and for the opportunity to examine and photograph several of these tufts of plaited hair. My own contribution to this romantic legend is depressingly prosaic. I instituted some inquiries among my horsey friends, and within a few days a package arrived from the Manning family living in Sarratt, Hertfordshire, containing several switches of mane from an aged gelding who lives in retirement in the open on their estate, exposed to the wind and other vicissitudes. The twisting of the hairs and the knots (half-hitches) were *precisely* as in the Azerbaydjan specimen. (I have since seen the animal and confirmed the phenomenon.) I think there is little doubt that the so-called plaiting is produced by the effect of the wind on a long mane which is continuously being whipped and twisted.

11. Richard Bernheimer. *Wild Men in the Middle Ages*. Cambridge, Mass.: Harvard University Press, 1952.

12. R. H. Van Gulik. *The Gibbon in China*. Leiden: E. J. Brill, 1967. Van Gulik is known to millions who care little about gibbons as the creator of that classic mandarin detective, Judge Dee.

13. W. E. Swinton. *Giants Past and Present*. London: Robert Hale, 1966.

2. Bigfoot in Asia

1. S. J. Stone. *In and Beyond the Himalayas*. London: Edward Arnold, 1896, pp. 6 and 60.

2. B. H. Hodgson. On the Mammalia of Nepal. *J. Asiat. Soc. Bengal*, **1**. 1832.

3. L. A. Waddell. *Among the Himalayas*. London: Constable, 1899.

4. According to Toni Hagen, author of *Nepal: Königreich am Himalaya* (Bern: Kummerly und Frey. Geographischer Verlag, 1960), the Sherpas are quick to call any footprints those of the Yeti. Hagen recalls that while on the glacier of Annapurna-Kette he and his Sherpa came upon a track in the snow. Hagen asked, 'What is that track?' The Sherpa replied, 'It is the Yeti, sir.' 'Why', asked Hagen, 'are you so sure?' The Sherpa disarmingly replied, 'Nobody else here, sir!' Several other examples of the cheerful cooperativeness of Sherpas are recounted in the present text.

5. C. K. Howard-Bury, *Mount Everest*. London: E. Arnold, 19, p. 141.

6. N. A. Tombazi, F.R.G.S. *Account of a photographic expedition to the southern glaciers of Kanchenjunga in the Sikkim Himalaya*. Bombay: Maxwell Press, 1925.

7. *The Statesman*. Friday, June 5th, 1959.

8. *Bihar and Orissa Research Soc.*, **26**. 1940.

9. T. S. Blakeney. *Alpine Journal*, **61**. 419–21, 1956. Eric Shipton. *Geographical Journal*, **122**. 370–72, 1956.

10. Slawomir Rawicz. *The Long Walk*. New York: Harper & Row, 1956.

11. A term devised by the American anthropologist, Russell Tuttle, to describe the gait of African apes on the ground. See: Knuckle-walking and the problem of human origins. *Science*, **166**. 953–61, 1969.

12. Ivan T. Sanderson. *Abominable Snowmen: Legend come to life*; Odette Tchernine. *The Yeti*. London: Neville Spearman, 1970.

13. *Genus*, **18**. 1962.

14. Odette Tchernine. *The Yeti*. Miss Tchernine's earlier work *The Snowman and Company* was published by Robert Hale in 1961.

15. Michel Peissel. The Abominable Snowman Hoax. *Weekend*, January 1961. Also, *Mustang, a lost Tibetan Kingdom*, New York: E. P. Dutton & Co., 1967.

16. Bernard Heuvelmans. *On the track of unknown animals*, New York: Hill & Wang, 1965. Rupert-Hart-Davis, 1958; Ivan T. Sanderson. *Abominable Snowmen: Legend come to life;* Odette Tchernine. *The Snowman and Company* and *The Yeti*.

17. One of the immediate results of the publicity given to Shipton's photograph was a letter to the Director of the Natural History Museum. The letter throws no specific light on the nature of the footprint, but it is so unequivocal, so clearly uninfluenced by any damned nonsense about native myths, that it is worth quoting in its entirety. The letter might have come from a retired British Army colonel ('Disgusted') living in Sussex, but in fact it was written by A. P. Hansen, a citizen of Denmark: 'I cannot understand the noise [*sic*] about the terrible Snowman of the Himalayas. The tracks that Mr E. Shipton photographed must be those of the huge brown bear.'

18. Norman Hardie. *In Highest Nepal*. London: Allen and Unwin, 1957.

19. P. Bordet. Traces de Yeti dans l'Himalaya. *Bull. Mus. Nat. D'Hist. Natur.*, **27**. 433–9, 1955.
20. Charles Stonor. *The Sherpa and the Snowman*. London: Hollis and Carter, 1955.
21. Charles Stonor's *The Sherpa and the Snowman*, and Ralph Izzard's *The Abominable Snowman Adventure*. London: Hodder & Stoughton, 1955.
22. G. O. Dyrenfurth. *American Alpine Journal*, **11**. 324–5, 1959.
23. John Hunt. *The Ascent of Everest*. London: Hodder and Stoughton, 1953, pp. 78–9.
24. F. W. Holiday. *The Great Orm of Loch Ness*. New York: W. W. Norton, 1969.
25. G. S. Kirk. *Myth, its meaning and functions in ancient and other cultures.* Berkeley: University of California Press, 1970.
26. See Barry Bishop's account of this expedition: Wintering on the Roof of the World. *National Geographic*, October 1962.
27. Sri Swami Pranavanandra. *Indian Geog.J.*, **30**. 1955.
28. See Appendix in Ivan T. Sanderson's *Abominable Snowmen: Legend come to life.*
29. *The Times*, June 8th, 1970; *The Sunday Express*, September 6th, 1970.
30. Chris Bonnington. *Annapurna South Face*. London: Cassell, 1971.
31. J. Marques-Rivière. *L'Inde Secrète et sa magie*. Paris, 1937.
32. Personal communication.
33. Toni Hagen tells much the same story. Freely translated, the Sherpa's reply to Hagen's question as to whether he had ever seen the Yeti was, 'No, I myself have never seen the Yeti; it was the father of my cousin and he lived beyond the mountains and died two years ago.'
34. Hilaire Belloc. 'The Yak'. *Cautionary Tales*. New York: Alfred Knopf, 1941.
35. A. G. Pronin. Abominable Snowman in the Pamirs? *Soviet Weekly*, January 23rd, 1958.
36. Gordon Creighton's valuable list of synonyms of 'Wild men' and man-like monsters appears as an appendix to Odette Tchernine's book *The Yeti*.
37. According to the Russian zoologist S. I. Ognev (1931) Przewalski's man-beast, or Khun-Guresu, was nothing more exciting than a Tibetan blue bear (*Ursus arctos pruinosus*).

38. This and the following quotation are a précis of descriptions given by V. A. Khaklov to Boris Porshnev. Quoted in Ivan T. Sanderson's *Abominable Snowmen: Legend come to life*, pp. 314–17, and Odette Tchernine's *The Yeti*, pp. 43–4.

3. Bigfoot in America

1. Ivan T. Sanderson. *Abominable Snowmen: Legend come to life*.
2. Bacil F. Kirtley, Unknown Hominids and New World Legends.
3. John Green. *The Year of the Sasquatch*. Agassiz, B.C.: Cheam Publications Ltd., 1970.
4. Olaus Murie. *A Guide to animal tracks*, 1954. William Henry Burt. *A field guide to mammals*, 1952. Both published in The Peterson Field Guide Series. Boston: Houghton Mifflin Co.
5. John Green. *On the track of the Sasquatch*. Agassiz, B.C.: Cheam Publications Ltd., 1968.
6. George R. Rumney. *Climatology*. Toronto: The Macmillan Co., 1968.
7. Quoted with the permission of the Minister for Recreation and Conservation, British Columbia, and Frank L. Beebe.
8. Extract from John Green. *On the track of the Sasquatch*, p. 59.
9. *The Vancouver Province*. Monday, October 6th, 1958.
10. Charles Stonor. *The Sherpa and the Snowman*, p. 157.
11. George H. Harrison. On the track of Bigfoot. *National Wildlife*, October–November 1970.
12. The film has been shown twice in the U.K. The first occasion was in 1968 in a B.B.C. 2 series, *The World About Us*, in a programme called *The Californian Bigfoot*; the second occasion was during the Royal Institution Christmas Lectures, called 'Monkeys without Tails', shown on B.B.C. 2, in January and again in September 1971. The author presented the film on both occasions.
13. The step is defined as the distance between the same point of successive footprints of opposite sides, i.e.: from the back of the right heel to the back of the left heel.
14. A sad epilogue to this affair was the death of Roger Patterson at a relatively early age in February 1972.
15. Ivan T. Sanderson. Wisconsin's Abominable Snowman. *Argosy* Magazine, April 1961.

4. Tales from the Minnesota Woods

1. Ivan T. Sanderson. Preliminary description of the external morphology of what appeared to be the fresh corpse of a hitherto unknown form of living hominid. *Genus*, **25**. 249–78, 1969.
2. *Siberskoye* is an artificial word. Roughly translated, 'Siberskoye man' means 'man from Siberia'.
3. See J. R. and P. H. Napier. *A Handbook of Living Primates.* London–New York: Academic Press, 1967.
4. Ivan Sanderson had in fact informed the New Jersey Office of the F.B.I. on his own account during January sometime earlier and received a dusty answer.

5. The Evidence of the Footprints

1. John Napier. The antiquity of human walking. *Sci. Amer.*, **216**. 56–66, 1967.
2. The photos of the Bossburg footprints have been submitted to two eminent British orthopaedic surgeons, who as well as expressing their own view, consulted a number of their colleagues. The consensus opinion is that the abnormal appearance of the right foot could well be due to a club-foot deformity.
3. Maurice Tripp. *Humboldt Times* (Eureka, Calif.). October 11th, 1960.
4. These photographs were sent to me by Dr Grover S. Krantz, an anthropologist of Washington State University, who has made many valuable contributions to the Sasquatch problem, including a fascinating report on some so-called Sasquatch hand prints from the Bossburg area found during the summer of 1970. See *Northwest Anthropological Research Notes*, **5**. 145–51, 1970.
5. Bernard Heuvelmans. *On the track of unknown animals.* New York: Hill & Wang, 1965.
6. Marcel Couturier. *L'Ours brun.* Grenoble, 1954.
7. Edmund Hillary and Desmond Doig. *High in the Thin Cold Air.* London: Hodder and Stoughton, 1962, pp. 65–7.
8. Not, as one might infer, the Everest after whom the mountain was named. This honour belongs to Sir George Everest, the distinguished surveyor-general of India, who directed the triangulation that in 1859 led to the estimate of the height of the mountain.

9. Edmund Hillary and Desmond Doig. *High in the Thin Cold Air.*
10. Eric Shipton. *That untravelled world.* New York: Charles Scribner's and Sons, 1969.

6. The Evidence of Natural History

1. Douglas Hill. *Man, Myth and Magic.* Part 8. London: B.P.C. Publications Ltd., 1970.
2. Professor Scott Russell recounts in his book *Mountain Prospect,* London: Chatto and Windus, 1946, how he came across footprints in the Karakorams. His photograph indicates a footprint with a very narrow heel. Clearly this is the print of a bear (*U. arctos isabellinus,* probably) in which the toe- and claw-prints have been obliterated by melting. Professor Scott Russell reports an important general observation that the normal double track of a bear reverts to a single line-ahead track in certain terrains (see Williams's track, plate 2).
3. Frederick Markham. *Shooting in the Himalayas.* London, 1854.
4. John Pollard. Letter to editor of *Country Life,* July 23rd, 1970.
5. S. J. Stone. *In and Beyond the Himalayas.*
6. See Alexandra David-Neal's book *With Mystics and Magicians in Tibet* (1931).
7. Charles Stonor. *The Sherpa and the Snowman.* The extract below is from p. 12.
8. R. H. Van Gulik. *The Gibbon in China.* Leiden, Holland: E. J. Brill, 1967.
9. George Schaller. *The Mountain Gorilla.* Chicago University Press, 1963.
10. Colin P. Groves. *Gorillas.* New York: Arco, 1970.
11. Clifford J. Jolly. *Man,* 5, 5–26, 1970.
12. D. W. Yalden and G. R. Hosey, *J. zool. Lond.* 165. 513–20, 1971.

7. The Evidence of Fossils

1. There are of course numerous references to fossil hominids in the literature. Readers who are interested in this subject are referred to the following general works: *Early Man* by F. Clark Howell, New York: Life Nature Library, 1965; *Evolution of Man* by David Pilbeam, New York: Funk & Wagnalls, 1970; *The Emergence of Man* by John Pfeiffer, New York: Harper & Row, 1969; *The Roots of*

Mankind by John Napier, London: Allen and Unwin, 1971; *Guide to Fossil Man* by Michael Day, New York: Grosset & Dunlap, 1970.

2. You may well ask what possible role 'dragon's teeth' play in the pharmaceutical profession. You will be told that they are crushed up into a fine powder and taken three times a day after meals as a potent panacea for all diseases from psittacosis to porphyria.

3. E. L. Simons and P. E. Ettell. Gigantopithecus. *Sci. Amer.*, **222.** 76–85, 1970.

4. W. Tschernezky. A reconstruction of the foot of the Abominable Snowman. *Nature*, May 7th, 1960.

5. Simons and Ettell (n. 3) do not seem to have taken allometry into account. They state that *Gigantopithecus* must have weighed 300 lb (acceptable) and stood nearly 9 foot tall (unacceptable).

6. John Pfeiffer, *The Emergence of Man*. New York: Harper & Row, 1969, p. 162.

7. W. L. Straus, Jr, and A. J. E. Cave. *Quart. Rev. Biol.*, December 1957.

8. Carleton S. Coon. *The Origin of Races.* New York: Alfred Knopf, 1962.

9. T. D. Stewart. American Neanderthalers. *Quart. Rev. Biol.*, **32.** 364–9. 1957.

Conclusions

1. Maurice Burton. Is this the Surrey Puma? *Animals*, December 1966.

2. G. O. Dyrenfurth. *To the third pole.* London: Werner Laurie, 1955.

3. W. L. Straus, Jr, Abominable Snowman. *Science*, **123.** 1024–5, 1956.

4. Philologists will no doubt be interested in the name, the Mahalangur Himal, given in Nepali maps for the Nuptse-Lhotse range. Translated this means the abode of the great snow langur. There is, however, no reason to suppose that the name has a direct zoological relevance any more than does Houndsditch, London, or Tiger, Wash., U.S.A. The langur is the sacred monkey of India, the reincarnation of the God Hanuman after whom the range is named.

5. Major Tilman, writing in 1955 in the *Alpine Journal*, was obviously impressed by the ape-man theory of Tschernezky (Nature of the Abominable Snowman. *Manchester Guardian:* February 20th, 1954. Tschernezky subsequently developed his theory in an appendix to Izzard's book *The Abominable Snowman Adventure*. London: Hodder and Stoughton, 1955).

6. Don Abbott. *The Reader's Digest*, January 1969.

Index

Index